Catch Phrases, Clichés and Idioms

Catch Phrases, Clichés and Idioms

A Dictionary of Familiar Expressions

Compiled by
Doris Craig

McFarland & Company, Inc., Publishers
Jefferson, North Carolina, and London

British Library Cataloguing-in-Publication data are available

Library of Congress Cataloguing-in-Publication Data

Craig, Doris.
    Catch phrases, clichés and idioms : a dictionary of familiar
expressions / Doris Craig.
        p. cm.
    ISBN 0-89950-467-1 (lib. bdg. : 50# alk. paper) ∞
    1. English language—Terms and phrases. 2. English language—
Idioms—Dictionaries. I. Title.
PE1689.C74 1990
423'.1—dc20   89-43644
                                                               CIP

Manufactured in the United States of America

McFarland & Company, Inc., Publishers
    Box 611, Jefferson, North Carolina 28640

This book is dedicated to my son

Andrew Emerson Craig

who is not a cliché at all,
but the most viable person I know

Introduction

Catch phrases of the day such as "shop till you drop," clichés like "life begins at forty" and idioms like "talk the hind leg off a donkey" have long been enriching the English language in both spoken and written form. *Catch Phrases, Clichés and Idioms* is a collection of thousands of these colorful expressions that is designed to be an invaluable aid to advertising copywriters, song lyricists, feature newspaper caption and headline writers and speech writers. It is not, however, a dictionary of slang. Slang terms appear only when they are an integral part of the catch phrase, cliché or idiom tabulated.

Each phrase is listed and cross-referenced alphabetically by KEY WORD. Thus, "raining cats and dogs," for example, appears under CAT, DOG and RAIN as well. In most cases, various forms of the word are listed under the root word. So under RUN you will find not only sayings that include the word RUN, but also those that include RUNNING, RUNNETH, RUNNER and RUNAROUND.

The phrases are not defined as to meaning or origin; the concept being that if the term is so obscure it demands explanation, it is of little value in broad communication. However, to an advertising copywriter working on a campaign for, say, a granola-peanut health snack product, the instantly-recognizable phrase "energy crunch" becomes a clever, informative headline.

To the casual student of the English language, this book will provide many interesting and entertaining moments. To the professional writer, it is a treasure trove of idea-starters that will make for more imaginative creative writing.

D.C.

1

The Dictionary

A

A

Get "A" for effort
Everything from A to Z
As easy/simple as ABC
Learn/know one's ABCs
Everything is A-OK

Abandon

Abandon the ship
Abandon hope all ye who enter
  here

Abhor

Nature abhors a vacuum

Able

Be ready, willing and able

About

Bring something about
Beat about the bush
Do an about-face on something
That's about the size of it!
It's about time!

Above

Above and beyond/over and
  above the call of duty
Someone/something is above
  suspicion
Someone is above the law

Someone/something is a cut
  above someone/something
Rise above something
Keep one's head above water
Be in something above one's head
Sit above the salt
Keep everything/be open and
  aboveboard

Absence

Absence makes the heart grow
  fonder
Be conspicuous by one's absence

Accident

Look like an accident on its way
  to happen
Accidents will happen
Do something accidentally on
  purpose

Accord

According to Hoyle

Account

Bring/call someone to account
Give a good account of oneself
Take something into account
Have an account to settle with
  someone

Ace • Add 3

On no account
Square accounts with someone
There's no accounting for taste
All present and accounted for
Someone is a no-account

Ace

Ace someone out of something
Be within an ace of something
Have an ace in the hole
Black as the ace of spades
Have an ace up one's sleeve
Hold all the aces

Ache

Feel an aching void
Oh, my achin' back!
My achin' heart!

Achilles

Have an Achilles heel

Acid

Take/fail/pass the acid test
Drop acid
Have an acid tongue
Acid-head

Acorn

Great oaks from little acorns
grow

Acquaintance

Have a nodding/passing acquaintance with someone/something

Across

Across the board
Live/go across the tracks
Come across with something
Put/get something across
Hands across the table
Something/someone cuts across
the grain

Act

Act like someone from the ice age

Act the goat
Act up
Act on something before the ink
is dry
Act like an alley cat
Put on an act
Never follow a trained dog act
Do a balancing act
Catch someone in the act
Read someone the riot act
Get into the act
Someone/something is a tough
act to follow
Get one's act together
Someone/something is a class act
Be a bad actor
Everybody wants to get into the
act!
Act your age!
Catch your act later!

Action

Get/have a piece of the action
Go where the action is
Clear the decks for action
Actions speak louder than words
Where's the action?

Activity

Something is a beehive/hotbed of
activity

Adam

Not know someone from Adam
Not since Adam was a boy
Someone/something is as old as
Adam
Madam, I'm Adam!

Add

Add insult to injury
Add fuel to the flames/fire
Something just doesn't add up
It all adds up!

Advantage

Have the advantage
Give someone the advantage
Take advantage of someone/
  something
Something is to someone's advan-
  tage

Advocate

Play the devil's advocate

Afire

Go like a house afire

Afraid

Be afraid of the dark
Be afraid of one's own shadow
Who's afraid of the big, bad
  wolf?

After

After all is said and done
Do something after a fashion
A man after one's own heart
The morning after

Again

On again, off again
Time and again
If at first you don't succeed, try,
  try again
Go back to the well again
Hit me again!
You can say that again!
Come again?

Against

Against one's better judgment
Against insurmountable odds
Be up against it
Be/race against the clock
Swim against the current
Hope against hope
Go against the grain
Be up against a brick wall

Have the cards stacked against
  one
Have one's back against the wall

Age

Age before beauty
Age of innocence
Age of reason
Live to a ripe old age
Act like someone from the ice age
The age of miracles is/is not past
Come of age
Haven't seen someone in a dog's/
  donkey's/coon's age
In this day and age!
Act your age!

Agree

Agree to disagree
Couldn't agree with someone/
  something more
Gentleman's agreement

Ahead

Be ahead of the game
Be ahead of one's time
Quit while you're ahead
Be one jump ahead of the sheriff/
  someone
Be ahead of the crowd
Full steam ahead!
Straight ahead and strive for
  tone!

Air

Air one's dirty linen in public
Take the air
Leave someone/something up in
  the air
Clear the air
Grab a handful of air
Walk/float on air
Be full of hot air
Pull something out of thin air
Give someone the air

Come up for air
Build castles in the air
Vanish into thin air
Smell money in the air
Have one's nose in the air
Be left up in the air about something
Someone/something is like a breath of fresh air
Someone's language makes the air turn blue
Put on airs

Aisle

Walk down the aisle
Knock/lay 'em in the aisles

Alarm

Someone/something is cause for alarm
False alarm
Sound the alarm!

Alert

Be on the alert for someone/something
Red alert!

Alike

Alike as two peas in a pod
Share and share alike
Great minds think alike

Alive

Alive and well and living in

————

Bury someone alive
Skin someone alive
Be alive and kicking
Look alive!
Bring 'em back alive!
Sakes alive!

All

All in the line of duty
All in the same boat
All hell breaks loose
All in all
All present and accounted for
All in the family
All in good time
All the traffic will bear
All good things must come to an end
All roads lead to Rome
All in the same breath
All dressed up and no place to go
All in a day's work
All sweetness and light
All wool and a yard wide
All over but the shouting
All in one piece
All or nothing at all
All that glitters is not gold
All work and no play makes Jack a dull boy
Get/be all fired up
Something is all for the best
Something is a bit of all right
Someone gets all the breaks
Something is all well and good
Something is all over the lot
Something is not all it's cracked up to be
Something is all to the good
Go all out for something
Give someone/something all one's got
Go all the way
For good and all
Go on all fours
Be all things to all men
Do/get something at all costs
Someone is all heart
Get/be all bent out of shape
Be all buttoned up
Be all stressed out
Be all man
Be all business

Be all wrapped up in someone/
  something
Be all steamed up about some-
  thing
Be all ears/eyes
Be all thumbs
Be/get all worked up over some-
  one/something
The kindest/unkindest cut of all
It's all in the mind
Have/know all the moves
Get it all together
For once and for all
Put/have all one's eggs in one
  basket
Laugh/cry all the way to the
  bank
After/when all is said and done
Get/be all shook up
Hold all the aces
It all boils down to something
Get away from it all
Have something all wrapped up
Be all wrapped up in something/
  someone
Touch all the bases
Have all one's buttons/marbles
Life's not all beer and skittles/
  pretzels
Hold all the cards
Lay/put all one's cards on the
  table
Have something written all over
  one's face
Something/someone is the daddy
  of them all
See one, you've seen 'em all
Be all smiles
It's all in the wrist
Know all the answers
Someone/something is all wet
The be-all and end-all of some-
  thing
All systems are go!

Not for all the tea in China!
And that's not all!
Come home, all is forgiven!
In all my born days!
That's all she wrote!
Hang it all!
Don't that beat/hang all?

Alley

Go up/down a blind alley
Someone/something is right up
  one's alley
Act like an alley cat

Alligator

Cry alligator tears
Dig/see you later, alligator!

Allow

Allow as something is so
Whatever someone/something allow
Make allowances for someone/
  something

Almighty

The almighty dollar
Something is in the hands of the
  Almighty

Alone

He who travels fastest travels
  alone
Let/leave well enough alone
Man cannot live by bread
  alone
Go it alone

Along

Go along for the ride
String along with someone/some-
  thing
Something is coming along
Getting along in years
String someone along

Also

Be an also-ran

Altar

Be left standing at the altar

Always

Always a bridesmaid, never a
bride
The customer is always right
The grass is always greener on
the other side of the fence
First, last and always
It's always darkest before the
dawn
You always hurt the one you love

Ambulance

Ambulance chaser

American

As American as apple pie
Miss American pie
The American way
America first!

Ambition

Blind ambition

Amount

Not amount to a hill of beans

And

No ifs, ands or buts!
And that's not all!

Angel

Be an angel of mercy
Sing like an angel
Be on the side of the angels
Fools rush in where angels fear to
tread
He/she's no angel!

Anger

Someone is slow to anger

Angle

Get an angle on something
Everybody's got an angle
What's your angle?

Animal

The male animal
Someone is a party animal

Another

Another nail in one's coffin
Another day, another dollar
Another country heard from
Just another pretty face
Just another face in the crowd
One man's meat is another man's
poison
Something/someone is a horse of
another color
Dance to another tune
Tomorrow's another day
You've got another think coming!

Answer

Have a pat answer for everything
Ask a silly question, get a silly
answer
Someone/something is the answer
to one's prayers
The answer man
Not dignify something with an
answer
Know all the answers

Ant

Have ants in the pants
Get antsy about something

Ante

Jack up the ante
Ante up!

Any

Any port in a storm
Any day of the week

Do/get something at any cost
Go to any lengths
Be anything but
Anything for a laugh
Anything that can go wrong, will
Anything worth doing is worth
  doing well
Something is anybody's guess
Steal anything that's not nailed
  down
Any way you slice it!
Call me anything but late for
  breakfast!
Anything goes!

Apart

All joking/kidding apart
Be miles/poles apart on something
No telling apart
Come apart at the seams

Ape

Go ape over someone/something

Appear

Speak of the devil and he's sure
  to appear
Appearances can be deceiving
Keep up appearances
Put in an appearance

Apple

Be the apple of someone's eye
The apple doesn't fall far from
  the tree
As American as apple pie
Polish the apple
There's a rotten apple in every
  barrel
An apple a day keeps the doctor
  away
The apple of discord
The Big Apple
Compare apples and oranges
Sure as God made little green
  apples

Upset the applecart
Have everything in apple-pie order
How do you like them apples?

Apron

Be tied/hang on to one's mother's
  apron strings

Area

Comb the area
Police the area
Cruise the area
Blanket the area
Something is a gray area

Arm

Bend one's arm
Be someone's right arm
Twist someone's arm
Break an arm for someone/some-
  thing
Put the arm on someone
The long arm of the law
Get a shot in the arm
Give one's right arm for some-
  one/something
Cost/pay an arm and a leg
Greet someone/something with
  open arms
Be in the arms of Morpheus
Be up in arms about something
With arms akimbo
Keep someone/something at arm's
  length
Be armed to the teeth
Armchair quarterback
One-armed bandit
As busy as a one-armed
  paperhanger
Go arm-in-arm with someone/
  something

Armor

Knight in shining armor

Have a chink in one's armor

Army

Have an army of friends/enemies
An army travels/marches on its
  stomach

Around

Lead someone around by the
  nose
The second time around
What goes around, comes around
Know one's way around
Sleep around
Beat around the bush
Drive someone around the bend
Love/money makes the world go
  around
Go around the clock
Poke around
Someone has been around the
  block once or twice
Run circles around someone
Bum around with someone
Go/run around every which way
Not have room enough to turn
  around
Bring someone around
Go/run around in circles
Every time one turns around
Buzz around someone
Push/jerk someone around
Screw/kid/fool/horse around
Mess/play/fiddle around

Arrow

Be narrow as an arrow
Be a straight arrow
Suffer the slings and arrows of
  someone/something

Art

Art for art's sake
I don't know art, but I know
  what I like!

Article

Someone/something is the genu-
  ine article

As

As the story goes
As luck would have it
As the crow flies
As ye sow, so shall ye reap

Ash

Ashes to ashes, dust to dust
Haul someone's ashes
Wear sackcloth and ashes

Aside

All kidding aside

Ask

Ask a burning question
Ask a silly question, get a silly
  answer
Ask for trouble
Ask for the moon
Give no quarter and ask none
Have something for the asking
I ask you!
Ask me no questions, I'll tell you
  no lies!
You asked for it!

Asleep

Asleep in the deep
Asleep at the switch
Asleep on the job

Attendance

Dance attendance on someone

Attention

Be the center of attention

Attitude

Strike an attitude
Cop an attitude

Have an attitude
Have a devil-may-care attitude
Have a high-and-mighty attitude
Have a holier-than-thou attitude

Attract

Opposites attract
Be the center of attraction
What's the big attraction?

Avenue

Explore every avenue

Avoid

Avoid someone/something like
the plague

Awakening

Get a rude awakening

Awash

Awash in red ink

Away

Get something all squared away
Get away with murder
Dry up and blow away
Give the show/game away
Get carried away

Salt/sock something away
An apple a day keeps the doctor
away
Blow someone away
Get blown away by someone/
something
Get away from it all
When the cat's away, the mice
will play
Pack/fold up one's tent and steal
away
Someone/something takes one's
breath away
Be a stone's throw away from
something
Someone/something is far and
away the best/worst
Do away with someone/something
Old soldiers never die, they just
fade away
Go away closer!

Ax

Get the ax
Give someone the ax
Have an ax to grind with some-
one
Like peeling a grape with an ax

B

Baby

Sleep like a baby
Cry/bawl like a baby
Throw the baby out with the
bathwater
Be left holding the baby
Easy as taking candy from a baby

Be as helpless as a baby
The baby boom
Bouncing baby boy/girl
Bottle baby
Be a babe in the woods
As innocent as a new-born
babe

Out of the mouths of babes
Baby needs a new pair of shoes!

Back

Back to the salt mines
Back to the drawing board
Back to square one
Back to chapter one
Back someone into a corner
Back down/off
Back the wrong horse
Do something behind someone's
back
Pay someone back with interest
Get on/off someone's back
Be laid back
Set someone back on his ears/
heels
Know something like the back of
one's hand
Keep something on the back
burner
Give someone the back of one's
hand
Go to hell and back for some-
one/something
Be fed up to the back teeth with
someone/something
Someone is back in circulation
Come back down to earth
Bounce back
Come back in a flash
Go back to the well again
Shrink back in shame
Pay someone back in his own
coin
Get back to basics
Have one's back to/against the
wall
Have eyes in the back of one's
head
Someone/something is a back
number
Be back in the saddle

Something rolls right off one's
back
Give someone the shirt off one's
back
Fall back on something
With one hand tied behind one's
back
Get/give a pat/clap on the back
The straw that broke the camel's
back
Pin someone's ears back
Like water off a duck's back
Have a monkey on one's back
Get one's back up
Turn back the clock
Get back on one's feet
Put one's back to something
Take a back seat to someone
Turn one's back on someone/
something
Stab/knife someone in the back
Have a yellow stripe/streak down
one's back
Know someone from way back
Bend over backwards for some-
one/something
Know something/someone back-
wards and forwards
Stay in one's own backyard
Back-to-back
Back-seat driver
Back-handed compliment
Lay back and enjoy it!
Oh, my achin' back!
Bring 'em back alive!
You scratch my back, I'll scratch
yours!

Bacon

Bring home the bacon

Bad

Bad money drives out good
Good, bad or indifferent

Someone/something is a bad lot
A bad excuse is better than none
Want something so bad you can
  taste it
Three on a match is bad luck
Something is a bad scene
Get bad vibes from someone/
  something
Get off to a bad start
Someone/something looks like a
  bad joke
Give someone a bad time
Go from bad to worse
Something leaves a bad taste in
  one's mouth
Throw good money after bad
Turn up like a bad penny
Someone/something is not half
  bad
Get on someone's bad side
Be a bad actor
Be a bad egg/hat/lot
Someone/something is bad news
Be in someone's bad books
Pass bad paper
Have bad blood between you and
  someone
Take a bad turn
Have a stroke/run of bad luck
Be the bearer of bad news/tidings
Peck's bad boy
Bad-mouth someone
Who's afraid of the big, bad wolf?

Badger

Badger someone to death
Bald as a badger

Bag

Bag of tricks
Bag and baggage
Be a bag of bones
Flea bag
Be left holding the bag

Let the cat out of the bag
Someone can't punch/fight one's
  way out of a paper bag
Something is a mixed bag
Someone is an old bag
Put on the feedbag
Brown-bag it
It's in the bag!
That's my bag!

Baling

Put together with chewing gum
  and baling wire

Bait

Bait the hook
Rise to the bait
Swallow/take the bait
Someone is jailbait
Fish or cut bait!

Bake

Baker's dozen
Someone/something is only half-
  baked

Balance

Something hangs in the balance
Strike a balance
Get caught/catch someone off-
  balance
Do a balancing act

Bald

Bald as a badger
Bald as a billiard ball
Bald as a peeled egg
Bald as a coot
Go at something bald-headed
Tell a bald-faced lie

Ball

Ball something up
Have a ball
Be someone's ball and chain

The whole ball of wax
Play ball with someone
Get/start/keep the ball rolling
Have something on the ball
Play hard/guts ball
Keep one's eye on the ball
Carry the ball
Drop the ball
Something is a whole new ball
  game
Gaze into one's crystal ball
Be behind the eight ball
Bald as a billiard ball
Be a ball of fire
Be belle of the ball
Play catch-up ball
Play heads-up ball
Something starts to snowball
Not have a snowball's chance in
  hell
Give/get a ballpark figure
Greaseball
Blackball someone
Ballin' the Jack
The ball's in your court!
That's the way the ball bounces!

Balloon

Stick a pin in/burst someone's
  balloon
Something/someone goes over
  like a lead balloon
Send up a trial balloon
When does the balloon go up?

Ballot

Stuff the ballot box

Banana

Be top banana
Play second banana
Go bananas over someone/some-
  thing
Drive someone bananas
Banana oil!

Band

Lead a brass band
To beat the band
Jump/climb on the bandwagon

Bandbox

Look like one just stepped out of
  a bandbox

Bandit

Make out like a bandit
One-armed bandit

Bane

Someone is the bane of someone's
  existence

Bang

Bang one's head against the wall
Get more bang for the buck
Someone/something goes over
  with a bang
Get a bang out of someone/some-
  thing
Do a bang-up job

Bank

Something is money in the bank
Laugh/cry all the way to the
  bank
Break the bank
Keep banker's hours
You can bank on it!

Bar

Bar fly
Belly up to the bar
Be behind bars
No holds barred
Beat me daddy, eight to the bar!

Bare

Bare one's soul
Give someone only the bare
  bones of something

Have the bare necessities
Tell a bare-faced lie

Bargain

Someone/something is no bargain
Drive a hard bargain
Strike a bargain
Make/strike a bargain with the
   devil
Get more than one bargained for
Have a bargaining chip

Bark

Bark up the wrong tree
Bark at the moon
Someone's bark is worse than his
   bite
Barking dogs seldom bite

Barn

Lock the barn door after the
   horse has been stolen
Can't hit the broad side of a barn
Were you born in a barn?

Barrel

There's a rotten apple in every
   barrel
Scrape the bottom of the barrel
Someone/something is a barrel of
   fun
More fun than a barrel of mon-
   keys
Like shooting fish in a barrel
Buy something lock, stock and
   barrel
Get/have someone over a barrel
Give someone both barrels
Pay cash on the barrelhead

Base

Be way off base
Can't get to first base with some-
   one
Touch all the bases

Bashful

As bashful as a schoolgirl
As bashful as a bride

Basic

Get back to basics

Basket

Be a basket case
Put/have all one's eggs in one
   basket
Be bound for hell in a handbasket

Bat

Bat the breeze with someone
Bat one's eyes/eyelashes at some-
   one
Bat one's gums
Bat a thousand
In the bat of an eye
Someone doesn't bat an eye at
   something
Go to bat for someone
Blind as a bat
Do something right off the bat
Fly off the bat
Go like a bat out of hell
Someone is an old bat
Have bats in the belfry
Batting zero
Batten down the hatches!

Bath

Take a bath on something
Throw the baby out with the
   bathwater

Battle

Draw the battle lines
Have a battle royal
Something is only half the battle
Something is an uphill battle
Win the battle but lose the war

Bawl

Bawl like a baby
Bawl someone out

Bay

Bay at the moon
Bring someone to bay

Be

Be that as it may
To be or not to be
The be-all and end-all of some-
thing

Beach

Someone is not the only pebble
on the beach
Something is not exactly a day at
the beach

Bead

Draw/get a bead on someone/
something
Count one's beads

Beam

Be broad in the beam
Be on/off the beam
Beam me up, Scotty!

Bean

Use one's bean
Someone doesn't know beans
about something
Be full of beans
Know one's beans
Spill the beans
Not amount to a hill of beans

Bear

Bear up under something
Bear with someone
Bear something in mind
Bear a grudge
Bear down on someone/some-
thing
Bear the brunt of something
Bear the expense
Bear the heat of something
Bear false witness
Everyone has his cross to bear
Bring pressure to bear
Grin and bear it
All the traffic will bear
Have a bear by the tail
Be loaded for bear
Be a bear for punishment
As cross as a bear
Be the bearer of bad news/tidings
Beware of Greeks bearing gifts
Something has no bearing on
something
Get/keep/lose one's bearings

Beard

Beard the lion in his den
Play the beard
Laugh in one's beard

Beast

The nature of the beast
Something is not fit for man nor
beast

Beat

Beat the drum for something
Beat one's gums/chops
Beat one's head against the wall
Beat the tar/stuffing out of some-
one
Beat the rap
Beat swords into plowshares
Beat the game
Beat someone's time
Beat someone to the punch/draw
Beat someone by a country mile
Beat someone all hollow
Beat something into the ground
Beat the pants off someone
Beat one's brains out
Beat someone fair and square

Beat a hasty retreat
Beat the living daylights out of
  someone
Beat the bushes for something
Beat a path to someone's door
Beat about/around the bush
Beat a dead horse
Beat someone to a pulp
Beat oneself up over someone/
  something
One's heart skips a beat
You can't beat the system
To beat the band
Get beaten black and blue
Off the beaten path/track
If you can't beat 'em, join 'em!
Beats me!
Beat me daddy, eight to the
  bar!
Don't that beat the Dutch?
Don't that beat all?

Beauty

Beauty is truth
Beauty is only skin deep
Beauty is in the eye of the be-
  holder
Beauty is as beauty does
Get one's beauty sleep
Age before beauty
A thing of beauty is a joy for-
  ever
Make beautiful music together
Black is beautiful
All brides are beautiful

Beaver

Busy as a beaver
Work like a beaver
Someone is an eager beaver
Have a beaver-bite

Beck

Be at someone's beck and call

Bed

Get up on the wrong side of the
  bed
Go to bed with the chickens
Should have stayed/stood in bed
Something is no bed of roses
Early to bed and early to rise
  makes a man healthy, wealthy
  and wise
Put something to bed
Make one's bed and lie in it
Go to bed in one's boots
Have a good bedside manner
Politics make strange bedfellows
Something is a hotbed of activity

Bedbug

Crazy as a bedbug
Cute as a bedbug
Tight as a bedbug
Don't let the bedbugs bite!

Bee

Busy as a bee
Have a bee in one's bonnet
The birds and the bees
Someone/something is the bee's
  knees
Something is a beehive of activity
Make a bee-line for someone/
  something
None of your beeswax!

Beef

Beef something up
Have a beef with someone
Make a beef about something
Beefcake
Where's the beef?

Beer

Cry in one's beer
Want an egg in one's beer
Have a champagne taste on a
  beer pocketbook

Life's not all beer and skittles/
  pretzels
Break out the beer
Someone/something is small beer

Beet

As red as a beet

Before

Before you can say Jack Robinson
Cast pearls before swine
Don't count your chickens before
  they're hatched
Look before you leap
Don't cry before you're hurt
Put the cart before the horse
Pride goeth before a fall
Before you know it!

Beg

Beg to differ with someone
Beg for mercy
Beg, borrow or steal something
Beg the question
Beggers can't be choosers
Something beggers description
Go begging for something

Begin

Can't begin to tell someone some-
  thing
The beginning of the end
Make a new beginning

Behavior

Be on one's best behavior

Behind

Behind closed doors
Not be dry behind the ears
With one hand tied behind one's
  back
Be behind bars
Do something behind someone's
  back

Be behind the eight ball
Be behind the scenes
The power behind the throne
Be behind someone/something 110
  percent
Be behind the times
Burn one's bridges behind one
Put something behind one

Behold

Beauty is in the eye of the beholder
Lo, and behold!

Belfry

Have bats in the belfry

Believe

Make believe
Have good reason to believe
  someone/something
Something's hard to believe
Don't believe everything you
  read/hear
Can't believe one's ears/eyes
Beyond belief
To the best of one's belief
Seeing is believing
Make a believer out of some-
  one
Believe it or not!
You better believe it!
Believe it!
Believe you me!

Bell

Bell the cat
Saved by the bell
Something rings a bell
Something is/sounds clear as a
  bell
Be there with bells on

Belle

Be the belle of the ball

Belly

Belly up to the bar
Go belly up
Someone is lower than a snake's belly
Have a bellyful of someone/something
Go belly-to-belly with someone/something
Yellow-bellied
Quit your bellyachin'!

Below

Hit below the belt
Sit below the salt

Belt

Belt out a tune
Hit below the belt
Tighten one's belt
Have something under one's belt
Have a good, stiff belt
Get a belt in the chops

Bench

Sit/be on the bench
Warm the bench

Bend

Bend the rules
Bend over backwards for someone/something
Bend someone's ear
Bend one's elbow
Bend someone's arm
Bend someone/something to one's will
Drive someone around the bend
On bended knee

Beneath

Something is beneath one's dignity
Someone is beneath contempt

Benefit

Be to one's benefit
Give someone the benefit of the doubt
Without benefit of clergy

Bent

Have a bent for something
Be all bent out of shape
As the twig is bent, so grows the tree
Be hell-bent for leather

Berry

As brown as a berry
The blacker the berry, the sweeter the juice

Berth

Give a wide berth to someone/something

Beside

Be beside oneself
Something is beside the point
Something is beside the mark

Best

Best by test
Best bib and tucker
Someone/something is far and away the best
Honesty is the best policy
Have the best intentions
Make the best of something
Laughter is the best medicine
Save the best for last
Give something one's best shot
Living well is the best revenge
Bring out the best butter
Do one's level best
The best defense is a good offense
Something/someone is the best thing since sliced bread
Be someone's new best friend

Be the best in the business
Get the best of someone
Do as best one can
Put one's best foot forward
He who laughs last, laughs best
To the best of one's knowledge/
  belief
Something is all for the best
Have someone's best interests at
  heart
Keep up with the best of them
Man's best friend
Have the best of both worlds
Wear one's Sunday best
Be on one's best behavior
Experience is the best teacher
The best things in life are free
Diamonds are a girl's best friend
Come off second-best
The best-laid schemes...
Best of luck!

Bet

Bet one's bottom dollar
Bet one's shirt
Bet dollars to donuts
Hedge one's bet
Call in one's bets
Don't bet the farm!
You bet your boots!
You bet your life!
You bet your bippy!

Better

Better late than never
Better dead than Red
Better than a sharp poke in the
  eye
Better safe than sorry
The sooner the better
Take a turn for the better
A bad excuse is better than none
Discretion is the better part of
  valor

Go someone one better
Against one's better judgment
Half a loaf is better than none
For better or worse
Think better of something
Two heads are better than one
One's better half
Get the better of someone
Someone/something has seen bet-
  ter days
Old enough to know better
Better luck next time!
You better believe it!

Between

Between the devil and the deep
  blue sea
Between a rock and a hard place
Between two fires
Between life and death
Have one's tail between one's
  legs
Take the bit between one's teeth
Betwixt and between
Few and far between
Read between the lines
Just between you, me and the
  lamp post
There's many a slip between the
  cup and the lip
Something falls between the
  cracks
The shortest distance between
  two points is a straight line
Hit someone right between the
  eyes
No love lost between you and
  someone
Bad blood between you and
  someone

Beware

Beware of Greeks bearing gifts
Let the buyer beware

Beyond

Beyond the shadow of a doubt
Beyond one's depth/scope
Beyond one's comprehension/ken
Beyond measure/price
Beyond the pale
Beyond belief
Someone/something is beyond
  compare
Above and beyond the call of
  duty
One step beyond
Not see beyond one's nose

Bib

Best bib and tucker

Bible

Swear to something on a stack of
  bibles
Someone wrote the bible on
  something

Bide

Bide one's time

Big

Big fat zero
Big as all outdoors
Big as a house
Big talk/talk big
Big cheese/wheel/magoo/shot/
  noise/wig
Big man on campus
Big as an elephant/whale
Big daddy
Big as life and twice as natural
Big brother is watching
Roll the big dice
The Big Apple
Something big is going down
Look at the big picture
Someone/something goes over big
The last of the big spenders

Make a big deal/thing/produc-
  tion out of something
Have a big mouth
Little pitchers have big ears
Have a heart as big as all out-
  doors
Someone is Mr. Big/the big
  man
Call out the big guns
Someone is too big for his
  britches/boots
Make/raise a big stink about
  something
Hit the big time/leagues
Be a big fish in a little pond
As big as you please
Be in the big house
Speak softly and carry a big stick
Have a roll/wad big enough to
  choke a horse
Get/have the big idea
Go for someone/something in a
  big way
Something is big box-office
Have bigger fish to fry
Something is bigger than a bread-
  box
The bigger they come, the harder
  they fall
Have eyes bigger than one's
  stomach
Big deal!
What's the big deal?
What's the big idea?
What's the big attraction?

Bill

Bill and coo
Fill the bill
Foot the bill
Get a clean bill of health
As queer/phony as a three-dollar
  bill
Sell someone a bill of goods

Bind

Be in a bind
Something makes the cheese
  more binding

Bird

Eat like a bird
Fly/sing like a bird
Be happy as a bird
Someone is a rare bird
The early bird catches the worm
Be free as a bird
The bird has flown
A bird in the hand is worth two
  in the bush
A bird of ill omen
Give someone the bird
Someone/something is strictly for
  the birds
Birds of a feather flock together
The birds and the bees
Charm the birds out of the trees
Kill two birds with one stone
Fine feathers do not make fine
  birds
Be naked as a jaybird
Bird-dog the situation
Bird-brained idea
Bird's-eye view
Be in the cat-bird seat

Birth

Be in one's birthday suit
Be the birthday boy/girl
Make a birthday wish
Sell one's birthright

Bit

Do one's bit
Get there bit by bit
Champ at the bit
Have a hair of the dog that bit
  one
Someone/something is a bit of all
  right

Not know something if it bit one
Lay something on a bit thick
Something is a bit thick
Take the bit in/between one's
  teeth
Be thrilled to bits
Someone is a two-bit operator
This won't hurt a bit!
Shave and a haircut, six bits!

Bite

Bite one's lip
Bite the dust
Bite someone's head off
Bite the hand that feeds one
Bite off more than one can chew
Bite the bullet
Put the bite on someone
Someone's bark is worse than his
  bite
Barking dogs seldom bite
Once bitten, twice shy
Have a beaver-bite
Don't let the bedbugs bite!
What's biting you?
Man bites dog!

Bitter

Take the bitter with the sweet
Something is the bitter end
Fight/stay to the bitter end
Something is a bitter pill to swal-
  low
The bitter truth
Something leaves a bitter taste in
  one's mouth

Black

Black as the ace of spades
Black is beautiful
Black as a crow/pitch/ink
Black hole in space
See something in black and white
Be the black sheep in the family
Things look black

Give someone/something a black
    eye
The pot calling the kettle black
Get beaten black and blue
Give someone a black look
Have a black mark against one
Little black book
The blacker the berry, the
    sweeter the juice
Media blackout
Blacklist/blackball someone

Blank

Draw a blank about something
Give someone a blank check
Give someone a blank look
Shoot blanks
Do something point-blank

Blanket

Blanket the area
Be a wet blanket
Throw a wet blanket on some-
    thing
Born on the wrong side of the
    blanket
Need a security blanket
Someone/something is as thin as
    a boarding-house blanket

Blarney

Be full of blarney
Kiss the Blarney Stone

Blast

Have a blast
Go full blast
Blast off!

Blaze

Blaze new trails
Go out in the blaze of glory
Go like blazes
Go to blazes!
What in blue blazes?
Like blazes you say?

Bleed

Bleed someone white/dry
Bleed like a stuck pig
Bleeding heart
My heart bleeds for you!

Bless

Blessed event
Something is a mixed blessing
Something is a blessing in dis-
    guise
Count one's blessings
Bless my soul!
Bless my stars!

Blind

Blind impulse
Blind as a bat
Blind, lame and halt
Blind ambition
Fly blind
Turn a blind eye to something
Would steal a dead fly from a
    blind spider
Like the blind leading the blind
Justice is blind
Love is blind
Go up/down a blind alley
Have a blind spot about some-
    one/something
Get/be blind drunk
Get/be in a blind rage
Rob/steal someone blind
Be color blind
Be deaf, dumb and blind about
    someone/something
Someone is blind in one eye and
    can't see out of the other
Have blinders on
Strike me blind!

Blink

Something is on the blink
Not blink an eye at something

In the blink of an eye
Have one's blinkers on

Bliss

Ignorance is bliss

Block

Knock someone's block off
Be the new kid on the block
A chip off the old block
Have a block for a head
Have a mental block about some-
one/something
Writer's block
Put one's head on the chopping
block
Someone has been around the
block once or twice
Put the blocks to someone
Hit a stumbling-block

Blonde

Blonde bombshell
Dishwater blonde
Bottle blonde
Ditsy/dizzy/dumb blonde
Incendiary blonde
Gentlemen prefer blondes
Do blondes have more fun?

Blood

Blood is thicker than water
Blood and thunder
Blood, toil, sweat and tears
Something is in/runs in one's
blood
Draw first blood
Something makes one's blood boil
Be someone's blood brother
Break a blood vessel
Something/someone makes one's
blood run cold
Hire new blood
Do something in cold blood
Something/someone is too rich
for one's blood
Be out for blood
Sweat blood
Someone/something warms one's
blood
Can't get blood from a stone/
turnip
Have sporting blood
One's own flesh and blood
Pay blood money
Something/someone turns one's
blood to ice
Bad blood between you and
someone
Smell blood
Blueblood
Bloody one's hands
Scream bloody murder
Hot-blooded
Blood-curdling yell
What do you want, blood?

Blot

Blot something out of one's mind
Blot one's copybook

Blow

Blow hot and cold
Blow someone a kiss
Blow one's credibility
Blow a fuse/gasket
Blow one's stack/top
Blow one's cool
Blow one's cover
Blow something sky-high
Blow one's chances
Blow off steam
Blow into town
Blow the whistle on someone
Blow something to kingdom come
Blow one's own horn
Blow someone's brains out
Blow one's lines
Blow one's mind

Blow someone away
Blow the lid off something
Blow one's cork
Deal someone a crushing blow
Something is not worth the pow-
  der to blow it up
Return blow for blow
Something will blow over
Dry up and blow away
Give/get a low blow
See which way the wind blows
It's an ill wind that blows nobody
  good
Come to blows with someone
  over something
Someone is just blowing smoke
Get blown out of the water
Blow off!
Blow it out your ear!
That's the way the wind blows!

Blue

Blue Monday
Feel blue
Get beaten black and blue
From out of the blue
Once in a blue moon
Out of a clear blue sky
Be true blue
Be blue around the gills
Talk/swear a blue streak
Talk until one is blue in the face
Like a bolt from the blue
Between the devil and the deep
  blue sea
Be in a blue funk
The boys in blue
Scream blue murder
Someone's language makes the air
  turn blue
Cryin' the blues
Sing the blues
Blueblood
Bluestocking

Blue-chip stock
Blue-ribbon jury
Blue-collar job
Blue-pencil something out
What in blue blazes?

Bluff

Call someone's bluff

Blush

Blush of youth
At first blush
Blushing bride

Board

Across the board
Stiff as a board
Back to the drawing board
Be on the boards
Something goes by the boards
Sweep the boards
Keep everything aboveboard
Boarding-house reach
Someone/something is as thin as
  a boarding-house blanket

Boat

Miss the boat
All in the same boat
Hot off the boat
Burn one's boats
A rising tide lifts all boats
Don't rock the boat!
Did you just get off the boat?

Body

Body English/language
Not have a nerve in one's body
Break every bone in someone's
  body
Your body is a temple
A sound mind in a healthy body
Keep body and soul together
Know where all the bodies are
  buried
Over my dead body!

Bog

Get bogged down
Something boggles the mind
Have a mind-boggling experience

Boil

Boil over
Something comes to a boil
Let the pot boil awhile
Something makes one's blood boil
It all boils down to something
A watched pot never boils
Keep the pot boiling
Be at one's boiling point
Work in a boiler room
Boiler-plate contract
Be hard-boiled about something
Something is a pot-boiler

Bold

Be bold as brass
Put a bold face on something
Make a bold stroke
With one bold stroke

Bolt

Cut from the same bolt of cloth
Make a bolt for it
Like a bolt from the blue
Shoot one's bolt
Something is a bucket of bolts
The nuts and bolts of something

Bomb

Bomb out
Someone/something is a real
  bomb
Drop a bombshell
Blonde bombshell

Bone

Bone up on something
Be bone idle
Be bone weary/tired
Something is a bone of contention

Break every bone in someone's
  body
Be dry as a bone
Like a dog worrying a bone
Work one's fingers to the bone
Have a bone to pick with some-
  one
A rag, a bone, a hank of hair
Throw someone a bone
Be chilled to the bone
Tickle someone's funny bone
Cut someone/something to the
  bone
Cut/slice near the bone
The nearer the bone, the sweeter
  the meat
Have a fever in your bones for
  someone
Jump someone's bones
Be all skin and bones
Make no bones about something
Know/feel something in one's
  bones
Give someone only the bare
  bones of something
Pull a boner

Bonnet

Have a bee in one's bonnet

Boo

Can't say "boo" to a goose
Not hear "boo" from anyone

Boob

Boob tube
Booby trap
Booby prize
Booby hatch

Boogie

Go full-tilt boogie
Born to boogie
Turn on the boogie box

Book

The Good Book
Little Black Book
Someone wrote the book on
  something
Throw the book at someone
Something is a closed book
Go/play by the book
Read someone like a book
One's life is an open book
Make book on something
Can't judge a book by its cover
Take a page/leaf from someone's
  book
Hit/crack the books
Something/someone is one for
  the books
Doctor/cook the books
Be in someone's bad/good books
Time to close the books
Blot one's copybook

Boom

Boom town
Baby boom
Lower the boom on
  someone/something

Boost

Give someone a boost

Boot

Boot someone out
Get a boot out of
  someone/something
Give/get the boot
Lick someone's boots
Wear concrete boots
Someone is too big for his boots
Die with one's boots on
As tough as old boots
Have one's heart in one's boots
Shake in one's boots
Go to bed in one's boots

Pull oneself up by the bootstraps
You bet your boots!
And there's more to boot!

Border

Make a run for the border
Something borders on lunacy
Someone/something is a border-
  line case

Bore

Be a crashing bore
Bored stiff/to death/to tears

Born

Born with a silver spoon in one's
  mouth
Born on the wrong side of the
  blanket
Born to boogie
Born and bred in _____
Born to the purple
Born on the sunny side of the
  hedge
Born under a lucky/dark star
Born into the world owing two
  dollars
There's a sucker born every min-
  ute
Someone was not born yester-
  day
To the manor/manner born
Be a born loser
Innocent as a newborn babe
In all my born days!
Were you born in a barn?

Borrow

Borrow trouble
Borrow from Peter to pay Paul
Beg, borrow or steal something
Live on borrowed time
Neither a borrower nor a lender
  be

Bosom

Bosom buddies
Cradle an asp to one's bosom

Both

Have both feet on the ground
The door swings both ways
Have the best of both worlds
Jump into something with both
   feet
Make both ends meet
Something cuts both ways
Have/can't have it both ways
Burn the candle at both ends
Give someone both barrels
Play both ends against the middle
Have both hands on the table
Butter one's bread on both sides
Work both sides of the street
Have both oars in the water
A plague on both your houses!

Bother

Be/get all hot and bothered
   about something/someone

Bottle

Bottle blonde
Bottle baby
Bottle something up inside
Hit the bottle
Be chief cook and bottle washer
Something is old wine in new
   bottles
Hit a bottleneck

Bottom

Bottom out
Have the bottom fall out of some-
   thing
Get to the bottom of something
From the bottom of one's heart
Hit rock bottom
Sink to the bottom

Bet one's bottom dollar
Deal off the bottom of the deck
Scrape the bottom of the barrel
Get to/read the bottom line
Someone is at the bottom of
   something
Bottomless pit
Rock-bottom price
Bottoms up!

Bounce

Bounce off the walls
Bounce back
Give someone the bounce
Get more bounce to the ounce
Bouncing baby boy/girl
That's the way the ball bounces!

Bound

Bound for hell in a handbasket
Be bound to pay
Be bound and gagged
Be out of bounds
By leaps and bounds
Someone knows no bounds

Bow

Bow and scrape
Bow out of something
Someone is a real bow-wow
Take a bow!

Bowl

Bowl someone over
Life is just a bowl of cherries
Live in a goldfish bowl

Box

Box someone's ears
First crack out of the box
Stuff the ballot box
Go home in a box
Open Pandora's box
Dumber than a box of rocks
Look like someone just stepped
   out of a bandbox

Someone/something is big box-
office
Turn on the boogie-box
Something is bigger than a breadbox

Boy

All work and no play makes Jack
a dull boy
Someone is a mama's boy
Someone is someone's fair-haired
boy
Golden boy
Be someone's whipping boy
Be a good old boy
Be the birthday boy
Not since Adam was a boy
Peck's bad boy
Bouncing baby boy
You can take the boy out of the
country, but you can't take the
country out of the boy
Boys will be boys
Be one of the boys
Separate the men from the boys
The boys in blue
The boys of summer
The old-boy network
Be boy-crazy

Brace

Brace yourself!
Brace up!

Brag

Something/someone is nothing to
brag about

Brain

Pick someone's brain
Have a brain the size of a pea
The brain drain
Lame brain
Brainchild
Braintwister

Brainstorming session
Brainwash
Blow someone's brains out
Wrack/rack one's brains
Someone doesn't use the brains
God gave him
Beat/pound one's brains out
Get one's brains fried
Pickle one's brains
Not have the brains God gave a
goose
Wear a brain-bucket
Feather-brained person
Hare-brained idea

Branch

Branch out
Offer someone the olive branch

Brand

Put one's brand on something
Something is brand-spanking new

Brass

Brass hat
Get down to brass tacks
Be bold as brass
Lead a brass band
Double in brass
Top brass

Brave

Brave something out
Put on a brave face/front

Brazen

Brazen something out
Brazen hussy

Bread

Bread is the staff of life
Bread always falls on its buttered
side
Take the bread out of someone's
mouth

Break bread together
Earn the bread
Cast bread upon the waters
Something is the best thing since sliced bread
Man cannot live by bread alone
Know which side one's bread is buttered on
Something is one's bread and butter
Butter one's bread on both sides
A jug of wine, a loaf of bread and thou
Be on the breadline
Be the breadwinner
Something is bigger than a breadbox

Break

Break someone's neck
Break one's neck for someone/something
Break someone's heart
Break out in a cold sweat
Break bread together
Break a blood vessel
Break new ground
Break into a smile/grin
Break into tears
Break an arm for someone/something
Break the ice
Break even
Break the habit
Break the bank
Break every bone in someone's body
Break up laughing
Break one's word
Break the news
Break the record
Break out the beer
Break someone up
Break someone/something in

Never give a sucker an even break
Make a break for it
Something will make or break someone/something
Someone gets all the breaks
All hell breaks loose
Can't make an omelet without breaking some eggs
Go at breakneck speed
Break it up!
You break me up!
Give me a break!
Break a leg!

Breakfast

Have breakfast with the chickens
Power breakfast
Call me anything but late for breakfast

Breast

Music hath charms to soothe the savage breast
Make a clean breast of something

Breath

Hold one's breath
Say something under one's breath
Catch one's breath
Draw one's last breath
Someone/something takes one's breath away
All in the same breath
Wait with bated breath
Someone/something is like a breath of fresh air
Don't hold your breath!
Don't waste your breath!
Save your breath!

Breathe

Breathe one's last
Breathe fire and brimstone
Breathe easy

Breathe fire
Breathe new life into something
Breathe down someone's neck
Not breathe a word of something
Have room to breathe
Take a breather
As I live and breathe!

Breed

The new breed
Someone/something is a different
  breed of cat
Familiarity breeds contempt
Born and bred in _____

Breeze

Breeze into town
Win in a breeze
Bat/shoot the breeze with some-
  one
Free as the breeze
Breezin' along with the breeze

Brew

Something is brewing

Brick

Something hits someone like a
  ton of bricks
Drop a brick
Come down on someone like a
  ton of bricks
Fall for someone like a ton of
  bricks
Try to make bricks without straw
Be up against a brick wall
Busy as a cat on hot bricks
Be one brick short of a load
Built like a brick outhouse
Hurl brickbats at someone
Goldbrick
You're a brick!

Bride

As bashful as a bride

Always a bridesmaid, never a
  bride
Child bride
Blushing bride
All brides are beautiful

Bridge

Something is water under the
  bridge
Cross that bridge when one
  comes to it
Burn one's bridges behind one

Brief

Hold no brief for someone/some-
  thing
One brief, shining moment
Get debriefed on something
Brevity is the soul of wit

Bright

Bright as day
Bright as a button
Bright as a new penny
Bright and early
Look on the bright side
Be bright-eyed and bushy-tailed
Brighten up!

Brimstone

Breathe fire and brimstone

Bring

Bring out the best butter
Bring down the house
Bring someone to heel
Bring someone to his knees
Bring something to light
Bring someone to bay
Bring home the bacon
Bring something into play
Bring someone up short
Bring something about
Bring someone to account
Bring something to a head

Bring someone down
Bring something out into the
open
Bring someone to his senses
Bring someone up to date/speed
Bring up the rear
Bring pressure to bear
Bring to mind
Bring on the dancing girls!
Bring 'em back alive!

Britches

Someone is too big for his
britches
Tan someone's britches

Broad

In broad daylight
Be broad in the beam
Can't hit the broad side of a barn
Be broad-minded

Broke

Be dead/flat/stone broke
Go for broke
The straw that broke the camel's
back
If it ain't broke, don't fix it
After they made someone, they
broke the mold
Leave a trail of broken hearts
There's a broken heart for every
light on Broadway
There's a broken light for every
heart on Broadway
Sound like a broken record

Broom

A new broom sweeps clean
Jump over the broomstick
Broom it!

Broth

Too many cooks spoil the broth
A fine broth of a lad

Brother

Big brother is watching
Everybody and his brother
Be someone's blood brother
He ain't heavy, he's my brother!
Am I my brother's keeper?
Brother, can you spare a dime?

Brow

By the sweat of one's brow
Knit one's brows
Someone is a high-brow

Brown

As brown as a berry
Be in a brown study
Do something up brown
Make brownie points
Brown-bag it
Be a brown-nose
How now, brown cow?

Bruise

Someone is a big bruiser
Be cruisin' for a bruisin'

Brunt

Bear the brunt of something

Brush

Brush up on something
Be tarred with the same brush
Give/get the brush/brushoff
Have a close brush with some-
one/something
Have a brush with greatness

Brute

Brute force

Bubble

Burst someone's bubble
Someone is a bubblehead
Bubble-gum rock

Buck

Buck for a raise
Get more bang for the buck
Make a fast buck
Pass the buck
The buck stops here
Have buck fever
Feel/look like a million bucks
Be buck-naked
Buck up!

Bucket

Kick the bucket
Something is a bucket of bolts
Can't carry a tune in a bucket
Rain buckets
Wear a brain-bucket
For cryin' in the bucket!

Buckle

Buckle down
Buckle up!

Bud

Nip something in the bud

Buddy

Use the buddy system
Bosom buddies

Buff

Be in the buff

Bug

Cute as a bug/bug's ear
Snug as a bug in a rug
Put a bug in someone's ear
Catch a bug
Get the bugs out of something
Go bughouse
Send someone to the bughouse
Be bug-eyed over someone/something
Don't let the bedbugs bite!
Bug off!

Buggy

Horse and buggy days
Still trying to sell buggywhips

Build

Build a house of cards
Build castles in Spain/the sand/
the air
Build a fire under someone
Build up a head of steam
Rome wasn't built in a day
Built like a brick outhouse
Something is jerry-built

Bull

Something is like a red rag to a
bull
Shoot/throw/sling the bull
Take the bull by the horns
Like a bull in a china shop
Someone is strong as a bull
Have a bull session
Hit the bullseye
Be waiting in the bullpen
Cock-and-bull story
Bully for you!

Bullet

Bite the bullet
A bullet with one's name on it
Faster than a speeding bullet

Bum

Bum around with someone
Get a bum steer
Get a bum rap
Be on the bum
Shiftless bum
Give/get the bum's rush
Have a bummer
Someone/something is a bummer
Hallelujah, I'm a bum!

Bump

Bump someone off

Bump up something
Sit there like a bump on a log
Have a bumper crop

Bun

Have a bun in the oven
Honeybun
Someone has great buns

Bundle

Bundle of energy
Bundle of nerves
Bundle of joy
Make/drop a bundle on something
Bundle up!

Bunk

Do a bunk
That's all bunk!

Burden

The burden of proof is on someone

Burn

Burn one's boats
Burn rubber
Burn up the road
Burn daylight
Burn one's bridges behind one
Burn the candle at both ends
Burn the midnight oil
Burn out
Have money to burn
Do a slow burn
Have time to burn
Money burns a hole in one's pocket
Fiddle while Rome burns
Get one's fingers burned
Get burned
Be burned up
Once burned, twice shy
Cook on all four/the front burners

Keep something on the back burner
Keep the home fires burning
Ask a burning question
Someone's ears are burning
Get a burnt offering

Burst

Burst at the seams
Burst someone's bubble/balloon
Burst into tears
Burst into laughter
Burst into song
Be bursting with good health
Be bursting with good news

Bury

Bury the hatchet
Bury someone alive
Bury oneself in something
Bury one's head in the sand
Let the dead bury the dead
Doctors can bury their mistakes
Know where all the bodies are buried

Bush

Bush telegraph
Beat around/about the bush
A bird in the hand is worth two in the bush
Beat the bushes with something
Be bushed
Someone/something is strictly bush-league
Something is a lot of bush-wa
Be bright-eyed and bushy-tailed

Bushel

Hide one's light under a bushel

Business

Business as usual
Drum up business

Give someone the business
Go like nobody's business
The business end of a gun
Be the best in the business
Make something someone's business
Be all business
Take care of business
Funny/monkey business
There's no business like show business
Something is a risky business
Do a land-office business
Run a vest-pocket business
Cloak-and-dagger business
That's show business/biz!
I mean business!
Mind your own business!
None of your business!

Bust

Bust a gut
Bust someone's balloon
Bust one's buttons
Bust one's chops
Be so proud one could bust
Go bust
Come on like gangbusters

Busy

Busy as a beaver/bee
Busy as a cat on a hot tin roof/ hot bricks
Busy as a one-armed paperhanger
Make busy-work

But

There, but for the grace of God, go I
Be anything but
No ifs, ands or buts

Butt

Butt one's head up against the wall

Be the butt of a joke
Work one's butt off
Butt out!

Butter

Butter someone up
Butter wouldn't melt in someone's mouth
Butter one's bread on both sides
Something is one's bread and butter
Bring out the best butter
Go like a hot knife through butter
Know which side one's bread is buttered on
Bread always falls on its buttered side
Be a butter-fingers
Butter-and-egg money

Butterflies

Butterflies are free
Have butterflies in one's stomach
Chase butterflies

Button

Button up one's mouth
Button something up
Button one's lip
Bright as a button
Push the panic button
Cute as a button
Hit something/be right on the button
Bust one's buttons
Be missing a few buttons
Have all one's buttons
Know how to push someone's buttons
Be all buttoned up
Buttonhole someone

Buy

Buy something off the rack

Buy now, pay later
Buy something lock, stock and
  barrel
Buy the cherry farm
Buy something for a song
Buy a pig in a poke
Buy someone off
Buy and sell someone
Buy/not buy someone's story
Money can't buy happiness/love
Let the buyer beware
I'll buy that!
Why buy the cow when the milk
  is free?

Buzz

Buzz around someone
Give someone a buzz
Get a buzz on
Buzzword
Buzz off!

By

By word of mouth

By and large
By all means
By the same token
By the sweat of one's brow
By guess and by golly/God
By rule of thumb
By fits and starts
By hook or by crook
By leaps and bounds
By the skin of one's teeth
Someone/something goes by the
  boards
Not by a long shot/chalk
Shine someone on by
Play something by ear
Go/play by the book
Go by the numbers
Hear by the grapevine
Fly by the seat of one's
  pants
Let bygones be bygones
In the sweet bye-and-bye
Bye-the-bye

C

Cabbage

Always chew your cabbage twice
Have a whole lot of cabbage
My little cabbage!

Cabin

Cabin fever

Caboodle

The whole kit and caboodle

Cage

Rattle someone's cage

Cahoots

Be in cahoots with someone

Cake

Get a slice/piece of the cake
Something is a piece of cake
Eat one's cake and have it too
Someone/something takes the
  cake
Something is icing on the cake
Someone earns long cake
Sell like hotcakes

Nutty as a fruitcake
Beefcake/cheesecake

Calf

Kill the fatted calf

Call

Call a spade a spade
Call someone's hand
Call in one's markers/bets
Call it square
Call it a day
Call someone/something into
　question
Call someone on the carpet
Call it quits/curtains
Call it off
Call names
Call the law on someone
Call someone's bluff
Call the shots
Call the tune
Call to the colors
Call me anything but late for
　breakfast
Call a halt to something
Call of nature
Call something into play
Call out the big guns
Call off the dogs
Call someone to account
Be at someone's beck and call
Something is too close to call
Be on call
Take a curtain call
Can't call your soul your own
Over and above/beyond the call
　of duty
The pot calling the kettle black
The piper/fiddler calls the tune
Many are called, but few are
　chosen
Something is uncalled for
Call me out!

Duty calls!
Don't call us, we'll call you!

Came

Came the dawn about some-
　thing

Camel

A camel is an elephant designed
　by a committee
The straw that broke the camel's
　back

Camp

Camp follower
Something/someone is high camp
Help send this kid to camp!
That's campy!

Campaign

Mud-slinging/smear campaign
Whispering campaign

Can

Open up a can of worms
Packed like sardines in a can
Kick the can
Give someone the can
Catch as catch can
Do as best one can
Canned laughter
Get canned
Can do!
Not if I can help it!

Canary

Look like the cat that swallowed
　the canary
Sing like a canary

Cancer

Need something like one needs
　cancer
Smoke a cancer stick

Candle

The game is worth the candle
Light a candle or curse the dark-
ness
Burn the candle at both ends
Someone/something can't hold a
candle to someone/something

Candy

Candy is dandy, but liquor is
quicker
Easy as taking candy from a baby
Like a kid in a candy store

Cannon

Someone/something is a loose
cannon

Canoe

Paddle one's own canoe

Can't

Can't beat the system
Can't take it with you
Can't live on love
Can't win for losing
Can't buy love/happiness
Can't see the forest for the trees
Can't hit the broad side of a barn
Can't make head nor tail out of
someone/something
Can't carry a tune in a bucket/
wheelbarrow
Can't believe one's ears/eyes
Can't make an omelet without
breaking some eggs
Can't help oneself
Can't make a silk purse out of a
sow's ear
Can't judge a book by its cover
Can't teach an old dog new tricks
Can't get there from here
Beggars can't be choosers
A zebra can't change its stripes

A leopard can't change its spots
If you can't beat 'em, join 'em

Canvas

Carry too much canvas

Cap

Set one's cap for someone
Have/get a feather in one's cap
Put on one's thinking cap
Put a cap on it!

Caper

Cut capers

Captain

Be the captain of one's soul
Be a captain of industry

Card

Play one's trump card
Have a card up one's sleeve
Play one's last card
Someone/something is the wild
card in the deck
Idiot card
Build a house of cards
Play one's cards close to the vest/
chest
Play one's cards right
Have the cards stacked against
one
Put/lay all one's cards on the
table
Hold all the cards
Something is/isn't in the cards
Can't tell the players without a
scorecard

Care

Handle with care
Not care a rap/fig for
someone/something
Not have a care in the world
Take care of business

Couldn't care less about some-
one/something
Watch your pennies and the dol-
lars will take care of themselves
Not care two hoots in hell
If you can't be good be careful
Have a devil-may-care attitude/
personality
Have a care!
Take care!

Carpet

Call someone on the carpet
Roll out the red carpet
Sweep something under the car-
pet

Carrot

Follow a carrot on a stick
Dangle the carrot
Carrot-top

Carry

Carry a grudge
Carry one's cross
Carry coals to Newcastle
Carry too much canvas
Carry one's own weight
Carry the ball
Carry the weight of the world on
one's shoulders
Carry a torch for someone
Carry something too far
Carry something off
Carry some weight with some-
one/something
Speak softly and carry a big stick
Fetch and carry for someone
Can't carry a tune in a bucket/
wheelbarrow
Cash and carry
Get carried away
Someone/something carries the day
Someone is carrying on about
something

Carry on!

Cart

Put the cart before the horse
Cart someone/something off
Upset the applecart

Case

Case of the tail wagging the dog
Case in point
Case the joint
Someone/something is a hard
case
Get on/off someone's case
Make a Federal case out of some-
thing
Have a case on someone
Be a basket/couch/mental case
Someone has a case of the cutes
Something is an open-and-shut
case
Just in case
In any case
Someone/something is a border-
line case
Get down to cases
Case closed!

Cash

Cash in on something
Cash and carry
Cash in one's chips
Pay cash on the barrelhead
Cold, hard cash
Put one's cash on the line
Be paper-rich and cash-poor

Cast

Cast pearls before swine
Cast aspersions on someone/
something
Cast in one's lot with someone
Cast sheep's eyes at someone
Cast a long shadow
Cast out devils

Cast one's eyes on someone/
  something
Cast bread upon the waters
Someone/something is cast in the
  same mold
Cast a pall over something
Let he who is without sin cast the
  first stone
Have a cast-iron stomach
The die is cast!

Castle

A man's home is his castle
Build castles in Spain/the air/the
  sand

Cat

Bell the cat
Let the cat out of the bag
Look like the cat that swallowed
  the canary
Have eyes like a cat
Play cat and mouse with some-
  one
There's more than one way to
  skin a cat
Someone/something is a different
  breed of cat
Let the old cat die
Act like an alley cat
Curiosity killed the cat
A cat has nine lives
As busy as a cat on a hot tin
  roof/hot bricks
Set a cat among the pigeons
Not have room enough to swing
  a cat
Grin like a Cheshire cat
As wary as a cat
Know which way the cat will
  jump
Be a cool cat
A cat can look on a king
As nervous as a long-tailed cat in

a roomful of rocking chairs
Look like something the cat
  dragged in
Rain cats and dogs
Fight like cats and dogs
All cats are gray in the dark
The fat cats
Be someone's cat's paw
When the cat's away, the mice
  will play
Someone/something is the cat's
  pajamas/meow/whiskers
Catnap
Fraidy-/scaredy-cat
Be in the cat-bird seat
Holy cats!
Look what the cat dragged in!
Jumpin' catfish!
Cat got your tongue?

Catch

Catch someone red-handed
Catch as catch can
Catch someone flat-footed
Catch the brass ring
Catch forty winks
Catch it in the neck
Catch one's death of cold
Catch one's breath
Catch a bug
Catch someone off-guard
Catch some Zzzzz's
Catch someone in the act
Catch someone napping
Catch someone with his pants
  down
Catch sight of something
Catch someone with his hand in
  the cookie jar/till
Catch someone off-balance
Catch the drift of something
It takes a thief to catch a thief
You can catch more flies with
  honey than with vinegar

The early bird catches the worm
Caught like a rat in a trap
Wouldn't be caught dead in
  something
Get caught in the crossfire
Catch-22
Play catch-up ball
Catch your act later!

Cause

Something/someone is cause for
  alarm
Have just cause
Someone/something is a lost
  cause
Just because

Caution

Throw caution to the wind
Someone is a caution

Cave

Have the roof cave in on one

Cease

Cease and desist!
Will wonders never cease?

Ceiling

Hit the ceiling

Cent

Do something for two cents
Feel like two cents
Put one's two cents in
Someone is a 10-percenter
Be behind someone/something 110
  percent
Not one red cent!

Center

Be the center of attention/attrac-
  tion
Be off-center
Front and center!

Ceremony

Stand on ceremony
Do something without ceremony

Certain

The certain feeling
That certain something
That certain someone

Chain

Chain reaction
Chain of events
Chain letter
Chain smoke
Chain store
Be the weak link in the chain
Someone's ball and chain
Pull/jerk someone's chain
The daisy chain

Chair

Sit on the edge of one's chair
Hang onto one's chair
Go to the chair
Something is as useless as re-
  arranging deck chairs on the
  Titanic
As nervous as a long-tailed cat in
  a roomful of rocking chairs
Armchair quarterback
Have a chair!

Chalk

Chalk talk
Chalk something up to experi-
  ence
Walk the chalk
Know the difference between
  chalk and cheese
Not by a long chalk!

Champ

Champ at the bit
Take something like a champ

Champagne

Have a champagne taste on a
beer pocketbook

Chance

Chance of a lifetime
Take a chance
Not stand a chance
Have a snowball's chance in hell
Have an outside chance
Not have a Chinaman's chance
Not have a fighting/sporting
chance
Not have a ghost of a chance
Wouldn't pay a dime for some-
one's chances
Blow one's chances
You pays your money and you
takes your chances!
Fat chance!

Change

Change one's tune
Change one's ways
Change of scene
Change of pace
Change of hands
Change horses in the middle of
the stream/midstream
Have a change of heart
A zebra can't change its stripes
A leopard can't change its spots
Earn a nice piece of change
The winds of change
Ring the changes

Chapter

Quote chapter and verse about
something
Someone wrote the chapter on
something
Back to chapter one

Charge

Charge something up to experience

Get a large charge out of someone

Charity

Charity begins at home

Charm

Charm the pants off someone
Charm the birds out of the trees
Something works like a charm
Third time is a charm
Music hath charms to soothe the
savage breast
Lead a charmed life
Meet one's Prince Charming

Chart

Something goes off the charts

Chase

Chase after something
Chase rainbows/butterflies
Chase up the wrong tree
Chase one's own tail
Lead someone a merry chase
Go on a wild-goose chase
Ambulance-chaser
Skirt-chaser
Go chase yourself!
Cut to the chase!

Cheap

Talk is cheap
Pull a cheap trick
Something is cheap at twice the
price
Get off cheap
Do something on the cheap
Something is dirt cheap
Get a cheap thrill
Take a cheap shot at someone/
something
Someone/something doesn't come
cheap
Cheapskate

Check

Check and double-check
Write a rubber check
Spring/pop for the check
Give someone a blank check
Take a rain check

Cheek

Turn the other cheek
Speak with tongue in cheek
Someone has a lot of cheek
Have roses in one's cheeks
Be cheek-by-jowl with someone

Cheer

Stand up and cheer
Be of good cheer
Bronx cheer
Give three cheers for someone/
    something
Cheer up, you'll soon be dead!

Cheese

Know the difference between
    chalk and cheese
Someone is the big cheese
Something makes the cheese
    more binding
Cheesecake
Someone/something is cheesy
Cheese it, the cops!
Hard cheese!

Chef

My compliments to the chef!

Cherry

Buy the cherry farm
Life is just a bowl of cherries

Chest

Something will put hair on one's
    chest
Get something off one's chest
Play one's cards close to the chest

Build a hope chest

Chestnut

Pull the chestnuts out of the fire
Someone/something is an old
    chestnut

Chew

Chew someone out
Chew the scenery
Chew the fat/cud/rag
Chew someone's ear off
Chew nails and spit rust
Bite off more than one can chew
Always chew your cabbage twice
Put together with chewing-gum
    and baling wire

Chicken

Chicken out of something
Someone is no spring chicken
Pull the chicken switch
Run around like a chicken with
    its head cut off
A chicken in every pot
Something is chicken feed
Chickens come home to roost
Don't count your chickens before
    they're hatched
Go to bed with the chickens
Have breakfast with the chickens
Be chicken-livered/hearted
Ain't nobody here but us chick-
    ens!
Which came first, the chicken or
    the egg?

Chief

Be chief cook and bottlewasher
Have all chiefs and no Indians

Child

Child bride
Spare the rod and spoil the child
Be with child

Be a child of nature
Be a child of the devil
Brainchild
Something is child's play
Children should be seen and not
  heard
Children and fools speak the
  truth
Be in one's second childhood
Women and children first!

Chill

Feel a sudden chill
Be chilled to the bone
Have a chilling experience
Chill out!

Chin

Keep one's chin up
Take it on the chin
Stick one's chin out
Chuck someone under the chin
Someone has more chins than a
  Chinese phone directory

China

Like a bull in a china shop
Not have a Chinaman's chance
Not for all the tea in China!

Chink

Have a chink in one's armor

Chip

Chip in
A chip off the old block
Have a chip on one's shoulder
Have a bargaining chip
Turn in one's chips
When the chips are down
Let the chips fall where they may
Cash in one's chips
Feel chipper
Blue-chip stock

Choice

You pays your money and you
  takes your choice
Hobson's choice

Choke

Choke someone off
Have a roll/wad big enough to
  choke a horse
Get all choked up about some-
  thing
Go choke on it!

Choose

Choose the lesser of two evils
Choose up sides
Pick and choose
Beggars can't be choosers
The chosen few
Many are called, but few are
  chosen

Chop

Be down in the chops
Beat one's chops
Lick one's chops
Get one's chops together
Someone has great chops
Get a belt in the chops
Bust one's chops
Put one's head on the chopping
  block
Get a klop in the chopper
What am I, chopped liver?

Chord

Something/someone strikes/
  touches a chord
The lost chord

Chow

Chow down
Chow line
Chow hound
Chowderhead

Chuck

Chuck someone under the chin
Chuck it all!

Chump

Someone is a chump

Church

Be poor as a churchmouse
See you in church!

Cigar

Silent as a cigar store Indian
Close, but no cigar!
What this country needs is a
   good five-cent cigar!
Cigarettes, whiskey and wild,
   wild women!

Cinch

Someone/something is a lead-pipe
   cinch
It's a cinch!

Circle

Something comes full circle
Vicious circle
Be in the inner circle
Run/go around in circles
Run circles around someone
Talk in circles
Someone/something is back in
   circulation

Circumstance

Under the circumstances...
Someone is in reduced circumstances

Circus

Something is a three-ring circus

City

City slicker
Have/get the keys to the city

You can't fight city hall
Panic city
Good-time city

Civil

Keep a civil tongue in one's head

Claim

Stake a claim on someone/some-
   thing
Jump someone's claim
Have no claim on someone/some-
   thing

Clam

Happy as a clam
Something is a clambake
Clam up!

Clamp

Put the clamps on someone/
   something

Clap

Clap eyes on someone/something
Give someone a clap on the back

Class

Class will tell
Someone/something is in a class
   by itself
Go to the head of the class
Someone/something is a class act
Someone has a classy chassis

Clay

Someone has feet of clay
Someone is a clay pigeon

Clean

Clean up the floor with someone
Clean up one's act
Clean someone's clock/plow
Clean forget something
Clean one's own house
Someone is Mr. Clean

A new broom sweeps clean
Be clean as a whistle
Make a clean breast of some-
thing
Have clean hands
Make a clean sweep of something
Show a clean pair of heels
Come clean
Have a clean slate
Keep one's nose clean
Get a clean bill of health
As clean as a hound's tooth
Take someone to the cleaners
Cleanliness is next to Godliness

Clear

Clear the decks for action
Clear the air
Something is/sounds clear as a
bell
Something is clear as mud
Steer clear of something
Be clear as crystal/glass
See one's way clear to do some-
thing
Something is clear as day
Get a clear signal from someone
Be in the clear
Out of a clear blue sky
The coast is clear
Have a clear conscience

Clergy

Without benefit of clergy

Clever

Someone is too clever by half

Climb

Climb the walls
Climb on the bandwagon
Go climb a tree!

Cling

Someone is a clinging vine

Clink

Throw someone in the clink
Someone/something is a clinker

Clip

Clip someone's wings
Clip one's words
Clip joint
Go at a fast clip

Cloak

Something/someone is cloaked in
mystery
Cloak-and-dagger business

Clobber

Haul off and clobber someone
Get clobbered

Clock

Clock watcher
Clean someone's clock
Someone has a face that would
stop a clock
Be against the clock
Go around the clock
Race against the clock
Turn back the clock
Something runs like a clock/
clockwork
Something is as regular as clock-
work

Close

Close on the heels of someone/
something
Close only counts in horse-
shoes
Play one's cards close to one's
chest/vest
Something is too close to call
Cut something close
Sail too close to the wind
Be in close quarters
Have a close call/shave

Have a close brush with some-
one/something
Something hits too close to home
Close, but no cigar!
Go away closer!

Close (vb)

Close the ranks
Close up shop
Close one's mind/eyes to some-
thing
Time to close the books
Can do something with one's eyes
closed
Something is a closed book
Behind closed doors
When one door closes, another
opens
Case closed!

Closet

Closet queen
Have a skeleton in one's closet
Come out of the closet
Something is like Fibber McGee's
closet

Cloth

Something is cut/made up from
whole cloth
Cut from the same bolt of cloth
A man of the cloth

Clothes

Clothes make the man
Wear one's best Sunday-go-to-
meeting clothes
Be a clothes horse
A wolf in sheep's clothing

Cloud

Be on cloud nine
Be under a cloud
Every cloud has a silver lining
Be in the clouds

Have one's head in the clouds

Clover

Be happy as a pig in clover
Be/live/roll in clover

Club

Club someone on the head with
something
Be clubby with someone
Join the club!
Welcome to the club!

Cluck

Cluck like a mother hen
Someone is a dumb cluck

Clue

Not have a clue about something
Give me a clue!

Clumsy

Clumsy as an ox

Clutch

Clutch at straws in the wind
Come through in the clutch
Have someone in one's clutches

Coal

Carry coals to Newcastle
Rake/haul someone over the
coals

Coast

Coast along on something
The coast is clear
From coast-to-coast

Coat

Give an old idea a new coat of
paint
Hang on to someone's coattails
Sugar-coat something

Cobbler

A cobbler should stick to his last

Cock

Cock one's ears
Cock one's eye at someone
Cock of the walk
Knock something into a cocked hat
Something is cockeyed
Cock-and-bull story
Be cock-sure of something
Go/be cock-a-hoop over someone/something
Go off half-cocked

Cockles

Warm the cockles of one's heart

Code

Crack the code
Dress code

Coffee

Wake up and smell the coffee

Coffin

Another nail in one's coffin
Smoke coffin nails/sticks

Coin

Coin money right and left/hand-over-fist
Coin of the realm
Two sides of the coin
The other side of the coin
Toss/flip a coin
To coin a phrase
Pay someone back in his own coin

Cold

Cold hands, warm heart
Cold hard cash
Be left out in the cold

Give/get the cold shoulder
Keep someone/something in cold storage
Play with/get a cold deck
Someone/something is neither hot nor cold
Run/blow hot and cold
Something/someone makes one's blood run cold
A cold day in hell
Do something in cold blood
Pass out cold
Be cold as a dead fish
Get/have cold feet
Stop cold
Dash/throw cold water on something
Give/get cold comfort
Catch one's death of cold
Have someone/something cold
Feed a cold, starve a fever
Break out in a cold sweat
See someone/something in the cold light of day
Knock someone cold
Quit/stop/go cold turkey
The dice are cold
Kiss a mule, cure a cold
Be stone-cold dead in the market

Collar

Collar a crook
Get/be hot under the collar
Roman collar

College

Give something the old college try
Joe College
Cow college

Color

See the color of someone's money
Not like the color of someone's money

Someone/something is a horse of
   another/a different color
Something lends local color to
   something
Call to the colors
Haul down one's colors
Sail under false colors
Show one's true colors
Come through with flying colors
Look at the world through rose-
   colored glasses
Off-color joke
Be color-blind

Colt

As frisky as a colt

Comb

Comb the area
Go over something with a fine-
   toothed comb

Come

Come through in the clutch
Come what may
Come across with something
Come off second-best
Come hell or high water
Come clean
Come to a screeching halt
Come out smelling like a rose
Come up and see someone's etch-
   ings
Come on strong
Come back into the flock
Come out of one's shell
Come down on someone like a
   ton of bricks
Come a cropper
Come apart at the seams
Come back down to earth
Come down hard on someone
Come by something honestly
Come up in the world

Come to blows with someone
Come to grips with something
Come to one's senses
Come to the point
Come up for air
Come on like gangbusters
Come to terms with something/
   someone
Come to blows with someone
   over something
Come of age
Come into one's own
Come through with flying colors
Come down the pike
Come out of the closet
Come up to snuff
Come out of the woodwork
Come to grief
Come to pass
Come in on a wing and a prayer
Come to think of it
Good things come in small pack-
   ages
Chickens come home to roost
Till the cows come home
Someday your prince will come
First come, first served
The bigger they come, the harder
   they fall
Easy come, easy go
Blow something to kingdom come
If Mohammed won't come to the
   mountain
Know enough to come in out of
   the rain
It'll all come out in the wash
Something/someone doesn't come
   up to scratch
All good things must come to an
   end
When one's ship comes in
Something comes from left field
Something comes to a head
Something comes to a boil

Cross that bridge when one
comes to it
If worse comes to worse
If push comes to shove
What goes around, comes around
Something/someone comes up to
the mark/marc
Something comes into play
Something comes to light
Something comes in handy
Something comes full circle
Something is coming along
Everything's coming up roses
Not know whether one is coming
or going
Get what's coming to one
Have it coming to one
Have something coming out of
one's ears
Know where someone is coming
from
Have no kick coming
Johnny-come-lately
Here I come, ready or not!
Come and get it!
Come off it!
Come up and see me sometime!
Come with me to the Casbah!
Come home, all is forgiven!
You've got another think coming!
Come again?

Comeuppance

Get one's/give someone his come-
uppance

Comfort

Give/get cold comfort
All the comforts of home
Creature comforts
Slip into something more com-
fortable
Someone/something is as com-
fortable as an old shoe

Command

Your wish is my command

Commission

Something/someone is out of
commission

Committee

Welcoming committee
A camel is an elephant designed
by a committee

Common

Common sense
Common garden variety
Have something/nothing in com-
mon with someone
Meet on common ground
Have the common touch
Something is common knowl-
edge

Companion

Fall in with evil companions

Company

Misery loves company
Be known by the company one
keeps
Be a company man
Two's company, three's a crowd
Keep company with someone

Compare

Compare apples and oranges
Someone/something is beyond
compare
As compared to what?

Complexion

Have a peaches-and-cream complexion
Have a schoolgirl complexion
That puts a different complexion
on it!

Compliment

Return the compliment
Give/get a left/back-handed com-
  pliment
Fish for compliments
My compliments to the chef!

Conclusion

Draw a conclusion
Something is a foregone conclu-
  sion
Jump to conclusions

Concrete

Concrete numbers
Wear concrete boots

Condition

Something is in mint condition
Someone is in a delicate condition

Confidence

Confidence game/trick
Take someone into one's confi-
  dence
Give/get a vote of confidence

Confound

Be confounded over someone/
  something
Confound it all!

Conk

Conk out

Connect

Someone is well connected

Conquer

Divide and conquer
Love conquers all
Hail the conquering hero!

Conscience

Have a clear conscience
Have a twinge of conscience
Pay conscience money

Consider

Consider the source
Take something under considera-
  tion

Contempt

Familiarity breeds contempt
Hold someone/something in contempt
Someone/something is beneath
  contempt

Content

Do something to one's heart's
  content
Be as contented as a cow

Contention

Something is a bone of contention
Something is someone's contention

Contract

Put out a contract on someone
Ink someone to a contract
Boiler-plate contract

Contradict

Contradict oneself
Something is a contradiction in
  terms

Conviction

Have the courage of one's convic-
  tions

Coo

Bill and coo

Cook

Cook someone's goose
Cook the books

Cook on all four/the front burn-
ers
Cook up something
Be chief cook and bottle-washer
Too many cooks spoil the broth
Take a Cook's Tour
Be cooking with gas
Live in a pressure cooker
What's cooking?

Cookie

Catch someone with his hand in
the cookie jar
Someone is a tough/smart cookie
Toss one's cookies
That's the way the cookie crum-
bles!

Cool

Cool down/off
Cool something/someone out
Cool one's heels
Be a cool cat
Play it cool
Be cool as a cucumber
Blow/lose/keep one's cool
Cool it!

Coon

Haven't seen someone/something
in a coon's age

Coop

Fly the coop
Be cooped up

Coot

Bald as a coot
Crazy as a coot
Someone is an old coot

Cop

Cop a plea
Cop out of something
Cop an attitude

Cop a feel
Cheese it, the cops!

Copy

Copycat
Blot one's copybook

Core

Be rotten to the core

Cork

Pop/blow one's cork
Someone/something is a corker
Put a cork in it!

Corn

Be full of corn
Tread on someone's corns
Be a cornball
For corn's sake!

Corner

Corner the market
Be driven into a corner
Be in a tight corner
Be in someone's corner
Paint oneself into a corner
Back someone into a corner
Turn the corner
See something/someone out of
the corner of one's eye
Cut corners
Go to the four corners of the
earth for someone/something

Corps

Drum someone out of the corps

Cost

Without counting the cost
Know the cost of everything and
the value of nothing
Do/get something at all/any cost
Something costs a pretty penny
Something costs an arm and a leg

Cotton

Be sitting on high cotton
Take the cotton out of one's
  ears
Do/don't cotton to someone/
  something
Cottonpicker
Keep your cotton-pickin' hands
  off!

Couch

Be a couch case
Be a couch potato

Cough

Cough something up

Couldn't

Couldn't care less about some-
  one/something
Couldn't agree with someone
  more
Couldn't hit the broad side of a
  barn
Couldn't punch/fight one's way
  out of a paper bag

Counsel

Keep one's own counsel

Count

Count sheep
Count noses
Count to ten
Count one's blessings
Count one's beads
Don't count your chickens before
  they're hatched
Be down for the count
It's the thought that counts
Close only counts in horseshoes
Stand up and be counted
Without counting the cost
Count me out!

Counter

Do something under the counter
Counterculture

Country

Another country heard from
A man without a country
You can take the boy out of the
  country, but you can't take the
  country out of the boy
Win/lose/beat someone by a
  country mile
One's country cousin
It's a free country!

Courage

Screw/pluck up one's courage
Get Dutch courage
Have the courage of one's convic-
  tions
Have raw courage

Course

As a matter of course
Let something run its course
Something is par for the course
Take a crash course in something
All in due course
Keep on course

Court

Be laughed out of court
Pay court to someone
Have one's day in court
Have a friend at court
Throw oneself on the mercy of
  the court
Kangaroo court
The ball's in your court!
See you in court!

Cousin

Kissin' cousin
Country cousin

Cover

Cover one's tracks
Cover a lot of ground
Cover story
Cover up for someone/something
Cover the waterfront
Work under cover
Run for cover
Can't judge a book by its cover
Have a good cover
Blow one's cover

Cow

Cow college
Be as contented as a cow
Sacred cow
Till the cows come home
Holy cow!
Why buy the cow when the milk is free?
How now, brown cow?

Cowboy

Drugstore cowboy
Rhinestone cowboy
Ride 'em, cowboy!

Crack

Crack a joke
Crack the whip
Crack the books
Crack someone up
Crack down on someone/something
Crack the code
Someone/something is a hard/tough nut to crack
First crack out of the box
Take a crack at something
Not crack a smile
At the crack of dawn
Someone/something's not all it's cracked up to be
Something falls between the cracks

Put paper over the cracks
Someone goes crackers
Crackpot idea
Get cracking!

Cradle

Cradle an asp to one's bosom
Rob the cradle
Rock the cradle
From the cradle to the grave
Cradled in the lap of luxury

Cram

Cram something down someone's throat
Cram something where the sun don't shine

Cramp

Cramp someone's style
Suffer writer's cramp

Crap

Crap out
Someone is full of crap
Feel crappy
Go to the crapper
Cut the crap!

Crash

Crash the gate
Crash out
Take a crash course in something
Find someplace to crash
Be a crashing bore

Crawl

Crawl out of the woodwork
Something/someone makes one's flesh crawl
You have to crawl before you can walk
Go on a pub crawl
The place is crawling with something

Give/get the creepie-crawlies

Crazy

Crazy like a fox
Go stir crazy
Something works/goes like crazy
Be crazy as a bedbug/coot/loon
Make someone crazy
Be boy/girl crazy
Someone is just a crazy, mixed-up kid
Crazy, man!

Cream

Cream rises to the top
Cream someone
The cream of the crop
Ice cream suit
I scream, you scream, we all scream for ice cream
Someone is a cream puff
Have a peaches-and-cream complexion

Creature

Creature comforts
Someone is a creature of habit

Credibility

Credibility gap
Blow one's credibility

Credit

Credit someone else for something
Give credit where credit is due
Take all the credit
Be a credit to someone/something
Something does one credit

Creek

Be up the creek without a paddle
If the Lord be willing and the creek don't rise

Creep

Something/someone creeps up on someone
Something/someone gives one the creeps
Give/get the creepie-crawlies

Cricket

Something/someone is not entirely cricket
As merry as a cricket

Crime

Crime does not pay
Something is a real crime
Let the punishment fit the crime

Crisp

Get burned to a crisp

Crocodile

Cry crocodile tears
After awhile, crocodile!

Crook

Crook the elbow
By hook or by crook
Collar a crook
Something/someone is crooked as a pretzel

Crop

The cream of the crop
Have a bumper crop
Something crops up
Come a cropper

Cross

Cross the line
Cross someone's path
Cross someone's palm with silver
Cross the T's and dot the I's
Cross that bridge when you come to it
Cross one's heart and hope to die

Cross swords with someone
Cross the Rubicon
Have one's cross to bear
Be as cross as two sticks/a bear
Carry one's cross
Nail someone to the cross
Get caught in the cross fire
Something crosses one's mind
Keep one's fingers crossed
Get/have one's wires crossed
Look cross-eyed at someone
Be at cross-purposes with some-
one/something
Double/triple-cross someone

Crow

Eat crow
Have something to crow about
As the crow flies
Black as a crow

Crowd

Be ahead of the crowd
Just another face in the crowd
Two's company, three's a crowd
Far from the madding crowd
There's one in every crowd!

Crown

Uneasy lies the head that wears
the crown
One's crowning glory

Cruise

Cruise the area
Shakedown cruise
Be cruisin' for a bruisin'

Crumble

That's the way the cookie crum-
bles!

Crush

Have a crush on someone
Deal someone a crushing blow

I'm crushed!

Crust

Someone has a lot of crust
The upper crust

Crutch

Something is about as funny as a
broken crutch
Need a crutch to remember something

Cry

Cry like a baby
Cry for the moon
Cry all the way to the bank
Cry one's eyes out
Cry one's heart out
Cry in one's beer
Cry uncle
Cry in the wilderness
Cry wolf
Cry alligator/crocodile tears
Cry for mercy
Be in full cry
Laugh until you cry
Something is a far cry from some-
thing
Don't cry over spilt milk
Don't cry before you're hurt
Need a shoulder to cry on
Hue and cry
Have a crying need for someone/
something
Something is a crying shame
Crying towel
Crying the blues
For crying out loud!
For crying in the bucket!
Cry havoc!

Crystal

Be clear as crystal
Gaze into one's crystal ball

Cucumber

Be cool as a cucumber

Cud

Chew the cud

Cudgel

Take up the cudgels for someone/
   something

Cue

Take one's cue from someone/
   something

Cuff

Cuff someone's ears
Talk/speak off the cuff
Something is off the cuff
Shoot one's cuffs

Culture

Culture vulture
Counterculture

Cup

Someone/something is/is not
   one's cup of tea
One's cup runneth over
There's many a slip between the
   cup and the lip
Have a cup of kindness
Be in one's cups
Something is a tempest in a tea-
   cup

Curdle

Give/get a look that would curdle milk
Blood-curdling yell

Cure

An ounce of prevention is worth
   a pound of cure
Something will either cure you or
   kill you

Take the cure
Kiss a mule, cure a cold

Curiosity

Curiosity killed the cat

Curl

Curl up and die
Something is enough to curl one's
   hair

Current

Swim against the current

Curry

Curry favor with someone

Curse

Light a candle or curse the dark-
   ness
Curses!

Curtain

Take a curtain call
Take one's final curtain
Ring down the curtain on some-
   one/something
Call it curtains
Something is curtains for some-
   one

Curve

Throw someone a curve

Customer

Someone is a tough customer
The customer is always right
Only one to a customer!

Cut

Cut someone off at the knees
Cut someone dead
Cut to the chase
Cut the Gordian knot
Cut up the pie
Cut one's own throat

Cut someone to the quick
Cut up rough
Cut off someone's water
Cut a long story short
Cut 'em off at the pass
Cut corners
Cut someone down to size
Cut one's eyeteeth on something
Cut the ground out from under
  someone
Cut off one's nose to spite one's
  face
Cut the mustard
Cut someone/something to the
  bone
Cut the wind out of someone's
  sails
Cut capers
Cut something fine/close
Cut a rug
Cut and run
Cut one's losses
Cut a swath
Cut near the bone
Cut a fine figure
Someone/something doesn't cut it
Someone is/isn't cut out for
  something
Someone/something is a cut
  above someone/something
Someone/something is cut from
  whole cloth

Something is cut and dried
Something is so thick you could
  cut it with a knife
Run around like a chicken with
  its head cut off
Like/not like the cut of someone's
  jib
Be cut from the same bolt of
  cloth
The kindest/unkindest cut of all
Have one's work cut out for one
Something is cut and dried
Something cuts across the grain
Something cuts no ice
Something cuts both ways
Be on the cutting edge of some-
  thing
Cutting remark
Cutthroat business
Cut it out!
Cut off my legs and call me
  Shorty!
Cut the crap!
Shave and a haircut, six bits!
Fish or cut bait!

Cute

Cute as a bug/bug's ear
Cute as a button
Cute as a bedbug
Someone has a case of the cutes
Someone/something is too cutesy

D

Dab

Be smack dab in the middle of
  something
A little dab'll do ya!

Daddy

Someone/something is the big
  daddy of them all
Be someone's sugar daddy

Beat me daddy, eight to the bar

Dagger

Look/stare daggers at someone
With daggers drawn
Cloak-and-dagger business

Daily

Do one's daily dozen
Play the daily double

Daisy

Fresh as a daisy
The Daisy Chain
Push up daisies

Dam

Something is water over the dam

Damn

Damn someone/something with
   faint praise
Not worth a tinker's damn
Not give a damn
Damn the torpedoes!

Damp

Dampen someone's spirits
Put the damper on something

Dance

Dance with the guy that brung
   ya
Dance attendance on someone
Dance to another/different tune
Dance at someone's funeral
Dance on someone's grave
Dance the night away
Give someone a song and dance
Don't dance on the table where
   you eat
If you dance, you have to pay the
   piper/fiddler
Put on one's dancing shoes
Bring on the dancing girls!

Dander

Get one's dander up

Dandy

Fine and dandy
Candy is dandy, but liquor is
   quicker

Danger

Defy danger
Something is fraught with danger
A little knowledge is a dangerous
   thing
Live dangerously

Dark

Born under a dark star
By dark of night
Be afraid of the dark
Take a shot in the dark
Tall, dark and handsome
As dark as a dungeon
Whistle in the dark
Keep someone in the dark
Be in the dark about something
Someone is a dark horse
It's always darkest before the
   dawn
Not darken one's door again
Light a candle or curse the dark-
   ness

Darn

You're darned if you do and
   darned if you don't
Darn tootin'!
Darned if I know!

Dash

Dash off a line to someone
Dash cold water on something
Dash someone's hopes
Make a dash for something
Dash it all!

Date

Date the stork
Have a heavy date
Bring someone up to date

Dawn

Be shot at dawn
It's always darkest before the
   dawn
At the crack of dawn
Came the dawn about something
Something finally dawns on
   someone

Day

Day in, day out
Day of reckoning
See something/someone in the
   cold light of day
Tomorrow's another day
Bright as day
Another day, another dollar
An apple a day keeps the doctor
   away
Be a day late and a dollar short
Someone/something has had its
   day
A little late in the day for some-
   thing
Take it one day at a time
As happy as the day is long
Something/someone carries the
   day
Have a field day with someone/
   something
Name the day
Just not one's day
Have one's day in court
The order of the day
See the light of day
Call it a day
Wouldn't give someone the time
   of day
Someone/something saves the

day
Something is clear/plain as day
Any day of the week
Something is not exactly a day at
   the beach
Dream the day away
As different as night and day
Forever and a day
Save for a rainy day
Every dog has his day
Make a day of it
Be as honest as the day is long
Pass the time of day
Rome wasn't built in a day
A cold day in hell
Today is the first day of the rest
   of your life
Have three squares a day
Live for the day
Be one's lucky day
Red-letter day
Fall on evil days
All in a day's work
Someone/something has seen bet-
   ter days
Someone's days are numbered
The good old days
Dog days
Salad days
Horse and buggy days
Scare/knock/beat the living day-
   lights out of someone
Nine/ninety-day wonder
Make my day!
That'll be the day!
In this day and age!
What a difference a day makes!
Great day in the morning!
Have a nice day!
In all my born days!

Dead

Dead as a doornail
Dead men tell no tales

Dead zone
Someone is a dead duck
Someone is dead meat
Cut someone dead
Run into a dead end
Someone is a dead ringer for
  someone
Be dead broke
Be dead on one's feet
Be dead tired
Be dead to the world
Be stone-cold dead in the market
Be dead in the water
Be dead drunk
Be cold as a dead fish
Be in dead earnest about some-
  thing
Better dead than Red
Beat/flog a dead horse
Loud enough to wake the dead
Wouldn't be caught dead in
  something
Would steal a dead fly from a
  blind spider
Stop dead in one's tracks
Someone/something is dead
  weight
Let the dead bury the dead
Someone/something is dead and
  gone
Someone is dead set on/against
  something
Step into dead men's shoes
Someone is a deadbeat
Deadpan look
Be dead-cold sober
Knock 'em dead!
Cheer up, you'll soon be dead!
Drop dead!
Over my dead body!

Deaf

Something falls on deaf ears
Turn a deaf ear to someone

Be deaf, dumb and blind about
  someone/something
Be deaf as a post
Be stone deaf
Be tone deaf

Deal

Deal someone a crushing blow
Deal off the bottom of the deck
Get a raw deal
Give/get a square/fair deal
Someone/something queers the
  deal
Give/get a sweetheart deal
Something is a done deal
Make a big deal out of something
Juice dealer
Double-dealing
Big deal!
What's the big deal?

Dear

Dear John letter
Run for dear life
The dear/dearly departed

Death

A fate worse than death
Be bored to death
Between life and death
Someone/something will be the
  death of one yet
Badger someone to death
Hang on like grim death
Something has been done to
  death
Nickel-and-dime someone to
  death
Be tickled to death
As sure as death and taxes
Catch one's death of cold
Sign one's own death warrant
A matter of life and death
Kiss of death

Look like death warmed over
Be sick to death of someone/
  something
Be at death's door
Death-defying feat

Deceive

What a tangled web we weave
  when first we practice to deceive
Appearances can be deceiving

Deck

Have the deck stacked against
  one
Something/someone is the joker/
  wild card in the deck
Load the deck
Something is as useless as rear-
  ranging deck chairs on the
  Titanic
Get/play with a cold deck
Deal off the bottom of the deck
Someone is not playing with a
  full deck
Clear the decks for action
Be all decked out in something
Hit the deck!

Deep

Give someone the deep freeze
Jump/go off the deep end
Between the devil and the deep
  blue sea
Be in something too deep
Still waters run deep
Be in deep water
Asleep in the deep
Beauty is only skin deep
Have deep pockets
Deep-six someone/something
Be knee-deep in something

Defeat

Snatch victory from the jaws of

defeat
The thrill of victory, the agony of
  defeat

Defense

The best defense is a good offense
Let one's defenses down
Be on the defensive

Defy

Defy danger
Death-defying feat

Degree

To the nth degree
Give/get the third degree
Something is only a matter of
  degrees

Delay

Justice delayed is justice denied

Delicate

Someone is in a delicate condition

Delight

Idiot's delight

Deliver

Deliver the goods
Signed, sealed and delivered

Den

Den of iniquity
Beard the lion in his den

Dent

Not make a dent in something

Deny

Justice delayed is justice denied

Depart

The dear/dearly departed

Depth

Be out of one's depth
Something is beyond one's depth

Deserve

One good turn deserves another

Design

Have designs on someone
A camel is an elephant designed
by a committee

Desire

One's heart's desire
Something/someone leaves a lot
to be desired

Desserts

Get one's just desserts

Device

Be left to one's own devices

Devil

Strike a bargain/make a pact
with the devil
Someone is full of the devil
Between the devil and the deep
blue sea
Have the devil to pay
Give the devil his due
Look like the devil
Let the devil take the hind-
most
Speak of the devil and he's sure
to appear
Be a child of the devil
Be in league with the devil
Cast out devils
Idle fingers/hands are the devil's
workshop
Have a devil-may-care attitude/
personality
Go to the devil!
The devil you say!

Dew

Fresh as the morning dew
Good old mountain dew
Dewy-eyed look

Dibs

Have dibs on something

Dice

The dice are cold/hot
Roll the big dice
Load the dice
No dice!

Die

Die with one's boots on
Die on the vine
Die laughing
Something is to die for
Let the old cat die
Old habits die hard
Never say die
Cross one's heart and hope to die
Do or die
Old soldiers never die, they just
fade away
Curl up and die
He who lives by the sword, dies
by the sword
Thought you'd died and gone to
heaven
The operation was a success but
the patient died
The die is cast!
Laugh, I thought I'd die!
Eat, drink and be merry, for
tomorrow you may die!

Different

Different strokes for different
folks
Sing/whistle a different tune
Take a different tack
Someone/something is a horse of
a different color

Dare to be different
As different as night and day
Dance to a different tune
Someone/something is a different
  breed of cat
March to a different drummer
The same but different
Beg to differ with someone
Split the difference
Same difference
What a difference a day makes!

Dig

Dig up the dirt on someone
Dig one's own grave
Dig in one's heels
Dig oneself into a hole
Gold-digger
Dig in!
Dig you later, alligator!
Plant you now, dig you later!
Hot diggety/diggety-dog!

Dignity

Something is beneath one's dignity
Stand on one's dignity
Not dignify something with an
  answer

Dilemma

Be on the horns of a dilemma

Dim

Take a dim view of someone/
  something
Someone is a little dim
Dimwit

Dime

Wouldn't pay a dime for someone's chances
Stop on a dime
Something/someone is a dime a
  dozen

Nickel-and-dime someone to
  death
Get off the dime!
Brother, can you spare a dime?

Dine

Wine and dine someone

Ding

Someone is a dingbat
Someone is a real ding-a-ling
Ring-a-ding-ding!

Dip

Dip into the till
Be a double-dipper
Go skinny-dipping
Well, I'll be dipped!

Dirt

Sweep the dirt under the rug/
  carpet
Dig up the dirt on someone
Hit pay dirt
Eat dirt
Something is dirt cheap
Dish the dirt
Do someone dirt
Treat someone like dirt
Do the quick and dirty to some-
  one
Play dirty pool
Give someone a dirty look
Pull a dirty trick
Get down and dirty
Wash/air one's dirty linen in
  public
Dirty one's hands
Do someone's dirty work
You dirty rat!
Hit the dirt!

Discretion

Discretion is the better part of
  valor

Throw discretion to the wind

Disguise

Something is a blessing in disguise

Dish

Dish the dirt
Take anything anyone can dish out
Something/someone is not/is one's dish of tea
Dishwater blonde
Dull as dishwater
Something tastes like dishwater

Disposition

Someone has an ugly disposition

Distance

Keep one's distance
Be within striking distance
The shortest distance between two points is a straight line

Ditch

Ditch someone
Fight to the last ditch
Make a last-ditch effort
Dull as ditch-water

Dive

Dive into something headfirst
Take a dive
Go into a nosedive
This place is a real dive

Divide

Divide and conquer

Divine

Divine intervention
To err is human, to forgive, divine

Dixie

Land of Dixie
You ain't just whistlin' Dixie!
Is it true what they say about Dixie?

Do

Do one's stuff
Do one's own thing
Do a number on someone
Do a double take
Do something for two pins/cents
Do a slow burn
Do as best one can
Do someone dirt
Do one's level best
Do something up brown
Do or die
Do away with something/someone
Do the trick
Do someone in
Do someone out of something
Do drugs
Do time/hard time
Do as I say, not as I do
When in Rome, do as the Romans do
Monkey see, monkey do
One's left hand doesn't know what one's right hand is doing
Anything worth doing is worth doing well
When all is said and done
Something is done to a turn
Handsome/beauty is as handsome/beauty does
Let George do it!
No can do!
Can do!
Nothing doing!

Doctor

Doctor the books

An apple a day keeps the doctor away
Doctors can bury their mistakes
Just what the doctor ordered!

Dodge

Dodge the issue
Time to get outta Dodge!

Dog

Dog days
Be sick as a dog
Every dog has his day
Work like a dog
Be top dog
Like a dog worrying a bone
Put on a dog and pony show
Have to see a man about a dog
Treat someone like a dog
A case of the tail wagging the dog
You can't teach an old dog new tricks
Love/like me, love/like my dog
Put on the dog
Have a hair of the dog that bit one
Older than God's dog
Someone is a dog in the manger
Something shouldn't happen to a dog
Never follow a dog act
Sea dog
Rain cats and dogs
Fight like cats and dogs
Go to the dogs
Barking dogs seldom bite
Call off the dogs
Let sleeping dogs lie
Lead a dog's life
Haven't seen someone in a dog's age
Have a hangdog look
Thick as ticks on a hounddog
Be in the doghouse

Dog-eat-dog world
Be dog-tired
Shaggy-dog story
Bird-dog the situation
Someone is a hot-dogger
Hot dog!
Hot diggety-dog!
Man bites dog!

Doll

Someone is a living doll
Get all dolled up

Dollar

The almighty dollar
Bet one's bottom dollar
Be sound as a dollar
Another day, another dollar
The sixty-four dollar question
A day late and a dollar short
Feel/look like a million dollars
Born into the world owing two dollars
Bet dollars to donuts
Watch your pennies and the dollars will take care of themselves
As hot as a two-dollar pistol
As phony/queer as a three-dollar bill

Done

Something has been done to death
After/when all is said and done
No sooner said than done
What's done is done
Something is a done deal
Someone is done for
Something is easier said than done
Man works from sun to sun, but woman's work is never done
Something is done to a turn
Something is over and done with

Donkey

Talk the hind leg off a donkey
Not see someone/something in
  donkey's years
When donkeys fly!

Donut

Keep your eye on the donut, not
  on the hole
Bet dollars to donuts

Door

When one door closes, another
  opens
The door swings both ways
Show someone the door
Be at death's door
Keep the wolf from the door
Not darken one's door again
Get a foot in the door
Lock the barn door after the
  horse is stolen
When the wolf is at the door,
  love flies out the window
Behind closed doors
Be a doormat
Something is right on one's door-
  step
Dead as a doornail

Dope

Dope something out
Get the inside dope on someone/
  something

Dose

Give someone a dose of his own
  medicine

Dot

Be right on the dot
Cross the T's and dot the I's

Double

Double or nothing
Double in brass

Do double duty
See double
Get/have double trouble
Give/get the double shuffle
Play the daily double
Do a double take
Give someone a double whammy
Something is double–Dutch to
  someone
Check and double-check
Double-dealing
Be a double-dipper
On the double!

Doubt

Plant the seeds of doubt
Beyond the shadow of a doubt
Give someone the benefit of the
  doubt
Be a doubting Thomas
No doubt about it!

Dough

Be rolling in dough

Down

Take a trip down memory lane
Go down with the ship
Batten down the hatches
Something big is going down
Have a down on someone
Play/tone something down
Sell someone down the river
Talk down to someone
Something suits someone right
  down to the ground/socks
Put one's foot down
Take someone down a peg
Bring down the house
Lay down the law
Cut someone down to size
Fall down on the job
Hit someone when he's down
Live something down
Be down at the heels

Be down and out
Be down on one's luck
Be down in the mouth/dumps/
  chops
Get down and dirty
Be down for the count
Pour money down the drain
Steal anything that's not nailed
  down
Back down
Come back down to earth
Bear down on someone/some-
  thing
Let one's hair down
Go down to the wire
When the chips are down
Get down to brass tacks
Win hands down
Breathe down someone's neck
Water something down
Get bogged down in something
Turn thumbs down on some-
  thing/someone
Go down a blind alley
It all boils down to something
Come down the pike
Bring someone down
Jump down someone's throat
Be down so long it looks like up
Wolf down one's food
Get down to cases
Something/someone goes down
  the tubes/drain
Look down one's nose at some-
  one/something
Go down swinging
Have something down pat
Pick 'em up and lay 'em down
Come down on someone like a
  ton of bricks
You can't keep a good man down
Catch someone with his pants
  down
Buckle/knuckle down

Garbage/chow down
Come down hard on someone
Bring/ring the curtain down on
  someone/something
Let one's defenses down
Get down to the short strokes
Let someone down easy
Cram/force/shove something
  down someone's throat
Turn the place upside down
Go down to the sea in ships
Get down to the nitty-gritty
Shake someone down
Slap someone down
Send shivers down one's spine
Haul down one's colors
Take something lying down
Something is a downer
Everything's going down-hill
Be down-to-earth
Get the low-down on someone/
  something
Give someone a dressing-down
Knock-down, drag-out fight
Down the hatch!
Pipe down!

Dozen

Do one's daily dozen
Baker's dozen
Something/someone is a dime a
  dozen
Talk nineteen to the dozen
Something is six of one and half-
  a-dozen of the other

Drag

Drag one's feet/heels/tail
Drag someone's name through
  the mud
Wild horses couldn't drag someone away from something
Someone/something is a real
  drag

Main drag
Look like something the cat
    dragged in
Knock-down, drag-out fight
Look what the cat dragged in!

Drain

Pour money down the drain
Something/someone goes down
    the drain
The brain drain

Draw

Draw the battle lines
Draw a blank about something
Draw a bead on someone
Draw the line at something
Draw first blood
Draw the purse strings
Draw in one's horns
Draw one's last breath
Draw a conclusion
Beat someone to the draw
The luck of the draw
Be quick on the draw
Have to draw someone a picture
Win, lose or draw
With daggers drawn
Back to the drawing board
Draw-and-quarter someone

Dream

Dream up something
Dream the day away
Something goes like a dream
Pipe dream
You're a dreamer!
What are you, dreaming?

Dress

Dress for success
Dress code
Dressed to the nines/hilt
Dressed to kill

All dressed up and no place to go
Give someone a dressing-down

Drift

Drift off to dreamland
Get the drift of something
As pure as the driven snow

Drink

Drink like a fish
Drink something in
Drink someone under the table
Something is meat and drink to
    someone
Drive someone to drink
You can lead a horse to water,
    but you can't make him drink
Eat, drink and be merry, for
    tomorrow you may die!

Drive.

Drive someone bananas
Drive someone around the bend
Drive someone to drink
Drive a hard bargain
Drive like a madman
Drive home a point
Drive someone to the wall
Bad money drives out good
Be driven into a tight corner
Sunday driver
Slave driver
Backseat driver
Be in the driver's seat

Drop

Drop a bombshell
Drop a brick
Drop the ball
Drop someone/something like a
    hot potato
Drop in one's tracks
Drop like flies
Drop a bundle on something
Drop acid

Wait for the other shoe to drop
Get the drop on someone
At the drop of a hat
Quiet enough to hear a pin drop
Bop/shop till you drop
Someone/something drops off the
  face of the earth
Name-dropper
Drop dead!

Drown

Drown one's sorrows/troubles
Look like a drowned rat
Throw water on a drowning man

Drug

Something is a drug on the mar-
  ket
Do drugs
Drugstore cowboy

Drum

Drum up business
Drum someone out of the corps
Something/someone is tight as a
  drum
Beat the drum for something
March to a different drummer

Drunk

Be blind/roaring/dead drunk
Be drunk as a skunk/lord
Spend money like a drunken
  sailor/Indian
Be punch-drunk

Dry

Dry as a bone
Dry as dust
Dry up and blow away
Not a dry eye in the house
Hang someone out to dry
Leave someone high and dry
Keep one's powder dry
Not be dry behind the ears

You never miss the water till the
  well runs dry
Bleed someone dry
Act on something before the ink
  is dry
Something is cut and dried

Duck

Someone is a sitting duck
Someone is a dead duck
Someone is a lame duck
Someone is a queer duck
Something is duck soup
Like a duck takes to water
Like water off a duck's back
Get/have one's ducks in a row
Play ducks and drakes
Everything is just ducky!
Nice weather for ducks!

Due

Give the devil his due
With all due respect
All in due course
Give credit where credit is due
Pay one's dues

Duke

Duke the waiter
Put up one's dukes

Dull

Dull as dish/ditch water
Never a dull moment
All work and no play makes Jack
  a dull boy

Dumb

Dumb like a fox
Dumb as a doorpost
Dumb blonde
Someone is a dumb bunny/cluck
Be deaf, dumb and blind about
  something/someone
Play dumb

Be dumber than a box of rocks
Dumb, rotten luck!
Dummy up!

Dump

Dump all over someone
Be down in the dumps

Dust

When the dust settles
Bite the dust
Dry as dust
Shake the dust from one's feet
Ashes to ashes, dust to dust
Pardon/watch my dust!

Dutch

Dutch treat
Get Dutch courage
Go Dutch
Have/be a Dutch uncle
Something is double-Dutch to
    someone
Don't that beat the Dutch?

Duty

Over/above and beyond the call
    of duty
Do double duty
All in the line of duty
Duty calls!

E

E

Get "E" for effort

Each

To each his own
Be at each other's throats
Made for each other
At each and every turn

Eager

Someone is an eager beaver

Eagle

Have/keep an eagle eye out for
    something
Someone is a legal eagle/beagle

Ear

Lend an ear
Put a bug in someone's ear

Set someone back on his ear
Bend someone's ear
Grin from ear to ear
Something goes in one ear and
    out the other
Have an ear for something
Turn a deaf ear to someone
Have/keep one's ear to the
    ground
Talk/chew someone's ear off
Cute as a bug's ear
Put a flea in someone's ear
Play something by ear
Throw someone out on his ear
You can't make a silk purse out
    of a sow's ear
Not be dry behind the ears
Get one's ears lowered
Be all ears

Can't believe one's ears
Be up to one's ears in something
Walls have ears
Something is music to one's ears
Little pitchers have big ears
Have something coming out of
  one's ears
Something falls on deaf ears
Have cauliflower ears
Someone's ears are burning
Have one's ears on
Box/cuff someone's ears
Take the cotton out of one's ears
Rabbit ears
Blow it out your ear!

Early

Early to bed and early to rise,
  makes a man healthy, wealthy
  and wise
Bright and early
You have to get up pretty early
  in the morning to...
The early bird gets/catches the
  worm
Vote early and often

Earn

Earn one's keep
Earn a nice piece of change
Earn the wages of sin
Earn the bread
Earn one's wings/spurs/salt
Learn and earn
A penny saved is a penny earned

Earnest

Be in dead earnest about something

Earth

Someone is the salt of the earth
Go to the four corners of the
  earth for someone/something
Someone/something drops off the
face of the earth
Move heaven and earth for some-
  one/something
Someone is the scum of the earth
Come back down to earth
Something is heaven on earth
Someone is hell on earth
Run someone/something to earth
Pay the earth for something
Be down-to-earth
What on God's green earth?

Ease

Ease off
Be ill at ease

East

East is east and west is west

Easy

Easy as ABC/pie
Easy come, easy go
Easy money
Easy does it
Something is easy pickin's
Someone is easy on the eyes
Be free and easy
Be on easy street
As easy as falling off a log
As easy as taking candy from a
  baby
Breathe easy
Get off easy
Let someone down easy
Easier said than done

Eat

Eat the forbidden fruit
Eat like a horse/pig
Eat one's words
Eat someone out of house and
  home
Eat high off the hog
Eat crow/dirt/humble pie
Eat like a bird

Eat one's cake and have it too
Eat one's hat
Eat one's heart out
You are what you eat
Don't dance on the table where
　you eat
Hungry enough to eat a horse
Have someone eating out of your
　hand
The proof of the pudding is in
　the eating
Dog-eat-dog world
Moth-eaten
Eat, drink and be merry, for
　tomorrow you may die!
Go eat worms!
What's eating you?

Edge

Be on the cutting edge of some-
　thing
Have an edge on someone/some-
　thing
Something/someone sets one's
　teeth on edge
Sit on the edge of one's chair
Live on the edge
Be on the razor's edge
Can't get a word in edgewise

Eel

Slippery as an eel
Wriggle like an eel

Effort

Get "E"/"A" for effort
Make a last-ditch effort

Egg

Egg someone on
Lay an egg
Be a bad/good egg
Want an egg in one's beer
Have egg on one's face
Bald as a peeled egg

Goose egg
Nest egg
Put/have all one's eggs in one's
　basket
Walk on eggs/eggshells
Kill the goose that lays the
　golden eggs
Can't make an omelet without
　breaking some eggs
Sure as eggs is eggs
Butter-and-egg money
Go suck eggs!
Last one in the pool is a rotten
　egg!
Which came first, the chicken or
　the egg!

Eight

Be behind the eight ball
Beat me daddy, eight to the bar!

Elbow

Elbow grease
Elbow room
Crook/bend one's elbow
Not know one's ass from his
　elbow
Be out at the elbows
Rub elbows with someone

Element

Be in one's element
Elementary, my dear Watson!

Elephant

An elephant never forgets
Have a memory like an elephant
As big as an elephant
A camel is an elephant designed
　by a committee
White elephant

End

End it or mend it
Run into a dead end

Stay/fight to the bitter end
Something is the bitter end
Jump/go off the deep end
Hold up one's end
Someone/something is the living
end
Something makes one's hair stand
on end
Be at wits' end
The business end of a gun
The end of the road
Be at the end of one's rope/tether
Get the short end of the stick
Not know which end is up
The beginning of the end
The end of the line
See a ray of light at the end of
the tunnel
The end justifies the means
The end of the rainbow
All's well that ends well
Burn the candle at both ends
Make both ends meet
Be at loose ends
Play both ends against the middle
The be-all and end-all of some-
thing

Enemy

Be one's own worst enemy
Have an army of enemies
With friends like you, who needs
enemies?

Energy

Energy crunch/crisis
Bundle of energy

Enjoy

Lay back and enjoy it

Enough

Old enough to know better
Give someone enough rope and
he'll hang himself

Something looks good enough to
eat
Not know enough to come in out
of the rain
Something is not enough to stick
in one's eye
Hungry enough to eat a horse
Something is enough to make
someone turn over in his grave
Leave/let well enough alone
Enough said!
Enough is enough!

Envy

Be green with envy

Err

To err is human, to forgive,
divine
Know/learn the error of one's
ways
By trial and error

Essence

Time is of the essence

Etch

Something is/isn't etched in stone
Come up and see someone's etch-
ings

Eternal

Hope springs eternal
The eternal triangle

Even

Break even
Keep on an even keel

Evening

The shank of the evening
Ladies of the evening

Event

Blessed event
Chain of events

Every

Every man has his price
Every cloud has a silver lining
Every dog has his day
Every inch a king/lady
Every now and then
Every time one turns around
There's a rotten apple in every barrel
There's one in every crowd
Run around/go every which way
Everybody and his brother
Everybody loves a lover
Everything but the kitchen sink
There's a first time for every-thing
Know the cost of everything and the value of nothing
Everything's coming up roses
Every man for himself!
Everybody wants to get into the act!

Evil

Money is the root of all evil
Fall in with evil companions
Give someone the evil eye
Something/someone is a neces-sary evil
Hear/see/speak no evil
Fall on evil days
Choose the lesser of two evils

Example

Set a good example
Make an example of someone/something

Excuse

A bad excuse is better than none
Ignorance of the law is no ex-cuse
Lame/flimsy excuse
What's your excuse for living?

Existence

Someone is the bane of one's existence

Expense

Bear the expense
Spare no expense

Experience

Experience is the best teacher
Have a chilling experience
Charge/chalk something up to experience
Have a mind-boggling experience
Have a hair-raising experience

Explore

Explore every avenue

Extra.

Go the extra mile
Find a little something extra in the pay envelope

Eye

As far as the eye can see
Keep your eye on the sparrow
Give someone the evil eye
In the bat of an eye
Someone doesn't bat an eye at something
Give someone the fish eye
Sleep with one eye open
Give someone a black eye
In the twinkling of an eye
See eye to eye with someone
An eye for an eye, a tooth for a tooth
Have fire in one's eye
Have/keep an eagle eye out for someone/something
Be in the public eye
More to something than meets the eye

Keep your eye on the donut, not on the hole

Beauty is in the eye of the beholder

Turn a blind eye to something

Not blink an eye

See something out of the corner of one's eye

Better than a sharp poke in the eye

In the blink of an eye

The hand is quicker than the eye

Have an eye for something

Cock one's eye at someone

Give someone the glad eye

Could see something with half an eye

Not a dry eye in the house

Keep one's eye on the ball

Keep a weather eye out

Look/can't look someone straight in the eye

To the naked eye

Look at something with a jaundiced eye

Someone is blind in one eye and can't see out of the other

Eyes are the windows to the soul

Bat one's eyes at someone

Someone/something is easy on the eyes

Hit someone right between the eyes

Have eyes bigger than one's stomach

Can't believe one's eyes

Make eyes at someone

Make/cast sheep's eyes at someone

Someone/something is a sight for sore eyes

Close one's eyes to something

Keep one's eyes peeled

Feast one's eyes on someone/something

With eyes wide open

Have eyes like saucers

Have stars in one's eyes

Have eyes in the back of one's head

Something/someone makes one's eyes pop

Have eyes like a cat

Clap/cast eyes on someone/something

Do something with one's eyes closed

Someone/something is a sight for sore eyes

Knock someone's eyes out

Set eyes on someone/something

Eyeball something/someone

Raise one's eyebrows

Cut one's eyeteeth on something

Give one's eyeteeth for something

Something is an eyesore

Something is eye-wash

Look cross-eyed at someone

Bright-eyed and bushy-tailed

Grab some shut-eye

Green-eyed monster

Bird's-eye view

Dewy-eyed look

Steely-eyed

Hit the bull's eye

In a pig's eye!

Here's mud in your eye!

F

Face

Face the music
Have egg on one's face
Not just another pretty face
Put a bold/good face on some-
thing
Have/wear a long face
Have a face that would stop a
clock
Feed one's face
Have something staring one right
in the face
Take someone/something at face
value
Wear a poker face
Laugh on the other side of one's
face
Cut off one's nose to spite one's
face
Keep a straight face
Talk until one is blue in the face
Throw something in someone's
face
Something is a slap in the face
Put one's face on
Rub someone's face in something
The face that launched a thou-
sand ships
Fly in the face of something
Put on a brave face
Have something written all over
one's face
Just another face in the crowd
Put on a happy face
Hide one's face
Save/lose face
Show one's face
Rearrange someone's face
A face only a mother could love

Do an about-face on something
Bare/bald-faced lie
Someone is two-faced
Get out of my face!
Shut your face!

Fact

The fact of the matter
As a matter of fact
The facts of life
Just the facts, Ma'am!

Fade

Old soldiers never die, they just
fade away
Something/someone is only a
faded memory

Fail

Fail the acid test
Words fail me!

Faint

Faint heart ne'er won fair
maiden/lady
Damn someone/something with
faint praise

Fair

Fair is fair
Fair, fat and forty
Play fair
Someone/something is fair game
Beat someone fair and square
Give/get a fair shake/deal
Turnabout is fair play
All's fair in love and war
By fair means or foul
Faint heart ne'er won fair
maiden/lady

Someone is someone's fair-haired boy
Someone is a fair-weather friend
Something is fair-to-middling
No fair!
Who's the fairest of them all?

Faith

Keep the faith

Fall

Fall a rung lower on the ladder
Fall all over oneself
Fall flat on one's face
Fall for something/someone like a ton of bricks
Fall on evil days
Fall on hard times
Fall off the wagon
Fall in with evil companions
Fall down on the job
Fall short of the mark
Fall from grace
Fall for someone/something
Fall into a slump
Fall head over heels in love
Fall back on something
Be heading for a fall
Have the bottom fall out of something
Into each life a little rain must fall
Have the roof fall in on someone
Ride for a fall
Let the chips fall where they may
The bigger they come, the harder they fall
Be the fall guy
Pride goeth before a fall
The apple doesn't fall far from the tree
Have something fall into one's lap
As easy as falling off a log
Something falls on deaf ears

Bread always falls on its buttered side
Something falls between the cracks
Have a falling-out with someone
How the mighty have fallen!

False

False alarm
Sail under false colors
Have false modesty
Bear false witness
Labor under a false impression

Family

All in the family
Be in the family way
Something runs in the family
Have a family feud
Someone is the black sheep in the family
Wear the pants in the family

Famine

Either a feast or a famine
Do something come fire, flood or famine

Famous

Famous last words
Get along famously with someone

Fan

Fan the flames/fire
Something hits the fan

Fancy

Fancy pants
Fancy Dan
Fancy lady
Something tickles one's fancy
Take a fancy to someone/something
Plain and fancy
Be footloose and fancy-free
Fancy that!

Far

Far from the madding crowd
Something is far and away the best/worst
Search far and wide for someone/ something
Spread something far and wide
As far as the eye can see
So near and yet so far
Push someone too far
Something is few and far between
Something is a far cry from something
Trust someone as far as you can throw him
The apple doesn't fall far from the tree
So far, so good
Far be it from me!
Far out!

Farm

Buy the farm/cherry farm
Send someone to the funny farm
Don't bet the farm!

Fashion

Do something after a fashion
Be a slave to fashion

Fast

Make a fast buck
Life in the fast lane
Pull a fast one on someone
Play fast and loose with someone/ something
As fast as greased lightning
Go/get nowhere fast
So fast it makes one's head swim
Get a fast shuffle from someone
Go at a fast clip
Faster than a speeding bullet
He travels fastest who travels alone
Hard-and-fast rule

Fat

Fat and sassy
The fat is in the fire
Fair, fat and forty
Chew the fat
Big fat zero
A fat lot of good something will do
Give someone a fat lip
Live off the fat of the land
It ain't over till the fat lady sings
The fat cats
Kill the fatted calf
Fat chance!

Fate

A fate worse than death
The fickle finger of fate

Father

Father figure
Like father, like son

Fault

Someone is generous to a fault

Favor

Curry favor with someone
Be an odds-on favorite

Fear

Put the fear of God into someone
Fools rush in where angels fear to tread
Have nothing to fear but fear itself
Have no fear, _____'s here!

Feast

Feast one's eyes on someone/ something
Either a feast or a famine
A moveable feast

Feat

Death-defying feat

Feather

Feather one's nest
Tar and feather someone
Could have knocked someone
  over with a feather
Light as a feather
Birds of a feather flock together
Get/have a feather in one's cap
Show the white feather
Fine feathers do not make fine
  birds
Ruffle someone's feathers
Make the feathers fly
Feather-brained person
Fine-feathered friend

Federal

Make a Federal case out of something

Feed

Feed someone a line
Feed one's face
Feed a cold, starve a fever
Feed the flames/fire
Be off one's feed
Bite the hand that feeds one
Something is like feeding time at
  the zoo
Put on the feedbag
Be fed up to the back teeth with
  someone/something
Spoon-feed something to someone
Something is chicken-feed

Feel

Feel blue
Feel out of sorts
Feel like a new man/woman
Feel fit as a fiddle
Feel the pinch
Feel one's oats
Feel something in one's bones
Feel fourteen kinds of a fool

Feel like a million bucks/dol-
  lars
Feel like two cents
Feel crappy
Feel in fine fettle
Feel an aching void
Feel a sudden chill
Feel chipper
Feel under par
Feel ten feet tall
Cop a feel
Feeling no pain
Feeling groovy
That certain feeling
Fellow feeling
Have a gut feeling

Feet

Get/have cold feet
Get back on one's feet
Someone has feet of clay
Stand on one's own two feet
Drag one's feet
Jump into something with both
  feet
Have two left feet
Not let any grass grow under
  one's feet
Keep/have both feet on the
  ground
Shake the dust from one's feet
Sweep someone off his/her feet
Get one's feet wet
Throw oneself at someone's feet
Be out/dead on one's feet
Get/have itchy feet
Take a load off one's feet
Think on one's feet
Go feet first into something
Feel ten feet tall

Fell

In one fell swoop
In one swell foop

Fellow

Fellow feeling
Fellow traveler
Hale fellow, well met
Politics make strange bedfellows

Fence

The grass is always greener on the other side of the fence
Straddle/sit on the fence
Someone is plain as a mud fence
Mend one's fences
Good fences make good neighbors

Fever

Feed a cold, starve a fever
Have a fever in one's bones for someone
Cabin fever
Buck fever
Spring fever

Few

Be a man of few words
The chosen few
Be few and far between
Be missing a few buttons
Many are called, but few are chosen
Win a few, lose a few

Fickle

The fickle finger of fate

Fiction

Truth is stranger than fiction

Fiddle

Fiddle while Rome burns
Fiddle around
Feel fit as a fiddle
The fiddler calls the tune
If you dance, you have to pay the fiddler

Fiddlesticks!

Field

Play the field
Be out in left field
Something comes from out of left field
Have a field day with someone/something

Fiend

Smoke like a fiend
Someone has a fiendish sense of humor

Fifth

Take the fifth

Fig

Someone/something is not worth a fig
Not care a fig for someone/something

Fight

Fight to the bitter end
Fight fire with fire
Fight like cats and dogs
Fight tooth and nail
Fight to the last ditch
Be spoiling for a fight
You can't fight city hall
Someone can't fight his way out of a paper bag
Knock-down, drag-out fight
Have/not have a fighting chance

Figure

Father/authority figure
Someone cuts a fine figure
A fine figure of a woman
Give/get a ballpark figure
Figures don't lie
Go figure!

File

The rank and file

Fill

Fill someone full of lead
Fill in for someone
Fill someone in
Fill one's pockets
Fill someone's shoes
Fill the bill
Bank and fill
Have one's fill of someone/something

Filthy

Filthy lucre
Be filthy rich

Final

Take one's final curtains

Find

Find streets paved with gold
Find a little something extra in the pay envelope
Find oneself
Find something out the hard way
Seek and ye shall find
Couldn't find one's own head if it wasn't screwed on
It's hard to find good help
A good man is hard to find
Finders keepers, losers weepers!

Fine

Fine feathers do not make fine birds
Cut something fine
Cut a fine figure
Something is a fine kettle of fish
A fine Italian hand
Feel in fine fettle
A fine figure of a woman
Read the fine print
Sew a fine seam
A fine broth of a lad
A fine-feathered friend
Go over something with a fine-toothed comb
Fine and dandy!
Fine by me!

Finger

Put one's finger on something
Give someone the finger
Point the finger at someone
Not lift a finger
The moving finger writes
Keep a finger on the pulse of something
Have more in one's little finger than _____
Wrap someone around one's little finger
The fickle finger of fate
Have a finger in every pie
Fingers were made before forks
Something/someone slips through one's fingers
Keep one's fingers crossed
Have sticky/itchy fingers
Work one's fingers to the bone
Snap one's fingers
Idle fingers are the devil's workshop
Have something at one's fingertips
Be a butterfingers
Be light-fingered

Finish

Finish someone off
Nice guys finish last

Fire

Set the world on fire
Be a ball of fire
Play with fire
Do something come fire, flood, or famine

Where there's smoke, there's fire
Pull the chestnuts out of the fire
Breathe fire and brimstone
Have fire in one's eye
Something is hanging fire
The fat is in the fire
Have too many irons in the fire
Get a baptism of fire
Out of the frying pan and into
 the fire
Go through fire and water for
 someone/something
Start/build a fire under someone
Add fuel to the fire
Fan the fire
Fight fire with fire
Be between two fires
Keep the home fires burning
Something fires the imagination
Hot as a firecracker
Something is a surefire thing
Great balls of fire!
Where's the fire?

First

First things first
First and foremost
First, last and always
First crack out of the box
First come, first served
Get to first base with someone
Draw first blood
At first blush
The first thing you know
Someone/something is of the first
 water
In the first place
Love at first sight
Today is the first day of the rest
 of your life
Let he who is without sin cast the
 first stone
There's a first time for everything
If at first you don't succeed, try,

try again
Go feet first into something
America first!
Women and children first!
See you in hell first!
Safety first!
Which came first, the chicken or
 the egg?

Fish

Fish for compliments
Fish in troubled waters
Have other/bigger fish to fry
As cold as a dead fish
Like shooting fish in a barrel
Swim like a fish
Drink like a fish
Like a fish out of water
Be neither fish nor fowl
Something is a fine kettle of fish
Give someone the fish eye
Tell a fish story
Someone is not the only fish in
 the sea
Go on a fishing expedition
Something/someone looks fishy
Fish or cut bait!
Ye gods and little fishes!
Jumpin' catfish!

Fist

Coin/make money hand over fist
An iron fist in a velvet glove
Be fight-fisted
Be two-fisted

Fit

Fit to be tied
Fit for a king
Look fit to kill
Something is not fit for man nor
 beast
Feel fit as a fiddle
Throw/have a fit

Something fits like a glove
Someone/something fits one to a
  T
If the shoe fits, wear it
By fits and starts
Give someone fits
One size fits all
Survival of the fittest

Five

Five will get you ten
Give someone five/the high five
Take five
Fifty million Frenchmen can't be
  wrong

Fix

Fix someone's wagon
The fix is in
If it ain't broke, don't fix it
Get a fix on someone/something

Flag

Wave the flag for someone/some-
  thing
Show the white flag
Rally around the flag
Lower one's flag
Run something up the flagpole

Flame

The keeper of the flame
Like a moth to the flame
One's old flame
Fan the flames
Feed/add fuel to the flames

Flap

Flap one's gums/jaws
Get into a flap about something

Flash

Quick as a flash
Something happens in a flash
Someone/something is a flash in
  the pan

Flat

Flat broke
As flat as a pancake
In no time flat
Leave someone flat
Fall flat on one's face
Tell someone something flat out
Catch someone flat-footed

Flattery

Flattery will get you nowhere/
  everywhere

Flea

Flea bag
Put a flea in someone's ear

Flee

Flee like rats from a sinking ship

Flesh

Flesh something out
The spirit is willing but the flesh
  is weak
Someone/something makes one's
  flesh crawl
Get one's pound of flesh
See someone in the flesh
One's own flesh and blood
Press the flesh
Be a thorn in someone's flesh
The way of all flesh
It's only a flesh wound!

Fling

Take a fling at something
Have a fling

Flip

Flip one's lid/wig
Flip out
Flip a coin

Float

Float a loan

Float on air
Can barely keep afloat

Flock

Birds of a feather flock together
Follow someone like a flock of
sheep
Come back into the flock

Flog

Don't flog a dead horse

Flood

Do something come fire, flood or
famine
Open the floodgates

Floor

Floor someone
Walk the floor over someone/
something
Get in on the ground floor of
something
Clean/wipe up/mop up the floor
with someone
I'm floored!

Flop

Flop house
Flop sweat
Something is a resounding flop
Do a belly flop

Flow

Go with the flow

Flower

Flower power
Hearts and flowers
Don't send me flowers!

Flush

Flush something/someone out
Four-flusher

Fly

Fly the coop

Fly like a bird
Fly off the handle/bat
Fly by the seat of one's pants
Fly blind
Would steal a dead fly from a
blind spider
Make sparks fly
Make the feathers/fur fly
Straighten up and fly right
A fly in the ointment
Someone wouldn't hurt a fly
Do something on the fly
When the wolf is at the door,
love flies out the window
You can catch more flies with
honey than vinegar
As the crow flies
No flies on someone
Drop like flies
Be off to a flying start
Come through with flying colors
Take a flying leap
Flying high
Flying saucer
Take a flyer
The bird has flown
Bar-fly
Fly-by-night operation
Go fly a kite!
When donkeys fly!

Foam

Foam at the mouth

Fog

Fog thick as pea soup
Be in a fog

Fold

Fold up one's tent and steal
away
Return to the fold
Have plenty of folding green
I'm folded!

Folks

Different strokes for different
  folks

Follow

Follow in someone's footsteps
Follow one's nose
Follow suit
Follow someone like a flock of
  sheep
Follow a carrot on a stick
Follow a well-traveled path
Never follow a dog act
Someone/something is a tough
  act to follow
Camp follower

Fond

Absence makes the heart grow
  fonder

Food

Food for thought
Wolf down one's food
Brain food

Fool

Fool around
Play the fool
There's no fool like an old fool
Make a fool of oneself
A fool and his money are soon
  parted
One can learn from any fool
Be nobody's fool
Be a prize fool
Feel fourteen kinds of a fool
Fools rush in where angels fear to
  tread
Not suffer fools gladly
Fool's gold
Fool's paradise
Children and fools speak the
  truth

Be penny-wise and pound-foolish

Foot

Foot the bill
Get/have a foot in the door
Wait on someone hand and foot
The shoe is on the other foot
Get off on the wrong/right foot
Put one's foot in it
Put one's foot in one's mouth
Shoot oneself in the foot
Put one's best foot forward
Put one's foot down
Have one foot in the grave
Give someone a hot foot
From head to foot
Lucky rabbit's foot
Follow in someone's footsteps
Have someone/something under-
  foot
Be footloose and fancy-free
Play footsie with someone
Hot-foot it somewhere
Have foot-in-mouth disease
Wouldn't touch something/some-
  one with a ten-foot pole
Catch someone flat-footed
Kiss my foot!

Forbid

Eat the forbidden fruit
God forbid!

Force

Force something down someone's
  throat
Force someone's hand
Someone/something is a force to
  be reckoned with
Someone/something is a moving
  force
Brute force

Forever

Forever and a day

Nothing is forever
A thing of beauty is a joy forever

Forget

Forgive and forget
Clean forget something
An elephant never forgets
Forget it!

Forgive

Forgive and forget
To err is human, to forgive divine
Come home, all is forgiven!

Fork

Fork something over
Fingers were made before forks
Speak with forked tongue

Form

Be at the top of one's form

Fort

Hold the fort

Forward

Put one's best foot forward
Know something backwards and
 forwards

Foul

Foul one's own nest
By fair means or foul

Four

Go to the four corners of the
 earth for something
Cook on all four burners
Go on all fours
Catch forty winks
Fair, fat and forty
Give someone forty lashes with a
 wet noodle
Feel fourteen kinds of a fool
The sixty-four dollar question
Four-letter word

Four-flusher

Fowl

Something is neither fish nor fowl

Fox

Crazy/dumb like a fox
Sly as a fox
Send a fox to guard the henhouse
Someone is a real fox
There's a fox in the henhouse
Foxy lady

Free

Free as the breeze/a bird
Free, white and twenty-one
The best things in life are free
Of one's own free will
Be free and easy
Have a free hand with something
The truth shall set you free
There's no such thing as a free
 lunch
Butterflies are free
Go scot-free
Be footloose and fancy-free
It's a free country!
Why buy the cow when the milk
 is free?

Freeze

Freeze someone out
Give someone the deep freeze
Something/someone makes one's
 blood freeze
Not till hell freezes over

Freight

Pay the freight

French

Take French leave
Fifty million Frenchmen can't be
 wrong
Pardon my French!

Fresh

Fresh as a daisy
Fresh as the morning dew
Someone/something is like a
  breath of fresh air
Have/get a fresh slant on some-
  thing
Be fresh out of something
Don't get/be fresh!

Friday

Girl/man Friday
Thank God it's Friday!

Friend

A friend in need is a friend in-
  deed
Diamonds are a girl's best friend
Be someone's new best friend
Man's best friend
Have a friend at court
Fair-weather friend
Fine-feathered friend
Have friends in high places
Have an army of friends
With friends like you, who needs
  enemies?

Fright

Look a fright
Get stage fright
Give someone a fright

Frisky

As frisky as a colt

Frog

Have a frog in one's throat
Turn a frog into a prince

From

From the word go
Know where someone is coming
  from

Front

Front money
Cook on the front burner
Put on a good/brave front
Front and center!

Fruit

Eat the forbidden fruit
The fruits of one's labors
Nutty as a fruitcake

Fry

Have other/bigger fish to fry
Out of the frying pan and into
  the fire
Get one's brains fried

Fuel

Add fuel to the flames/fire

Full

Someone is not playing with a
  full deck
Be in full swing with something
Have one's hands full
Be full of oneself
Fill someone full of lead
Something comes full circle
Be full of beans/prunes/hot air/
  crap
Be full of the devil/the Old Nick/
  the Old Scratch
Go full blast
Go at something full tilt
With a full head of steam
Be full of Blarney
Be in full cry
Go full-tilt boogie
Something is either half-empty or
  half-full

Fun

Getting there is half the fun
More fun than a barrel of monkeys

Make fun of someone/something
Have fun and games
Someone/something is a barrel of
  fun
Poke fun at someone/something
Tickle someone's funny bone
Something is about as funny as a
  broken crutch
Send someone to the funny farm
Funny money
Funny business
Funny you should mention it!
Funny peculiar or funny ha-ha?
Do blondes have more fun?

Funeral

Dance at someone's funeral
Someone would be late for his
  own funeral

It's your funeral!

Fur

Make the fur fly

Fury

Hell hath no fury like a woman
  scorned
Sound and fury

Fuse

Blow a fuse
Have a short fuse

Fuss

Kick up a fuss about something

Future

The wave of the future

G

Gab

Have a gift of gab

Gaff

Get/give a lot of gaff
Can't stand the gaff

Gag

Gag someone
Someone/something is enough to
  make one gag
Be bound and gagged

Gain

No pain, no gain
Nothing ventured, nothing gained

Your loss is my gain!

Gallery

Play to the gallery
Peanut gallery

Game

The name of the game
The game is/isn't worth the can-
  dle
Beat the game
Something is a whole new ball
  game
Play the numbers game
At this stage of the game
The only game in town

Be ahead of the game
Throw the game
It's not whether you win or lose,
   it's how you play the game
Someone/something is fair game
Give the game away
Confidence game
Play the waiting game
Games people play
Play mind games with someone
Have fun and games
Two can play that game!
It's only a game!

Gamut

Run the gamut
Run the gamut from "A" to "B"

Gander

Take a gander at someone/some-
   thing
What's sauce/good for the goose
   is sauce/good for the gander

Gang

Gang up on someone
Chain gang
Come on like gangbusters

Gap

Credibility gap
Generation gap

Gape

Gape at someone
Gaper's block

Garbage

Garbage in, garbage out
Something is nothing but garbage
Garbage down!

Garden

Lead someone down the garden
   path

Common garden variety
Promise someone a rose garden

Gas

Be full of gas
Run out of gas
Step on the gas
Be cooking with gas
Take the gas pipe
Gasbag

Gasket

Blow a gasket

Gate

Give someone the gate
Swing like a gate
Crash the gate
Be left at the gate
Pearly gates

Gather

Gather rosebuds while ye may
A rolling stone gathers no moss

Gauntlet

Run the gauntlet
Throw down the gauntlet

Gear

Throw something out of gear
Slip a gear
Shift into high gear
Get one's rear in gear
Get into high gear

Gentle

Gentle as a lamb
Gentlemen prefer blondes

Genuine

Someone/something is the genu-
   ine article

Get

Get to first base with someone

Get in on the ground floor of
  something
Get someone over a barrel
Get on/off someone's back
Get off the hook
Get up on the wrong side of the
  bed
Get on the ball
Get something off the ground
Get one's back/hackles up
Get a load of something/someone
Get in one's licks
Get one's teeth into something
Get a foot in the door
Get the shaft
Get one's dander up
Get into the act
Get into high gear
Get the hang of something
Get the show on the road
Get a fix on someone/something
Get on in years
Get a bang/boot/kick out of
  someone/something
Get a girl in trouble
Get the brush/brush-off
Get under one's skin
Get down to brass tacks
Get someone's goat
Get in someone's hair
Get a rise out of someone
Get a load on
Get the boot/ax/sack
Get a fast shuffle
Get away from it all
Get the inside story
Get blown out of the water
Get a clear signal from someone
Get mixed messages from some-
  one
Get something across
Get one's bearings
Get one's beauty sleep
Get the best of someone

Get more bounce to the ounce
Get off cheap
Get a piece of the action
Get back to basics
Get a pat on the back
Get off on the right/wrong foot
Get down to cases
Get a word in edgewise
Get down off/on one's high horse
Get into a lather/sweat
Get a cold deck
Get the ball rolling
Get away with murder
Get something off one's chest
Get nowhere fast
Get the upper hand
Get the drop on someone
Get back on one's feet
Get something through one's
  thick skull
Get more than one bargained for
Get all shook up
Get off the pot
Get it all together
Get along famously with someone
Get one's act together
Get it in the neck
Get off easy
Get what's coming to one
Get one's ducks in a row
Get one's rear in gear
Get one's brains fried
Get the goods on someone
Get the jump on someone/some-
  thing
Get to the bottom of something
Get to the bottom line
Get wind of something
Get one's feet wet
Get the green light
Get off to a good/bad start
Get one's house in order
You can't get blood from a stone/
  turnip

Tell someone where to get off
Five will get you ten
What you see is what you get
You have to get up pretty early
   in the morning to. . .
Get cracking!
Get the hook!
Get with it!
Get real!
Get lost!
Get a horse!
It gets me right here!

Ghost

Give up the ghost
Be as pale as a ghost
Not have a ghost of a chance
Look like someone has seen a
   ghost

Gift

Don't look a gift horse in the
   mouth
Someone thinks he's God's gift to
   someone/something
Have a gift of gab
Beware of Greeks bearing gifts

Gild

Gild the lily

Gill

Be loaded/stewed to the gills
Be green/blue around the gills
Be fed up to the gills with some-
   one/something

Girl

Girl Friday
Call girl
Get a girl in trouble
A girl in every port
Sweater/cover girl
Have your girl call my girl
Be the birthday girl

Bouncing baby girl
A mere slip of a girl
Heaven will protect the working
   girl
Men seldom make passes at girls
   who wear glasses
Diamonds are a girl's best friend
As bashful as a schoolgirl
Have a schoolgirl complexion
Be girl-crazy
Bring on the dancing girls!

Give

Give someone the gate/air
Give someone a song and dance
Give someone some skin/five
Give someone the cold shoulder
Give someone both barrels
Give someone the shirt off one's
   back
Give someone a tumble
Give someone the air
Give someone the business
Give someone a hand
Give someone a mouthful of
   knuckles
Give one's eyeteeth for something
Give someone a fat lip
Give someone a pain
Give someone the advantage
Give someone a bad/hard time
Give someone the finger
Give someone enough rope and
   he'll hang himself
Give someone/something the
   once-over
Give someone the brush/brush-
   off
Give the devil his due
Give a damn
Give someone the shaft
Give someone the back of one's
   hand
Give someone a turn

Give someone a run for his
  money
Give someone a snow job
Give someone a boost
Give someone the boot/bounce/
  ax/sack
Give someone the fish eye
Give no quarter and ask none
Give someone the needle
Give the game/show away
Give a wide berth to some-
  one
Give someone/something a black
  eye
Give someone/something a
  whirl
Give someone the works
Give someone an inch and he'll
  take a mile
Give someone the benefit of the
  doubt
Give someone the creeps
Give someone the glad eye
Give up the ghost
Give as good as one gets
Give someone fits
Give someone the heebie-jeebies
Give someone the high sign
Give one's right arm for some-
  one/something
Give something one's best shot
Give someone/something all one's
  got
Give someone a pat on the back
Wouldn't give someone the time
  of day
Wouldn't give a dime for one's
  chances
Not have the brains God gave a
  goose
Indian giver
Give it the gun!
Give me a break!
Give it a rest!

Glad

Give someone the glad eye
Put on one's glad rags
Give someone the glad hand
Not suffer fools gladly

Glass

Have a glass jaw
As smooth/clear as glass
People who live in glass houses
  shouldn't throw stones
Look at the world through rose-
  colored glasses
Men seldom make passes at girls
  who wear glasses

Glitter

All that glitters is not gold

Glory

Go out in a blaze of glory
One's crowning glory
Old glory
Glory be!

Glove

An iron fist in a velvet glove
Something fits like a glove
Handle someone/something with
  kid gloves
Hang up one's gloves
Take the gloves off
Go hand-in-glove with someone/
  something

Go

Go to seed/pot/the dogs
Go like a house afire
Go off one's rocker
Go down the drain/tubes
Go against the grain
Go like a bat out of hell
Go to bat for someone/something
Go begging for something
Go over like a lead balloon

Go from bad to worse
Go for broke
Go the limit
Go full blast
Go where the action is
Go places
Go into a tailspin
Go whistle for something
Go to the mat for someone/something
Go over with a bang
Go over one's head
Go like clockwork
Go off the deep end
Go through the motions
Go to town
Go like sixty
Go to hell in a handbasket
Go like blazes
Go out on a limb for someone
Go in one ear and out the other
Go to wrack/rack and ruin
Go up in smoke
Go someone better
Go around in circles
Go down to the wire
Go hog-wild over someone/something
Go home in a box
Go whole-hog over something
Go at something hammer and tongs
Go Dutch
Go overboard for someone/something
Go all the way
Go at something hot and heavy
Go into orbit over someone/something
Go over something with a fine-toothed comb
Go to any lengths
Go by the book
Go like nobody's business

Go through the mill
Go over the top
Go on all fours
Go it alone
Go the extra mile
Go with the flow
Go along for the ride
Go bananas/ape over someone/something
Make a go of something
Pay as you go
All dressed up and no place to go
Something is touch and go
All systems are go
There but for the grace of God, go I
Let oneself go
Be on the go
Easy come, easy go
Something goes by the boards
Something goes over one's head
Something goes without saying
Something goes over with a bang
As the story goes
What goes around, comes around
Not know whether someone's coming or going
Get out while the going's good
When the going gets tough, the tough get going
Something big is going down
To hell and gone
Here today, gone tomorrow
Be a gone goose
Go climb a tree!
Go soak your head!
Go fly a kite!
Go for it!
Go play in traffic!
Go to the devil!
Go peddle your papers!
Go to blazes!
Go suck eggs!
Anything goes!

Goat

Get someone's goat
Be/act the goat
Separate the sheep from the goats

God

God helps those who help them-
selves
Put the fear of God into someone
Sure as God made little green
apples
There, but for the grace of God,
go I
By guess and by God
Someone doesn't use the brains
God gave him
The mills of God grind slowly
Not have the brains God gave a
goose
Something is in the lap of the
gods
Someone/something is older than
God's dog
Someone thinks he's God's gift to
someone
Cleanliness is next to godliness
With God as my witness!
Honest to God!
So help me, God!
Ye gods and little fishes!
For God's sake!
Thank God it's Friday!
What on God's green earth?

Gold

Gold digger
Find streets paved with gold
All that glitters is not gold
Someone/something is as good as
gold
Someone has a heart of gold
Silver threads among the gold
Someone/something is worth its
weight in gold

Something is a gold mine
Fool's gold
Kill the goose that lays the
golden eggs
Golden opportunity
Golden boy
Silence is golden
Goldbrick

Golf

Golf widow

Golly

By guess and by golly
By golly!

Gone

Someone/something is dead and
gone
Someone/something is gone with
the wind
The thrill is gone
Here today, gone tomorrow
Someone is a gone goose
Someone is a goner

Good

Good fences make good neigh-
bors
Good, bad or indifferent
Good things come in small pack-
ages
Good riddance to bad rubbish
If you can't be good, be careful
Be of good cheer
Have a good cover
All good things must come to an
end
The best defense is a good offense
Set a good example
One good turn deserves another
Put in a good word for someone
So far, so good
Add one for good measure
It's hard to find good help

A good man is hard to find
It's an ill wind that blows nobody good
For good and all
Have a good mind to do something
As good as new
Someone/something is as good as gold
Be as good as one's word
Something looks good enough to eat
A miss is as good as a mile
In good faith
Someone/something is too good to be true
Someone/something is too much of a good thing
A fat lot of good something will do
Be/get on someone's good side
What's good for the goose is good for the gander
Be a good scout/egg/skate
Throw good money after bad
Bad money drives out good
The Good Book
All in good time
Something is all well and good, but. . .
Have a good head on one's shoulders
Be a good old boy
The road to hell is paved with good intentions
One never had it so good
Give a good account of oneself
Something is all to the good
Have someone on good authority
Get off to a good start
Be in someone's good books
Have a stroke of good luck
Have a good bedside manner
Be bursting with good news

The good old days
You can't keep a good man down
Give as good as one gets
Be up to no good
Let the good times roll
Get out while the getting is good
No news is good news
Put on a good front
Put a good face on something
Something does someone a world of good
Be a goodie two-shoes
This is as good as it gets!
Good gravy!
Good grief!
Your guess is as good as mine!
Goodie-goodie gumdrops!
What's the good word?

Goods

Deliver the goods
Sell someone a bill of goods
Get the goods on someone

Goose

Goose egg
Kill the goose that lays the golden eggs
Cook someone's goose
Call of the wild goose
Can't say "boo" to a goose
Someone is a gone goose
What's good/sauce for the goose is good/sauce for the gander
The goose hangs high
Be loose as a goose
Not have the brains God gave a goose
Go on a wild-goose chase

Got

Got someone's number
Got to hand it to someone
Give someone/something all you've got

You've got another think coming!
Cat got your tongue?

Grab

Grab a handful of air
Grab some shut-eye/forty winks
Something/everything is up for
  grabs
How does that grab you?

Grace

Fall from grace
Something is a saving grace
There, but for the grace of God,
  go I

Grade

Make the grade

Grain

Take something with a grain of
  salt
There's more than a grain of
  truth in something
Go against the grain
Someone/something cuts across
  the grain

Grand

Make a grandstand play

Grant

Take something for granted

Grape

Sour grapes
Hear something through/by the
  grapevine
Peel me a grape!

Grasp

Let your reach exceed your grasp

Grass

Grass widow
Snake in the grass

The grass is always greener on
  the other side of the fence
Let no grass grow under one's feet
Be knee-high to a grasshopper

Grave

Have one foot in the grave
Dig one's own grave
Someone/something is enough to
  make someone turn over in his
  grave
From the cradle to the grave
Dance on someone's grave
Swear to something on one's
  mother's grave
Work the graveyard shift

Gravy

Get on the gravy train
No guts, no gravy
Good gravy!

Grease

Grease someone's palm
Grease the wheels of something
Grease monkey
The squeaky wheel gets the grease
Elbow grease
Greasy spoon
As fast as greased lightning

Great

Great minds think alike
Great oaks from little acorns
  grow
The great unwashed
Going great guns
Someone/something is no great
  shakes
Have a brush with greatness
Great day in the morning!
Great balls of fire!

Greek

Beware of Greeks bearing gifts

It's all Greek to me!

Green

Be green with envy
Be green around the gills
Give/get the green light
Have plenty of folding green
As sure as God made little green
    apples
Have a green thumb
Long green
Lean, green machine
The grass is always greener on
    the other side of the fence
Green-eyed monster
What on God's green earth?

Greet

Greet someone with open arms

Grey

All cats are grey in the dark

Grief

Come to grief
Good grief!

Grim

Hang on like grim death

Grin

Grin from ear to ear
Grin and bear it
Grin like a Cheshire cat
Break into a grin

Grind

Grind to a halt
Have an ax to grind with some-
    one
The same old grind
The mills of God grind slowly
Put someone through the meat-
    grinder
Keep one's nose to the grindstone

Grip

Have a grip like a vice
Lose one's grip
Come to grips with something
Get a grip on yourself!

Grit

Grit one's teeth
True grit
Get down to the nitty-gritty

Groove

Get in the groove
Feeling groovy

Gross

Gross someone out
Someone/something is really
    gross

Ground

Stand one's ground
Break new ground
Have/keep one's ear to the
    ground
Meet on common ground
Beat something into the ground
Get in on the ground floor of
    something
Cut the ground out from under
    someone
Cover a lot of ground
Something suits someone right
    down the ground
Worship the ground someone
    walks on
Stay on middle ground
Know something from the ground
    up
Know the ground rules
Have both feet on the ground
Get something off the ground
Lose ground
Hit the ground running

Grow

Grow like a weed
Absence makes the heart grow
   fonder
Great oaks from little acorns
   grow
Money doesn't grow on trees
Not let any grass grow under
   one's feet
Someone/something grows on
   someone
Have growing pains
Grow up!

Grudge

Carry/bear a grudge

Guard

Guard something with your life
Send a fox to guard the henhouse
Keep your guard up
Catch someone off-guard

Guess

Something is anybody's guess
By guess and by golly/God
Second-guess someone
Guess-timate
Your guess is as good as mine!

Guilty

As guilty as sin
Innocent until proven guilty

Gum

Gum up the works
Beat/flap one's gums
Bubble-gum rock

Put together with chewing-gum
   and baling wire
Goodie, goodie gum-drops!

Gun

Gun one's motor
Jump the gun
Give it the gun
Go like a son of a gun
The business end of a gun
Hired gun
Be top gun
Stick to/stand by one's guns
Go great guns
Call out the big guns
Go gunning for someone
Shotgun wedding

Gut

Have a gut feeling
Bust a gut
No guts, no gravy
Have no guts
Play guts ball
Hate someone's guts
Someone has a lot of guts
Spill someone's guts

Guy

Dance with the guy that brung
   ya
Be the fall guy
Someone is a prince of a guy
Be a regular/stand-up guy
Nice guys finish last
Wise-guy
No more Mr. Nice Guy!

H

Habit

Kick the habit
Someone is a creature of habit
Old habits die hard

Hack

Hack writer
Someone can't hack something
Someone is an old hack
Get/have one's hackles up

Hail

Hail the conquering hero!

Hair

Win/lose by a hair
Tear one's hair out
Not turn a hair
Something hangs by a hair
Something is enough to curl one's
  hair
Wouldn't harm a hair on some-
  one's head
Something makes one's hair stand
  on end
Let one's hair down
Get in someone's hair
Have a hair of the dog that bit
  one
Wear a hair shirt
A rag, a bone, a hank of hair
See neither hide nor hair of
  someone/something
Something will put hair on one's
  chest
Split hairs
Have someone by the short hairs
Have a hair-raising experience
Have a hair-trigger temper

Someone is a fair-haired boy
Shave and a haircut, six bits!

Hale

Hale fellow, well met
Hale and hearty

Half

Half a loaf is better than none
Someone/something is a laugh
  and a half
Have half a mind to do some-
  thing
One's better half
Could see something with half an
  eye
Someone/something is not half
  bad
Getting there is half the fun
Something is only half of the
  battle
Take half measures
Someone is too clever by half
Something is either half empty or
  half full
Meet someone halfway
Something is six of one and half-
  a-dozen of the other
Go off half-cocked
Someone/something is half-baked
Half-past kissing time, time to kiss
  again!

Hall

You can't fight city hall

Halt

Call a halt to something
Grind to a halt

Come to a screeching halt
Blind, lame and halt

Hammer

Hammer away at something
Hammer something home
Hammer something out
Go at something hammer and
  tongs
Someone/something is as subtle
  as a sledge hammer

Hand

Hand something to someone on a
  silver platter
Hand someone a line
Live hand to mouth
Have someone/something in the
  palm of one's hand
Call someone's hand
Throw in one's hand
Know someone/something like
  the back of one's hand
One hand washes the other
With hat in hand
Have someone eating out of one's
  hand
Bite the hand that feeds one
Wait on someone hand and foot
A bird in the hand is worth two
  in the bush
Catch someone with his hand in
  the cookie jar/till
Tip one's hand
On the other hand
One's left hand doesn't know
  what one's right hand is doing
Give someone the glad hand
Give someone the back of one's
  hand
Get/have the upper hand
Put one's hand to the plow
Try/set one's hand at/to some-
  thing

Rule with an iron hand
Do something with a heavy hand
Hold the winning hand
Have to hand it to someone
A fine Italian hand
Do something with one hand tied
  behind one's back
Force someone's hand
Have a free hand with something
Give someone a hand
Lend a hand
Keep one's hand in
The hand is quicker than the eye
Hands across the table
Have a hit on one's hands
One's hands are tied
Dirty one's hands
Many hands make light work
Be on one's hands and knees
Have one's hands full
Play into someone's hands
Be putty in someone's hands
Wash one's hands of someone/
  something
Take the law into one's own
  hands
Win hands down
Have clean hands
Throw up one's hands
Sit on one's hands
In the hands of the Almighty
Have both hands on the table
Change of hands
Cold hands, warm heart
Bloody one's hands
Time hangs heavy on one's hands
Take one's life into one's own
  hands
Read the handwriting on the wall
Grab a handful of air
Bound for hell in a handbasket
Left/back-handed compliment
Coin/make money hand-over-fist
Catch someone red-handed

Go hand-in-glove with someone/
something
Hand-pick someone/something
Keep your cotton-pickin' hands
off!

Handle

Handle someone/something with
kid gloves
Handle with care
Someone/something is too hot to
handle
Fly off the handle
Get the handle on someone/
something

Handsome

Handsome is as handsome does
High, wide and handsome
Tall, dark and handsome

Hang

Hang up one's shingle
Hang on like grim death
Hang on to your hat/chair
Hang on to someone's coattails
Hang by a hair/thread
Hang one's hat on something
Hang someone out to dry
Hang on to one's mother's apron
strings
Hang up one's gloves
Hang in there
Hang one on
Hang tough
Get the hang of something
Find a hook to hang something
on
Give someone enough rope and
he'll hang himself
Let it all hang out
Something hangs in the balance
Thereby hangs a tale
Time hangs heavy on one's hands

The goose hangs high
Leave someone/something hang-
ing in the air
Hanging from the rafters
Have one's tongue hanging out
Something is hanging fire
Have a hangdog look
Get all hung-up on someone/
something
Have a hang-up about someone/
something
Hang it all!
Well, I'll be hanged!

Happen

Accidents will happen
Look like an accident on its way
to happen
Something shouldn't happen to a
dog
Something happens in a flash
What's happening?

Happy

Happy as a lark/clam/bird
Happy as a pig in clover
Happy as the day is long
Happy hunting ground
Money can't buy happiness
Happy-go-lucky
Slap-happy
Trigger-happy
Happy days are here again!

Hard

Hard as a rock
Play hard ball
Someone is hard as nails
Cold, hard cash
School of hard knocks
Something is a hard nut to crack
Someone/something is a hard
case
Something is a hard row to hoe

Give someone a hard time
Between a rock and a hard place
Be hard up for something
Drive a hard bargain
Something is hard to believe
Come down hard on someone
Old habits die hard
Do hard time
Fall on hard times
Find out something the hard way
It's hard to find good help
A good man is hard to find
The bigger they come, the harder
  they fall
Hard-and-fast rule
Something is hard-sledding
Be hard-boiled about something
Hard-luck story

Harm

Wouldn't harm a hair on someone's head
Be in/out of harm's way

Harp

Harp away on something

Hash

Hash something over/out
Hash up something
Hash house
Fix someone's hash
Sling hash
This'll settle your hash!

Haste

Haste makes waste
Make haste slowly
Marry in haste, repent at leisure
Beat a hasty retreat
Don't be hasty!

Hat

Something/someone is old hat
Pull rabbits out of a hat

Talk through one's hat
Eat one's hat
Be a bad hat
Hold/hang on to your hat
Put on one's high hat
Hang one's hat on something
Anyplace you hang your hat is
  home
Knock something into a cocked
  hat
Keep something under one's hat
At the drop of a hat
Toss/throw one's hat into the
  ring
Take one's hat off to someone
With hat in hand
Pass the hat
Brass hat
Be a man of many hats
Be mad as a hatter
Here's your hat, what's your
  hurry?

Hatch

Booby hatch
Don't count your chickens before
  they're hatched
Down the hatch!
Batten down the hatches!

Hatchet

Hatchet face
Hatchet man
Bury the hatchet
Do a hatchet job on someone/
  something

Hate

Hate someone/something like
  poison
Hate someone's guts
Love/hate relationship

Haul

Haul down one's colors

Haul someone's ashes
Haul someone over the coals
Haul in one's horns
Haul off and clobber someone
Over the long haul

Have

Have a bellyful of someone/something
Have the world on a string
Have a case/crush on someone
Have a foot in the door
Have a ball/blast
Have a screw loose
Have something down pat
Have rocks in one's head
Have something knocked/taped
Have a finger in every pie
Have the last laugh
Have someone/something in the palm of one's hand
Have two left feet
Have a good head on one's shoulders
Have an eye for something
Have a lot of mileage on one
Have a lot of crust
Have something coming to one
Have the time of one's life
Have one's back up
Have one's hands full
Have ants in the pants
Have cold feet
Have something up one's sleeve
Have it out with someone
Have one too many
Have to get married
Have what it takes
Have something under one's belt
Have no use for someone/something
Have all one's buttons/marbles
Have one's wires crossed
Have something written all over it

Have one's hands tied
Have one's nose to the grindstone
Have someone in stitches
Have someone's number
Have the world by the tail
Have a tiger by the tail
Have someone's hide
Have too many irons in the fire
Have someone/something in one's hip pocket
Have someone/something underfoot
Have someone over a barrel
Have two strikes against one
Have a go at something
Have a bone to pick with someone
Have an edge on something
Have dibs on something
Have it in for someone
Have money to burn
Have one's heart in the right place
Have one's hand in the till/cookie jar
Have one's work cut out for one
Have a hollow leg
Have a fit/kittens
Have something at one's fingertips
Have a good mind to do something
Have it made
Have one's ears lowered
Have fire in one's eye
Have someone's head on a platter
Have both hands on the table
Have a piece of the action
Have the advantage
Have all the moves
Have one's nose in the air
Have a monkey on one's back
Have someone dead to rights
Have one's head in the clouds
Have a hair of the dog that bit one

Have the last word
Have one's ear to the ground
Have a big mouth
Have the drop on someone
Have something on the ball
Have tux, will travel
Have all one's eggs in one basket
Have one's back against the wall
Have eyes in the back of one's head
Have a card/ace up one's sleeve
Have a field day with someone/something
Have one foot in the grave
To have and to hold
Let someone have it
Not have a prayer
Eat one's cake and have it too
As luck would have it
Have a heart!
Have a nice day!

Havoc

Raise havoc with someone/something
Cry havoc!

Hawk

Hawk the goods
Watch someone like a hawk

Hay

Make hay while the sun shines
Like looking for a needle in a haystack
Go haywire
That ain't hay!

Head

Head for the hills
Lose one's head
Have a block for a head
Can't make head nor tail out of someone/something

Keep a civil tongue in one's head
Club someone over the head with something
Uneasy lies the head that wears the crown
Be in over one's head
Someone is simple/soft in the head
From head to heels
Bring something to a head
Put one's head in the lion's mouth
Can't get something through someone's thick head
Build up/with a full head of steam
Get one's head shrunk
Something comes to a head
Get something into one's head
Have someone's head on a platter
From head to toe/foot
Someone/something will turn one's head
Keep one's head above water
Something rears its ugly head
Something goes over one's head
Have rocks in one's head
Have one's head in the clouds
Fall head over heels in love
Talk one's head off
So fast it'll make one's head swim
Be head and shoulders above someone/something
Couldn't find one's head if it wasn't screwed on
Have a swelled head
Butt/beat one's head against the wall
Laugh one's head off
Can't make head nor tail of something/someone
Something comes to a head
Something/someone gets into one's head

Bury one's head in the sand
Hold one's head up
Have a good head on one's shoulders
Give/get a kick in the head
Wouldn't harm a hair on someone's head
Put one's head in a noose
Have eyes in the back of one's head
Be sick in the head
Hit the nail right on the head
Have sawdust in one's head
Talk/speak off the top of one's head
Run around like a chicken with its head cut off
Need something like a hole in the head
Put one's head on the chopping block
Bite someone's head off
Have a price on one's head
Be in something above one's head
Go to the head of the class
Give someone his head
Have holes in one's head
Hit the nail on the head
Have a roof over one's head
Heads will roll!
Two heads are better than one
Put our heads together
Cash on the barrelhead
Chowderhead
Dive into something headfirst
Go head-to-head against someone/something
Play heads-up ball
Go at something bald-headed
Go soak your head!
Heads I win, tails you lose!

Heal

Time heals all wounds

Get/have a clean bill of health
A sound mind in a healthy body
Be bursting with health
Someone is the picture of health
Healthy as a horse
Early to bed and early to rise makes a man healthy, wealthy and wise
Physician, heal thyself!

Heap

The top of the heap

Hear

Hear something by/through the grapevine
Quiet enough to hear a pin drop
Can't hear oneself think
Not hear "boo" from anyone
Don't believe everything you hear
Children should be seen and not heard
Another country heard from
You ain't heard nothin' yet!

Heart

Heart and soul
Break someone's heart
Cry/eat one's heart out
Tear someone's heart out
Absence makes the heart grow fonder
There's a broken light for every heart on Broadway
There's a broken heart for every light on Broadway
Home is where the heart is
Warm the cockles of one's heart
Someone has a heart of gold
Wear one's heart on one's sleeve
From the bottom of one's heart
One's heart is in one's mouth
Do something to one's heart's content

Have a heart of stone
Have one's heart set on something
Have one's heart in the right place
A man after one's own heart
One's heart stands still
Cross one's heart and hope to die
Have someone's best interests at heart
Cold hands, warm heart
Have a heart as big as all outdoors
With a heavy heart
One's heart skips a beat
Someone is all heart
Have one's heart in one's boots
Have a change of heart
Faint heart ne'er won fair maiden
Learn/know something by heart
The way to a man's heart is through his stomach
Bleeding heart
Lose heart
Hearts and flowers
Leave a trail of broken hearts
Hale and hearty
Something tugs at one's heartstrings
Have a heart-to-heart talk
Be chicken-hearted
Have a heart!
My heart bleeds for you!
My achin' heart!

Heat

Turn on/up the heat on someone/something
Give someone heat about something
Bear the heat of something
It's not the heat, it's the humidity!
If you can't stand the heat, stay out of the kitchen!

Heaven

Heaven will protect the working girl
Move heaven and earth for someone/something
Someone/something is heaven on earth
Pennies from heaven
Be in seventh heaven
Thought you'd died and gone to heaven
A marriage made in heaven
Something stinks to high heaven
Heaven only knows!
Heavens to Betsy!
Thank heavens!
What in the name of heaven?

Heavy ·

Do something with a heavy hand
Someone is a heavy hitter
Have a heavy date
Play the heavy
Go at something hot and heavy
Time hangs heavy on one's hands
With a heavy heart
Be heavy-handed about something
He ain't heavy, he's my brother!
That's heavy, man!

Hector

Hector someone
Not since Hector was a pup

Hedge

Hedge one's bet
Born on the sunny side of the hedge

Heel

Have an Achilles heel
Turn on one's heel

Bring someone to heel
Time wounds all heels
Set someone back on his heels
Kick up one's heels
Cool one's heels
Show a clean pair of heels
Be close on the heels of someone/
  something
Drag one's heels
Dig in one's heels
Take to one's heels
Fall/be head-over-heels in love
  with someone
Someone is well-heeled

Hell

Hell hath no fury like a woman
  scorned
Hellcat
Not till hell freezes over
A cold day in hell
Go to hell and back for some-
  one/something
Go like a bat out of hell
All hell breaks loose
Be hell on wheels
Something is a living hell
Something is hotter than hell
The road to hell is paved with
  good intentions
Have hell to pay
Have a snowball's chance in hell
Come hell or high water
Go through hell and high water
  for someone
To hell and gone
Something is hell on earth
Not give two hoots in hell
Bound for hell in a handbasket
Be hell-bent for leather
See you in hell first!
War is hell!
What the hell?
Who the hell are you?

Help

Can't help oneself
Good help is hard to find
God helps those who help them-
  selves
Mother's little helper
Be as helpless as a baby/kitten
Help send this kid to camp!
Not if I can help it!
So help me, God!

Hen

Hen party
Mad as a wet hen
Cluck like a mother hen
Scarce as hens' teeth
There's a fox in the henhouse
Send a fox to guard the henhouse
Mother-hen someone/something

Herd

Ride herd on someone/something
Be off like a herd of turtles

Here

Here today, gone tomorrow
Here and now
Here, there and everywhere
The buck stops here
Something is neither here nor
  there
Abandon hope, all ye who enter
  here
Here goes nothing!
Same here!
Happy days are here again!
I'm outta here!
Have no fear, _____'s here!
Ain't nobody here but us chick-
  ens!
Here's hoping!

Hero

No man is a hero to his valet

Hail the conquering hero!
My hero!

Hesitate

He who hesitates is lost

Hide

Hide one's face
Hide one's head in the sand
Hide one's light under a bushel
See neither hide nor hair of
    someone/something
Will have someone's hide
Tan someone's hide
You can run, but you can't hide

High

High, wide and handsome
High as a kite
Search high and low for some-
    one/something
Come hell or high water
Go through hell and high water
    for someone
Hit the high spots
Leave someone high and dry
Get/be on/off one's high horse
Shift into high gear
Eat/live high on/off the hog
Give someone the high sign
Give someone a high five
Have friends in high places
Have juice in high places
Someone is a high roller
Take the high road
Someone/something is high camp
The goose hangs high
Something stinks to high heaven
You can only pile something on
    so high
Put on one's high hat
Get high
Be sitting on high cotton
Be higher than Jesus on stilts

Highjinks
Highway robbery
Be knee-high to a grasshopper
Blow something sky-high

Hike

Take a hike!

Hill

Be king of the hill
Someone is over the hill
Not amount to a hill of beans
Go over the hill
As old as the hills
Take to/head for the hills
Make a mountain out of a mole-
    hill
Everything's going downhill
What in Sam Hill?

Hip

Have something/someone in one's
    hip pocket
Shoot from the hip
Be so hip you're crippled
Someone/something is joined at
    the hip
A moment on the lips, a year on
    the hips
That's hip, man!

Hire

Hire new blood
Hired gun

History

History repeats itself
Someone/something is history

Hit

Hit the sauce/bottle
Hit the skids
Hit it off with someone
Hit someone when he's down
Hit someone where he lives

Hit the jackpot
Hit the ceiling/roof
Hit the road
Hit the sack
Hit the books
Hit pay dirt
Hit below the belt
Hit one's stride
Hit something right on the nose/
  button
Hit someone right in the puss
Hit the nail right on the head
Hit the big time/leagues
Hit a bottleneck
Hit bottom/rock bottom
Hit the high spots
Hit the ground running
Hit a stumbling block
Hit the wall
Hit man
Look like one was hit by a truck
Can't hit the broad side of a barn
Have a hit on one's hands
Something is hit or miss
Something hits one right between
  the eyes
Something hits close to home
Something hits the fan
Something hits the spot
Someone is a heavy hitter
Hit me again!
Hit the deck/dirt/silk!

Hitch

Hitch one's wagon to a star
Something goes off without a
  hitch
Something has a hitch in it some-
  where
Get hitched
What's the hitch?

Hob

Raise/play hob with someone/
something
Hob-nob with someone

Hog

Hog the spotlight
As independent as a hog on ice
Eat/live high off the hog
Road hog
Go whole-hog over someone/
  something
Go hog-wild over someone/some-
  thing

Hold

Hold one's breath
Hold up one's end
Hold one's peace
Hold onto one's hat
Hold one's tongue
Hold all the cards
Hold one's head up
Hold one's own
Hold the fort
Hold someone at bay
Hold all the aces
Hold one's temper
Hold the winning hand
Hold no brief for someone/some-
  thing
Hold the line
Hold something against someone
Hold out on someone
Get hold of oneself
Something won't/doesn't hold
  water
Someone/something can't hold a
  candle to someone/something
Someone can/can't hold his
  liquor
To have and to hold
No holds barred
Be left holding the bag/baby
Hold the phone!
Hold your horses!

Hold everything!
Don't hold your breath!

Hole

Hole up somewhere
Get out of the hole
Have an ace in the hole
Need someone/something like a
   hole in the head
Live in a hole in the wall
Money burns a hole in one's
   pocket
Be a square peg in a round hole
Keep your eye on the donut and
   not on the hole
Dig oneself into a hole
Stare a hole through someone
Black hole in space
Have holes in one's head
Buttonhole someone

Hollow

Have a hollow leg
Beat someone all hollow
Something is a hollow victory

Holy

By all that's holy
Someone is a holy terror
Have a holier-than-thou attitude
Holy cow!
Holy smoke!
Holy cats!
Holy mackeral!

Home

Home, sweet home
Home is where the heart is
Anyplace you hang your hat is
   home
As welcome as money from home
Drive home a point
Chickens come home to roost
Bring home the bacon
Hammer something home

Someone/something is nothing to
   write home about
Pick up one's marbles and go
   home
Eat someone out of house and
   home
Keep the home fires burning
Something hits close to home
A house is not a home
A man's home is his castle
Charity begins at home
Go home in a box
All the comforts of home
There's no place like home
It takes a heap of living to make
   a house a home
There's nobody home upstairs
Come home, all is forgiven!

Honest

Make an honest woman out of
   someone
Be as honest as the day is long
Honesty is the best policy
Honesty is its own reward
Come by something honestly
Honest Injun!
Honest to Pete/goodness/God!

Honey

Land of milk and honey
Someone/something is a honey
You can catch more flies with
   honey than with vinegar
Honeybun
Honeybunch
The honeymoon is over

Honor

There's no honor among thieves
Do the honors
Have honorable intentions
On my honor!
Scout's honor!

Hook

Bait the hook
Give someone the hook
By hook or by crook
Get off the hook
Swallow something hook, line
    and sinker
Find a hook to hang something
    on
Let someone off the hook
Be on the hook for something
Get the hook!

Hoop

Jump through hoops for some-
    one/something
Be/go cock-a-hoop over some-
    one/something

Hoot

Not give/care a hoot
Not give two hoots in hell

Hop

A hop, skip and a jump away
Be mad as hops
Be hopping mad
Be all hopped up
Hop to it!

Hope

Hope springs eternal
Hope against hope
Where there's life there's hope
Cross one's heart and hope to die
Abandon hope all ye who enter
    here
See a ray of hope
Dash someone's hopes
Get one's hopes up
Here's hoping!

Horn

Horn in on someone/something
Toot/blow one's own horn

Take the bull by the horns
Draw/pull in one's horns
Haul in one's horns
Lock horns with someone
Be on the horns of a dilemma

Hornet

Be mad as a hornet
Stir up a hornet's nest

Horse

Horse marines
Bet/back the wrong horse
Eat like a horse
Be healthy as a horse
Don't look a gift horse in the
    mouth
Don't flog/beat a dead horse
You can lead a horse to water,
    but you can't make him drink
Someone/something is a horse of
    another/different color
Lock the barn door after the
    horse is stolen
Hungry enough to eat a horse
Have a roll/wad big enough to
    choke a horse
Work like a horse
Get on/be on/get off one's high
    horse
Put the cart before the horse
Someone/something is a dark
    horse
Someone is a horse trader
Be a clothes horse
Have/not have horse sense
Change horses in midstream
Wild horses couldn't drag some-
    one away from something
Get something straight from the
    horse's mouth
Don't spare the horses
Close only counts in horseshoes
One-horse town

Horse-and-buggy days
Get a horse!
That's a horse on me!
Hold your horses!
That's what makes horse racing!

Hot

Hot as a firecracker
Hot as a two-dollar pistol
Hot off the boat
Hot to trot
Someone/something blows hot
  and cold
Drop someone/something like a
  hot potato
Busy as a cat on a hot tin roof/
  hot bricks
Someone/something is hot stuff
Make it hot for someone
Go like a hot knife through
  butter
Be full of hot air
Get/be hot under the collar
Strike while the iron is hot
Get/be all hot and bothered
  about someone/something
Go at something hot and heavy
Get into hot water
Give someone a hot foot
Someone/something is too hot to
  handle
Someone is a hot number
Be in the hot seat
Some like it hot
The dice are hot
Have the hots for someone
Have hot pants for someone
Something is hotter than hell
Sell like hotcakes
Something is a hotbed of activity
Hot-pillow hotel/motel
Hot-blooded
Last of the red-hot mamas
There'll be a hot time in the old

town tonight!
When you're hot, you're hot!
Hot dog/diggety-dog!

Hound

Hound someone for something
Chow hound
As thick as ticks on a hound dog
As clean as a hound's tooth

Hour

Zero hour
The eleventh hour
Every hour on the hour
Happy hour
H-hour
Keep bankers' hours
The wee small hours
Idle away the hours
After-hours joint

House

Eat someone out of house and
  home
Build a house of cards
Bring down the house
Go like a house afire
Not a dry eye in the house
Something is on the house
Someone is big as a house
Be in the big house
Clean one's house
Put one's house in order
A house is not a home
It takes a heap of living to make
  a house a home
Hash house
Sporting house
Flap house
People who live in glass houses
  shouldn't throw stones
Be in the doghouse
Shout something from the house-
  tops

Go bughouse
Boardinghouse reach
Something/someone is as thin as
   a boardinghouse blanket
A plague on both your houses!

Howl

Howl at the moon
Be a howling success

Human

To err is human, to forgive,
   divine
The milk of human kindness

Humble

Eat humble pie

Hung

Hung jury

Hunger

Someone/something is strictly
   from hunger
Lean, mean and hungry
Hungry enough to eat a horse

Hunk

Someone is a hunk of man
Hunker down
Everything's hunky-dory

Hunt

Hunt and peck
Witch hunt
Happy hunting ground

Hurry

Hurry up and wait
Here's your hat, what's your
   hurry?

Hurt

Don't cry before you're hurt
You always hurt the one you love
Someone wouldn't hurt a fly
What you don't know won't hurt
   you
The truth hurts
This won't hurt a bit!
This will hurt me more than it
   will hurt you!

I

I

Cross the T's and dot the I's

Ice

Ice cream suit
Put someone/something on ice
Something cuts no ice
Skate on thin ice
Break the ice
As independent as a hog on ice

Fire and ice
Something turns one's blood to
   ice
Someone has ice water in his
   veins
Act like someone from the ice age
Something is the icing on the
   cake
Something is only the tip of the
   iceberg

You scream, I scream, we all scream for ice cream!

Idea

Get the big idea
Give an old idea a new coat of paint
Hare/hair-brained idea
What's the big idea?

Idiot

Idiot box
Idiot card
Idiot's delight
Tales told by idiots

Idle

Idle fingers/hands are the devil's workshop
Idle away the hours
Be bone idle

If

No ifs, ands or buts
Something is iffy

Ignorance

Ignorance is bliss
Ignorance of the law is no excuse

Ill

Be ill at ease
It's an ill wind that blows nobody good
A bird of ill omen

Image

Work on one's image
Be the very image of someone/something
Someone is the spirit and image of someone
Someone is the spit/spittin' image of someone

Imagine

Something is a figment of one's imagination
Something fires one's imagination
Someone's imagination runs riot
Imagine that!

Impress

Be impressed with oneself
Labor under a false impression

Impulse

Blind impulse

In

In like a lamb, out like a lion
Be in like Flynn
Be in the doghouse
Be in a pickle/jam
Have it in for someone
Be in bad with someone
Be in league with the devil
Take something in one's stride
Do someone in
Be in over one's head
Know the ins and outs of something
Be in the inner circle
Out with the old, in with the new!
Last one in the pool is a rotten egg!

Inch

Give someone an inch and he'll take a mile
Within an inch of one's life
Every inch a king/lady
Kill someone by inches

Indian

Indian summer
Indian giver
Silent as a cigar-store Indian
Spend money like a drunken Indian
Have all chiefs and no Indians

Honest Injun!

Indifferent

Good, bad or indifferent

Influence

Be under the influence

Injury

Add insult to injury
An old football injury

Ink

Ink someone to a contract
As black as ink
Be awash in red ink
Act on something before the ink
is dry

Innocent

Innocent until proven guilty
Innocent as a lamb
Innocent as a newborn babe
The age of innocence

Inside

Know something/someone inside
out
Have the inside track
Turn something inside out
Something is an inside job
Get the inside story/dope
Something is an inside joke

Insult

Add insult to injury

Intention

The road to hell is paved with
good intentions
Have the best intentions
Have honorable intentions

Interest

Pay back someone with interest
Have someone's best interests at
heart

Invention

Necessity is the mother of invention

Iron

Iron something out with someone
Have an iron fist in a velvet glove
Rule with an iron hand
Have an iron constitution
Strike while the iron is hot
Have too many irons in the fire
Have a cast-iron stomach

Issue

Dodge the issue

Itch

Get/have an itch for something
Get the seven-year itch
Have an itchy palm
Have itchy feet
Have itchy fingers

Ivory

Sit in an ivory tower
Tickle the ivories

J

Jack

Jack up the ante/price
All work and no play makes Jack
    a dull boy
Before one can say Jack Robin-
son
Ballin' the jack
Every last manjack
Scared as a jackrabbit
Jackrabbit start
Hit the jackpot

Jail

Someone is jailbait

Jam

Jam session
Be in a jam
It must be jelly, cuz jam don't
    shake like that!

Jar

Catch someone with his hand in
    the cookie jar

Jaundice

Look at something with a jaundiced eye

Jaw

Have a glass jaw
Have a lantern jaw
Flap one's jaws
Snatch victory from the jaws of
    defeat

Jazz

Jazz something up
Jazz stick
And all that jazz!

Jelly

It must be jelly, cuz jam don't
    shake like that!

Jerk

Jerk someone's chain
Jerk someone around
Jerk around
Jerk off
Have the jerks
Jerk-water town
Tear-jerker

Jib

Not like the cut of someone's jib

Jig

Do something in jig time
The jig is up!

Job

Give someone a snow job
Something is an inside job
Asleep on the job
Fall down on the job
Do a hatchet job on someone
Do a job on someone
Do a bang-up job
Something is a put-up job

John

John Q. Public
Dear John letter
Put one's John Hancock on some-
    thing
Johnny-on-the-spot
Johnny-come-lately

Join

If you can't beat 'em, join 'em

Joined at the hip
Join the club!

Joint

Get/have one's nose out of joint
Case the joint
The joint is jumping
Smoke a joint
Clip/gyp joint
After-hours joint

Joke

Crack a joke
Someone can't take a joke
Someone/something looks like a
  bad joke
Be the butt of a joke
Something is an inside joke
Off-color joke
Someone/something is the joker
  in the deck
All joking aside/apart
Only joking!
No joking!
What is this, a joke?

Jowl

Be cheek-by-jowl with someone/
  something

Joy

Jump for joy
Be someone's pride and joy
A thing of beauty is a joy forever
Bundle of joy
Go for a joy ride
Joystick
Killjoy

Judge

Be sober/solemn as a judge
You can't judge a book by its
  cover
Sit in judgment on someone
Against one's better judgment

Here come de judge!

Jug

A jug of wine, a loaf of bread
  and thou

Juice

Juice dealer
The blacker the berry, the
  sweeter the juice
Stew in one's own juice
Pour on the juice
Have juice in high places
Get juiced

Jump

Jump through hoops for someone
Jump out of one's skin
Jump over the broomstick
Jump for joy
Jump off the deep end
Jump on the bandwagon
Jump the gun
Jump down someone's throat
Jump someone's bones
Jump someone's claim
Jump to conclusions
Get the jump on someone/some-
  thing
Not know which way to jump
Be one jump ahead of the sheriff
Know which way the cat will
  jump
A hop, skip and a jump away
Jumping-off place
Jumpin' catfish!
Go jump in the lake!

Jungle

It's a jungle out there

Jury

The jury is still out on something
Hung jury
Blue-ribbon jury

Just

Just for the hell of it
Just under the wire
Just for the record
Just the ticket
Just what the doctor ordered
Just one's meat
Just the same
Just one of those things
Just tell 'em Joe sent ya
Just another pretty face
Just another face in the crowd

Have just cause
Get one's just desserts
It just goes to show you
Just try and start something!

Justice

Justice is blind
Justice delayed is justice denied
Poetic justice
The end justifies the means
Monstrous injustice

K

Keel

Keel over
Be/keep on an even keel

Keep

Keep someone/something in cold
  storage
Keep everything aboveboard
Keep a straight face
Keep one's bearings
Keep up with the best of them
Keep someone in the dark
Keep one's head above water
Keep up appearances
Keep something on the back
  burner
Keep one's cool
Keep on course
Keep your eye on the donut, not
  on the hole
Keep one's distance
Keep the ball rolling

Keep a civil tongue in one's head
Keep your powder dry
Keep a stiff upper lip
Keep an ear to the ground
Keep one's nose clean
Keep someone in his place
Keep an eagle eye out for
  someone/something
Keep your eye on the sparrow
Keep one's eyes peeled
Keep an eye on someone/
  something
Keep the home fires burning
Keep one's nose out of something
Keep company with someone
Keep the wolf from the door
Keep your guard up
Keep on the straight and narrow
Keep on an even keel
Keep one's fingers crossed
Keep one's hand in
Keep one's chin up

Keep both feet on the ground
Keep something under one's hat
Keep up with the Joneses
Keep something under wraps
Keep one's own counsel
Keep on the good side of some-
one
Keep on one's toes
Keep someone posted
Keep body and soul together
Keep someone/something at arm's
length
Keep something in mind
Keep one's eye on the ball
Keep one's wits about one
Keep a weather eye out
Keep one's nose to the grind-
stone
Keep tabs on someone/something
Keep the faith
Keep bankers' hours
Keep the lid on something
Keep pace with someone/some-
thing
Keep the peace
Keep someone on the side
Keep the pot boiling
Keep a finger on the pulse of
something
You can't keep a good man down
Earn one's keep
Be known by the company one
keeps
Play for keeps
An apple a day keeps the doctor
away
Finders keepers, losers weepers
The keeper of the flame
Keep on truckin'!
Keep your shirt/pants on!
Keep your cotton-pickin' hands
off!
Keep pitching!
Am I my brother's keeper?

Keg

Sit on a powder keg

Kettle

Something is a pretty/fine kettle
of fish
The pot calling the kettle black

Key

Have the key to someone's heart
Get/have the keys to the city
Get/be all keyed up

Kick

Kick off
Kick the bucket/can
Kick the habit
Kick over the traces
Kick up one's heels
Kick oneself
Kick up a fuss/row
Kick someone when he's down
Kick something around
Kick in one's share
Get a kick out of someone/some-
thing
Get/give a swift kick in the pants
Get a kick in the head/teeth
Have no kick coming
Be alive and kicking
Here's the kicker!

Kid

Kid around
Handle someone/something with
kid gloves
Someone is just a crazy, mixed-up
kid
Be the new kid on the block
Like a kid in a candy store
Be kidding on the square
All kidding aside/apart
Help send this kid to camp!
I kid you not!

Kill

Kill someone by inches
Kill the fatted calf
Kill two birds with one stone
Kill the goose that lays the
   golden eggs
Kill time
Kill someone with kindness
If looks could kill
The urge to kill
Dressed to kill
Be in at the kill
Something will either cure you or
   kill you
Look fit to kill
Curiosity killed the cat
Made a killing in the market
Killjoy
Lady/man-killer

Kind

Two of a kind
Feel fourteen kinds of a fool
Milk of human kindness
Kill someone with kindness
Have a cup of kindness
The kindest/unkindest cut of all

King

Fit for a king
Be king of the hill
Live like a king
A cat can look on a king
Every inch a king
Pay a king's ransom for some-
   thing
Kingpin
Kingmaker
Get/have the keys to the king-
   dom
Blow something to kingdom come

Kiss

Kiss and make up

Kiss of death
Kiss something goodbye
Kiss the Blarney stone
Kiss someone/something off
Kiss a mule, cure a cold
Blow/throw someone a kiss
Half-past kissing time, time to kiss
   again
Kissin' cousins
Kiss my foot!

Kit

The whole kit and caboodle

Kitchen

Everything but the kitchen sink
If you can't stand the heat, stay
   out of the kitchen

Kite

Someone is high as a kite
Go fly a kite!

Kitten

Weak/helpless as a kitten
Soft as a kitten
Playful as a kitten
Have kittens
Give someone kittens

Knee

On bended knee
Cut someone off at the knees
Bring someone to his knees
Be on one's hands and knees
Someone/something is the bee's
   knees
Be knee-deep in something
Be knee-high to a grasshopper

Knickers

Get one's knickers in a twist

Knife

Knife someone in the back

Something is so thick you could
cut it with a knife
Go like a hot knife through butter

Knight

Knight in shining armor
Be someone's white knight

Knit

Knit one's brows
Stick to one's knitting
Close-knit group

Knock

Knock oneself out for someone/
something
Knock 'em in the aisles
Knock someone back on his
heels
Knock on wood
Knock something into a cocked
hat
Knock someone for a loop
Knock the living daylights out of
someone
Knock someone's block off
Knock someone's socks off
Knock the spots off someone
Knock someone up
Knock someone cold
Knock the tar out of someone
Knock someone's eyes out
Knock the stuffing out of some-
one
Opportunity knocks but once
The school of hard knocks
Have something knocked
Could have knocked someone
over with a feather
Someone is a knockout
Knock-down, drag-out fight
Knock it off!
Knock 'em dead!

Knot

Tie the knot
Cut the Gordian knot
Have one's stomach tied up in
knots

Know

Know someone from way back
Know which way the cat will
jump
Know all the answers
Know one's beans/onions
Know something from the ground
up
Know something like one's own
name
Know where it's at
Know where someone/something
is coming from
Know the cost of everything and
the value of nothing
Know all the moves
Know the ground rules
Know the ins and outs of some-
thing
Know one's place
Know the ropes
Know someone/something inside
out
Know something in one's bones
Know something/someone like
the back of one's hand
Know one's stuff
Know one's way around
Know something by heart
Know the score
Know which side one's bread is
buttered on
Know something backwards and
forwards
Know all the tricks of the trade
Know what's what
Know where all the bodies are
buried

To know one is to love him/her
Old enough to know better
It's not what you know, it's who
  you know
Someone doesn't know beans
  about something
Not know someone from Adam
Be in the know
One's left hand doesn't know
  what one's right hand is doing
Not know which way to jump
Not know enough to come in out
  of the rain
Not know which end/way is up
Not know what time it is
Not know whether one is coming
  or going
It takes one to know one
The first thing you know
Someone is a poet and doesn't
  know it
Something/someone knows no
bounds
Be known by the company one
  keeps
Knowledge is power
A little knowledge is a dangerous
  thing
To the best of one's knowledge
Something is public/common
  knowledge
What you don't know won't hurt
  you!
Darned if I know!
Goodness/heaven only knows!

Knuckle

Knuckle down
Knuckle under
Give someone a knuckle sand-
  wich
Have white knuckles
Give someone a mouthful of
  knuckles

L

Labor

Labor under a disadvantage
Labor under a false impression
Do hard labor
Something is a labor of love
The fruits of one's labors

Lad

A fine broth of a lad

Ladder

Move up the ladder of success
Fall/slip a rung lower on the
ladder
Don't walk under a ladder

Lady

Lady luck
Every inch a lady
It ain't over till the fat lady sings
Faint heart ne'er won fair lady
Fancy lady
Foxy lady
Ladies of the evening
Lady-killer
Lady-in-waiting

That was no lady, that was my
wife!

Lake

Go jump in the lake!

Lam

Be/take it on the lam

Lamb

Gentle/meek as a lamb
Like a lamb to the slaughter
Innocent as a lamb
In like a lamb, out like a lion
In two shakes of a lamb's tail
A wolf in lamb's clothing

Lame

Lame excuse
Someone is a lame duck
Blind, lame and halt
Lamebrain

Land

Land of milk and honey
Land of Dixie
Land of Nod
See how the land lies
Live off the fat of the land
Landslide victory
The Marines have landed!
For lands' sakes!

Lane

Life in the fast lane
Take a trip down memory lane

Language

Murder the language
Speak someone's language
One's language makes the air
turn blue

Lap

Lap something up

Be cradled/live in the lap of
luxury
Have something fall into one's lap
Something is in the lap of the
gods

Lard

Lard the wheels
Someone is a tub of lard

Large

Large as/larger than life
By and large
Get a large charge out of some-
one/something

Lark

Happy as a lark
Go on a lark

Lash

Lash out at someone
Give someone forty lashes with a
wet noodle
Bat one's eyelashes at someone
Give someone a tongue-lashing

Last

Last but not least
Last of the big spenders
Last of the red-hot mamas
Last resort
First, last and always
Have the last laugh
Have the last word
Something is the last straw
Be on one's last legs
Nice guys finish last
He who laughs last, laughs best
Someone/something is the last
word in something
Heading for the last roundup
Breathe one's last
Play one's last card
A cobbler should stick to his last

Fight to the last ditch
Every last manjack
Save the best for last
Make a last-ditch effort
At long last!
Last one in the pool is a rotten
egg!

Latch

Latch onto someone/something
Latchkey kid

Late

A day late and a dollar short
Better late than never
A little late in the day for some-
thing
Someone would be late for his
own funeral
Too little too late
Too soon old and too late smart
Sooner or later
Catch your act later
Johnny-come-lately
It's later than you think!
See/dig you later, alligator!
Plant you now, dig you later!
Call me anything but late for
breakfast!

Lather

Get oneself into a lather

Laugh

Laugh in one's beard
Laugh someone/something off
Laugh one's head off
Laugh up one's sleeve
Laugh until you cry
Laugh all the way to the bank
Laugh it up
Laugh oneself silly
Laugh out of the other side of
one's mouth

Laugh on the other side of one's
face
Something/someone is a laugh
and a half
Anything for a laugh
Have the last laugh
Someone/something is a laugh a
minute
Do something just for laughs
Something is no laughing matter
Break up laughing
Die laughing
Leave 'em laughing
Split one's sides laughing
Burst/break into laughter
Canned laughter
Laughter is the best medicine
Someone laughs like a hyena
Laugh, I thought I'd die!
The laugh's on me/you!

Laurels

Look to/rest on one's laurels

Law

Someone/something is above the
law
Possession is nine points of the
law
The letter of the law
The long arm of the law
Ignorance of the law is no excuse
Call the law on someone
Be a law unto oneself
Take the law into one's own
hands
Lay down the law
Someone's word is law
Need a Philadelphia lawyer

Lay

Lay an egg
Lay down the law
Lay 'em in the aisles

Lay back and enjoy it
Lay something on the line
Lay all one's cards on the table
Lay low
Lay something to rest
Pick 'em up and lay 'em down
Play it as it lays
Kill the goose that lays the
  golden eggs
Be laid back

Lead (vb)

Lead someone down the garden/
  primrose path
Lead a dog's life
Lead a charmed life
Lead someone around by the
  nose
Lead the way
Lead someone a merry chase
Lead a brass band
You can lead a horse to water,
  but you can't make him drink
All roads lead to Rome
Like the blind leading the blind
Take me to your leader!

Lead

Have lead in one's pants
Fill someone full of lead
Someone/something goes over
  like a lead balloon
Something will put lead in your
  pencil
Something is a lead-pipe cinch
Get the lead out!

Leaf

Shake/tremble like a leaf
Turn over a new leaf
Take a leaf from someone's book

League

Be in league with the devil/some-
  one

Something/someone is strictly
  bush league
Lunar league
Play in/hit the big leagues

Leak

Leak a story
Take a leak
Something springs a leak

Lean

Lean hard on someone/some-
  thing
Lean, green machine
Lean, mean and hungry

Leap

Look before you leap
Take a leap in the dark
By leaps and bounds
Leapin' lizards!
Go take a flying leap!

Learn

Learn something by heart
Learn the ropes
Learn and earn
Live and learn
One can learn from any fool
Listen and learn
Something is a lesson to be
  learned

Lease

Get a new lease on life

Least

Least said, soonest mended
Last, but not least
Someone/something is the least
  of one's worries

Leather

Someone/something is as tough
  as old leather

Be hell-bent for leather

Leave

Leave something/someone hang-
ing in the air
Leave no stone unturned
Leave someone in the lurch
Leave 'em laughing
Leave someone flat
Leave well enough alone
Leave someone high and dry
Leave someone holding the bag/
baby
Leave a trail of broken hearts
Take it or leave it
Take French leave
Take leave of one's senses
Love 'em and leave 'em
Something/someone leaves a lot
to be desired
Something/someone leaves a bad
taste in one's mouth
Someone/something leaves one
cold

Left

Be left at the altar/gate
Be left to one's own devices
Be left out in the cold
One's left hand doesn't know
what one's right hand is doing
Have two left feet
Something comes from left field
Make/coin money left and right
Left-handed compliment

Leg

Something costs/pay an arm and
a leg
Someone still gets into his pants
one leg at a time
Do leg work
Not have a leg to stand on
Have a hollow leg

Pull someone's leg
Give someone a leg up
Talk the hind leg off a donkey
Have one's tail between his legs
Be on one's last legs
Shake a leg!
Break a leg!
Cut off my legs and call me
Shorty!

Legal

Someone is a legal eagle/beagle
Make it legal

Legend

Someone is a legend in his own
time/mind

Lemon

Someone/something is a real
lemon
If you get a lemon, make lemon-
ade

Lend

Lend a hand
Lend an ear
Lend local color
Something lends itself to some-
one/something
Something lends color to some-
thing
Neither a borrower nor a lender
be

Length

Keep someone/something at arm's
length
Be on the same wavelength
Go to any/all lengths

Leopard

A leopard can't change its spots

Less

Less is more

In less than no time
More or less
Couldn't care less about some-
  one/something
Choose the lesser of two evils

Lesson

Teach someone a lesson
Something is a lesson to be
  learned

Let

Let one's defenses down
Let one's hair down
Let bygones be bygones
Let the chips fall where they may
Let the cat out of the bag
Let someone down easy
Let sleeping dogs lie
Let off steam
Let someone off the hook
Let the dead bury the dead
Let it all hang out
Let oneself go
Let it be
Let someone have it with both
  barrels
Let someone have it right be-
  tween the eyes
Let/leave well enough alone
Not let any grass grow under
  one's feet
Live and let live
Let George do it!
Let's not and say we did!
Let 'er rip!

Letter

The letter of the law
Be letter perfect
Open letter
Dear John letter
Chain letter
Poison-pen letter

Four-letter word
Red-letter day

Level

Level off
Be on the level
Do one's level best
Water seeks its own level
Put the leveler on someone

Lick

Lick one's wounds
Lick one's chops
Lick someone's boots
Lick something/someone into
  shape
Give something a lick and a
  promise
Get/put in one's licks
Hot licks
Lickety-split

Lid

Blow the lid off something
Flip one's lid
Keep the lid on something
Wear a skid-lid
Put a lid on it!

Lie

Lie through one's teeth
Lie low
Make one's bed and lie in it
Let sleeping dogs lie
Bald/bare-faced lie
Figures don't lie
See how the land lies
Tell little white lies
Ask me no questions, I'll tell you
  no lies
Uneasy lies the head that wears
  the crown
Take/not take something lying
  down

Life

Life is just a bowl of cherries
Life in the fast lane
Life begins at forty
Life is not all beer and skittles/
    pretzels
Live the life of Riley
To save one's life
A matter of life and death
Guard something with one's life
Where there's life, there's hope
Within an inch of one's life
Large as/larger than life
Variety is the spice of life
Be between life and death
Big as life and twice as natural
Run for dear life
One's life is an open book
Get a new lease on life
Have the time of one's life
Be the life of the party
The facts of life
Lead a charmed life
Lead a dog's life
Take one's life into one's own
    hands
Into each life a little rain must fall
Breathe new life into something
Light up someone's life
Be in the prime of life
The best things in life are free
Today is the first day of the rest
    of your life
Risk life and limb for someone/
    something
Something is a slice-of-life
You bet your life!
Not on your life!

Lift

A rising tide lifts all boats

Light

Light a candle or curse the dark-
ness
Light a fire under someone
Light as a feather
Light up someone's life
Bring something to light
Something comes to light
Trip the light fantastic
Something will never see the light
    of day
Be out like a light
All sweetness and light
Hide one's light under a bushel
Get the green light
See a ray of light at the end of
    the tunnel
Throw light on something
Many hands make light work
Travel light
There's a broken heart for every
    light on Broadway
There's a broken light for every
    heart on Broadway
Someone's pilot light is out
See something in the cold light of
    day
Someone has a few lights out in
    his marquee
Someone lights up like Times
    Square/a Christmas tree
As fast as greased lightning
Lightning never strikes in the
    same place twice
Be light-fingered

Like

Like father, like son
Like me, like my dog
Like it or lump it
There's no place like home
Someone up there likes me!
A likely story!
I don't know art, but I know
    what I like!
How do you like them apples?

Lily

Gild the lily
Someone is lily-white
Someone is lily-livered

Limb

Go/be out on a limb
Risk life and limb for someone/
  something

Limit

Limit one's losses
Go the limit
The sky's the limit!
Ain't that the limit?

Limp

Limp along
Be limp as a dishrag
Limp-wristed

Line

Line one's pockets
Cross the line
Tread/walk a thin line
Toe/walk the line
Put one's money/cash on the line
Read/get to the bottom line
Hold the line
Drop someone a line
Lay something on the line
The end of the line
Draw the line at something
Swallow something hook, line
  and sinker
Hand/feed someone a line
Walk a straight line
All in the line of duty
Dash off a line to someone
The shortest distance between
  two points is a straight line
Punch line
Chow line
Draw the battle lines
Read between the lines

Blow one's lines
Every cloud has a silver lining

Linen

Wash/air one's dirty linen in public

Link

The missing link
Be the weak link in the chain

Lion

Beard the lion in his den
Roar like a lion
In like a lamb, out like a lion
Get the lion's share of something
Put one's head in the lion's
  mouth
Throw someone to the lions

Lip

There's many a slip between the
  cup and the lip
A slip of the lip
Keep a stiff upper lip
Give someone a fat lip
Pay lip service to someone
Button one's lip
Bite one's lip
Zip one's lip
Loose lips sink ships
A moment on the lips, a year on
  the hips
Read my lips!
Zip your lip!

Liquor

Can/can't hold one's liquor
Candy is dandy, but liquor is
  quicker
Get all liquored up

Listen

Listen in on something
Listen and learn

Listen up!

Litter

The pick/runt of the litter
Litterbug

Little

Little pitchers have big ears
Little shaver
Little black book
Be a big fish in a little pond
Wrap someone around one's little
finger
A little bird told me
Into each life a little rain must
fall
Too little, too late
Someone is a little shaver
Sure as God made little green
apples
Have more in one's little finger
than _____
Great oaks from little acorns
grow
Tell little white lies
A little knowledge is a dangerous
thing
Mother's little helper
One's little red wagon
One's little black book
Live a little!
Ye gods and little fishes!

Live

Live something down
Live and let live
Live hand to mouth
Live off the fat of the land
Live in a goldfish bowl
Live in a pressure cooker
Live and learn
Live out in the sticks
Live to a ripe old age
Live out in the 'burbs/shrubs
Live it up

Live high off the hog
Live on borrowed time
Live the life of Riley
Live for the moment/day
Live by one's wits
Live like a king
Live dangerously
Live on the edge
Live in a hole in the wall
Live in the lap of luxury
Live across/on the wrong side of
the tracks
People who live in glass houses
shouldn't throw stones
Can't live without someone/
something
Can't live on love
Man cannot live by bread
alone
Someone is a live wire
Hit someone where he lives
He who lives by the sword, dies
by the sword
A cat has nine lives
Something is a living hell
Living well is the best revenge
Knock/scare/beat the living day-
lights out of someone
Someone/something is the living
end
Someone is a living doll
Alive and well and living
in _____
Live a little!
You only live once!
Pardon me for living!
Step lively!
What's your excuse for living?

Liver

Someone is chicken/yellow-
livered
Someone is lily-livered
What am I, chopped liver?

Load

Load the dice/deck
Be one brick short of a load
Take a load off one's feet
Get a load off one's mind
Get a load on
Get a load of something/someone
Loaded question
Be loaded for bear
Be loaded to the gills

Loaf

Half a loaf is better than none
A jug of wine, a loaf of bread
  and thou

Loan

Float a loan

Local

Local yokel
Lend local color
Think someone is a local when
  they're a fast express

Lock

Lock horns with someone
Lock the barn door after the
  horse is stolen
Buy something lock, stock and
  barrel
Have/get a lock on something
Have something all locked up

Log

As easy as falling off a log
Sit there like a bump on a log
Sleep like a log
Be at loggerheads with someone/
  something

Long

Long green
Happy as the day is long
Cut a long story short

Cast a long shadow
Have/wear a long face
Getting long in the tooth
As honest as the day is long
In the long run
Not by a long chalk/shot
Over the long haul
The long arm of the law
You're a long time dead
The long and short of some-
  thing
Someone earns long cake
Take a long shot
Something is someone's long suit
Nervous as a long-tailed cat in a
  roomful of rocking chairs
Long live the king/queen!
Long time no see!
You should live so long!
At long last!
Take a long walk off a short pier!

Look

Look a fright
Look like a drowned rat
Look like a million bucks/dollars
Look like death warmed over
Look like the devil
Look on the bright side
Look at the world through rose-
  colored glasses
Look like the cat that swallowed
  the canary
Look like something the cat
  dragged in
Look daggers at someone
Look cross-eyed at someone
Look before you leap
Look the other way
Look/can't look someone in the
  eye
Look to one's laurels
Look down one's nose at some-
  thing/someone

Look like one just stepped out of a bandbox
Look out for number one
Look like an accident on its way to happen
Look like someone has seen a ghost
Look at the big picture
Look like one was hit by a truck
Look at something with a jaundiced eye
A cat can look on a king
Don't look a gift horse in the mouth
Give someone a dirty look
Have a hangdog look
Give/get a blank look
Give/get a look that would curdle milk
Give/get a black look
A look that speaks volumes
If looks could kill
Something looks good enough to eat
Something/someone looks fishy
Someone looks fit to kill
Be down so long it looks like up
Like looking for a needle in a haystack
Things are looking up
Be on the lookout for someone/something
Have a look-see
Look alive/sharp!
Look ma, no hands!
Look what the cat dragged in!

Loon

Crazy as a loon
Send someone to the loony bin

Loop

Be thrown for a loop
Knock someone for a loop

Find a loophole

Loose

Loose lips sink ships
Play fast and loose with someone/something
Have a screw loose
All hell breaks loose
Someone/something is a loose cannon
Be on the loose
Be at loose ends
Be loose as a goose
Hang loose
Be footloose and fancy-free
Loosen up!

Lord

Lord it over someone
Be drunk as a lord
If the Lord be willin' and the creek don't rise
Lord only knows!

Lose

Lose by a nose/hair/whisker
Lose one's shirt
Lose one's bearings
Lose face
Lose ground
Lose one's grip
Lose all one's marbles
Lose sight of something
Lose heart
Lose one's head/cool
Lose track of someone/something
Lose by a country mile
Not lose any sleep over someone/something
Win a few, lose a few
Win, lose or draw
Win some, lose some
Heads I win, tails you lose
It's not whether you win or lose, it's how you play the game

Be a sore loser
Finders keepers, losers weepers
Can't win for losing
Use it or lose it!
Boozers are losers!

Loss

Be thrown for a loss
Be at a loss for words
Limit/cut one's losses
Your loss is my gain!

Lost

He who hesitates is lost
Someone/something gets lost in
  the shuffle
No love lost between you and
  someone
Something gets lost in the trans-
  lation
Be lost in thought
Someone/something is a lost cause
The lost chord
Make up for lost time
Get lost!

Lot

Someone is a bad lot
Someone has a lot of crust
Someone has a lot of mileage on
  him/her
Someone/something is all over
  the lot
Someone/something leaves a lot
  to be desired
Cast in one's lot with someone/
  something
A fat lot of good something will
  do

Loud

Loud enough to wake the dead
Think out loud
Read someone/something loud
  and clear

Actions speak louder than words
For crying out loud!

Love

Love at first sight
Love makes the world go around
Love me, love my dog
Love conquers all
Love 'em and leave 'em
Love is blind
Love not wisely, but too well
Love nest
Fall head over heels in love
True love never runs smooth
A face only a mother could love
All's fair in love and war
Money can't buy love
Can't live on love
To know someone is to love him/
  her
When the wolf is at the door,
  love flies out the window
No love lost between you and
  someone
Make love, not war
You always hurt the one you love
Something is a labor of love
Puppy love
Misery loves company
Someone is a vision of loveliness
Live-in lover
Love-hate relationship
For the love of Pete!

Low

Search high and low for some-
  one/something
Lay/lie low
Be low man on the totem pole
Give/get a low blow
Lower one's flag
Lower the boom on someone
Someone is lower than a snake's
  belly

Fall/slip a rung lower on the ladder
Get one's ears lowered
Get the low-down on someone/
something

Luck

Luck out with someone/some-
thing
Someone's luck runs out
Try one's luck
Be down on one's luck
Have a run/streak/stroke of
good/bad luck
The luck of the Irish
The luck of the draw
As luck would have it
Press one's luck
Three on a match is bad luck
Lady luck
Dumb, rotten luck
Get lucky
Be born under a lucky star
Thank one's lucky stars
Happy-go-lucky
Hard-luck story
Lotsa luck!

Best of luck!
Better luck next time!

Lump

Like it or lump it
Have a lump in one's throat
Take one's lumps

Lull

The lull before the storm

Lunacy

Something borders on lunacy

Lunch

There's no such thing as a free
lunch
Let's do lunch

Lung

At the top of one's lungs

Lurch

Leave someone in the lurch

Luxury

Live/cradled in the lap of luxury

M

Mad

Mad as hops
Mad as a hornet/wet hen
Mad as a hatter
Mad money
So mad one could spit
So mad one can't see straight

Go/be stark-raving mad
Go like mad
Be hopping mad
Have method to one's madness
Drive like a madman
Far from the madding crowd

Made

Made for each other
Made up of whole cloth
Sure as God made little green
  apples
Someone is not made of money
A marriage/match made in
  heaven

Main

Main drag
In the main
Be someone's main man
Be someone's main squeeze
Go at something with might and
  main

Make

Make a break for it
Make believe
Make someone sick
Make a last-ditch effort
Make it legal
Make an example of someone/
  something
Make a grandstand play
Make the nut
Make the feathers/fur fly
Make a long story short
Make a dent in something
Make a mountain out of a mole-
  hill
Make a fool out of someone
Make a go of something
Make one's bed and lie in it
Make a Federal case out of some-
  thing
Make a pass at someone
Make hay while the sun shines
Make the best of something
Make tracks
Make out like a bandit
Make a bargain/pact with the
  devil

Make beautiful music together
Make sheep's eyes at someone
Make no bones about something
Make a clean sweep of something
Make a clean breast of something
Make an honest woman out of
  someone
Make both ends meet
Make a monkey out of someone
Make the rounds
Make a spectacle of oneself
Make a big production/deal out
  of something
Make oneself scarce
Make the scene
Make a big stink about something
Make mincemeat out of someone
Make or break someone
Make a play for someone
Make money hand-over-fist
Make up for lost time
Make the grade
Make a fast buck
Make a splash
Make all the right moves
Make eyes at someone
Make a beeline for someone/
  something
Make a day/night of it
Make a bundle on something
Make someone an offer he can't
  refuse
Make a mint
Make short work of someone/
  something
Make a beef about something
Make a new beginning
Make a bolt/dash for it
Make book on something
Make it hot for someone
Make a scene
Make a killing in the market
Make busywork
Make whoopee

Make fun of someone/something
Be on the make
Two wrongs don't make a right
Something/someone is enough to
     make someone turn over in his
     grave
Can't make head nor tail out of
     something/someone
Kiss and make up
You can lead a horse to water,
     but you can't make him drink
One swallow does not a summer
     make
Can't make a silk purse out of a
     sow's ear
Politics make strange bedfellows
Can't make an omelet without
     breaking some eggs
Clothes make the man
Many hands make light work
Something/someone makes one's
     mouth water
Something/someone makes one's
     hair stand on end
Someone/something makes one's
     flesh crawl
Something/someone makes one's
     blood boil
Money/love makes the world go
     around
Something/someone makes one's
     blood run cold
What a difference a day makes
So fast it makes your head swim
What makes someone tick
Something/someone makes one's
     eyes pop
Meet one's maker
Kingmaker
Make it snappy!
Make no mistake about it!
Don't make me laugh!
Make my day!
Don't make waves!

That's what makes horse-racing!
Wanna make something of it?

Man

Man cannot live by bread alone
Man of the cloth
Man of the hour
Man after one's own heart
Man of means
Man about town
Man of the world
Man of parts
Man without a country
Man in/on the street
Man works from sun to sun, but
     woman's work is never done
Man Friday
Be all man
Be a man of few words
Be a man of purpose
Be someone's main man
A good man is hard to find
Be low man on the totem pole
No man is a hero to his valet
Every man has his price
Clothes make the man
Big man on campus
The answer man
Something is not fit for man nor
     beast
Have to see a man about a dog
Be all man
Be a company man
Be a man among men
Be a marked man
You can't keep a good man down
Throw water on a drowning man
Feel like a new man
Odd man out
The Man upstairs
Take something like a man
Macho man
Hatchet/hit man
Hunk of man

A mountie always gets his man
Meat-and-potatoes man
Every last manjack
Man's best friend
The way to a man's heart is
  through his stomach
Be all things to all men
Dead men tell no tales
Separate the men from the boys
Step into dead men's shoes
Someone is a one-man show
Have a man-to-man talk
Man bites dog!

Manger

Someone is a dog in the manger

Manner

To the manner born
Have a good bedside manner
Mind one's manners

Many

Many are called, but few are
  chosen
Many hands make light work
In so many words
Be a man of many hats
Too many cooks spoil the broth
Have one too many
Have too many irons in the fire

Map

Put something/someplace on the
  map

Marble

Have/lose all one's marbles
Pick up all the marbles
Pick up one's marbles and go
  home

March

March to a different drummer
Steal a march on someone

An army marches on its stomach

Mare

Ride shank's mare
Mare's nest

Marines

Horse Marines
Tell it to the Marines!
The Marines have landed!

Mark

Mark time
Fall short of/miss the mark
Something is beside the mark
Something/someone doesn't come
  up to the mark
Have a black mark against one
X marks the spot
Be a marked man
Call in one's markers
Mark my words!

Market

Be in the market for something
Be stone-cold dead in the market
Corner the market
Black market
Something is a drug on the mar-
  ket
Make a killing in the market

Marry

Marry in haste, repent at leisure
A marriage made in heaven
Have to get married

Mat

Go to the mat for someone/some-
  thing
Roll out the welcome mat
Be a doormat

Match

A match made in heaven

The whole shooting match
Play the rubber match
Meet one's match
Three on a match is bad luck

Matter

As a matter of fact
As a matter of course
A matter of life and death
A matter of record
No laughing matter
The fact of the matter
Mind over matter
It matters not
Not mince matters

May

Come what may
Let the chips fall where they may
Be that as it may
Queen of the May

Meal

Meal ticket
Square meal
Mealy-mouthed

Mean

Lean, mean and hungry
It don't mean a thing if it ain't
   got that swing
A man of means
By all means
Ways and means
By no means
By fair means or foul
The end justifies the means
I mean business!

Measure

Measure up to someone/some-
   thing
Beyond measure
One for good measure
Take someone's measure

Measure-for-measure
Take half-measures

Meat

Meat wagon
Mystery meat
Just one's meat
One's meat is another man's
   poison
Something is meat and drink to
   someone
Someone is dead meat
The nearer the bone, the sweeter
   the meat
Meat-and-potatoes man
Put someone through the meat-
   grinder
All that meat and no potatoes!

Medicine

Give someone a dose of his own
   medicine
Something is strong medicine
Take one's medicine
Laughter is the best medicine

Meek

Meek as a lamb
Meek as Milquetoast
The meek shall inherit the earth

Meet

Meet on common ground
Meet one's Waterloo
Meet one's maker
Meet someone halfway
Meet one's Prince Charming
Meet one's match
Make both ends meet
More to something than meets
   the eye
Hale fellow, well met
Wear one's best Sunday-go-meet-
   ing clothes

Melt

One look and one could melt
Butter wouldn't melt in someone's
  mouth

Memory

Someone/something is only a
  faded memory
Have a memory like an elephant
Jog someone's memory
Take a trip down memory lane

Mend

Mend one's fences
End it or mend it
Least said, soonest mended

Mental

Have a mental block
Be a mental case

Mercy

Mercy killing
Be an angel of mercy
Throw oneself on the mercy of
  the court
Be at the mercy of someone
Beg/cry for mercy
For mercy's sake!
Mercy me!

Merry

Lead someone a merry chase
Be merry as a cricket
Eat, drink and be merry, for
  tomorrow you may die
The more the merrier!

Mess

Mess around
Mess up
Mess of food
Another fine mess
Make a mess of something
Be in a mess

Don't mess with me!

Method

Have method to/in one's madness

Mettle

Prove one's mettle

Middle

Middle of the road
Change horses in the middle of
  the stream
Play both ends against the middle
Something is someone's middle
  name
Be/stay on middle ground
Be in the middle of nowhere
Be smack dab in the middle
Someone/something is fair-to-
  middling

Midnight

Burn the midnight oil

Might

Go at something with might and
  main
The pen is mightier than the
  sword
How the mighty have fallen
The almighty dollar
Have a high-and-mighty attitude

Mile

Walk a mile in another man's
  moccasins
Go the extra mile
Win/lose by a country mile
Give someone an inch and he'll
  take a mile
A miss is as good as a mile
Talk a mile a minute
Be miles apart on something
Someone has a lot of mileage on
  him/her

Milk

Milk something for all its worth
Milk of human kindness
Milk run
Don't cry over spilt milk
Land of milk and honey
Get/give a look that would curdle milk
Why buy the cow when the milk is free?

Mill

Grist for the mill
Go through the mill
Gin mill
The mills of God grind slowly
Have a millstone around one's neck
Run-of-the-mill

Million

Someone/something is one in a million
Look/feel like a million bucks/dollars
Fifty million Frenchmen can't be wrong

Mince

Not mince words
Not mince matters
Make mincemeat out of someone

Mind

Mind one's manners
Mind over matter
Mind one's P's and Q's
Have a mind like a steel trap
Have a good mind to do something
Read someone's mind
Someone's mind is in the gutter
Give someone a piece of one's mind

Be in/out of one's right mind
Something crosses one's mind
Keep something in mind
Bring something to mind
Have a one-track mind
Close one's mind to something/someone
Get a load off one's mind
Have half a mind to do something
Play mind games with someone
Someone/something has a mind of its own
A sound mind in a healthy body
Something boggles the mind
Out of sight, out of mind
Someone is a legend in his own mind
Blow one's mind
Bear something in mind
Great minds think alike
Be broad-minded
Have a mind-boggling experience
It's all in your mind!
Mind your own business!
Who's minding the store?

Mine

Something is a gold mine
What's yours is mine and what's mine is my own
Back to the salt mines
Your place or mine?

Mint

Mint money hand-over-fist
Make a mint
Something is in mint condition

Minute

There's a sucker born every minute
Someone/something is right up to the minute

Someone/something is a laugh/
thrill a minute
Talk a mile a minute

Miracle

Something is a minor miracle
The age of miracles is/is not past

Misery

Misery loves company
Put someone out of his misery

Miss

Miss the mark
Miss the boat
Miss something by a country mile
A miss is as good as a mile
Something is hit or miss
You never miss the water till the
well runs dry
Wouldn't miss something for the
world
Someone is missing a few buttons
The missing link

Mistake

Doctors can bury their mistakes
Make no mistake about it!

Mister

Someone is Mister Big
Someone is Mister Clean
Meet Mister Right
No more Mister Nice Guy!

Mix

Mix it up with someone
Oil and water don't mix
Get mixed up in something
Something is a mixed bag
Someone is just a crazy, mixed-up
kid
Mixed blessing

Molasses

As slow as molasses in January

Mold

Someone/something is cast in the
same mold
After they made someone, they
threw away the mold

Moment

Moment of truth
Live for the moment
Never a dull moment
Do something on the spur of the
moment
A moment on the lips, a year on
the hips
One brief, shining moment
One's moment in the sun
Unforgettable moment

Monday

Blue Monday
Monday-morning quarterback

Money

Money talks
Money is the root of all evil
Money makes the world go
around
Money can't buy love/happiness
Money burns a hole in one's
pocket
Money doesn't grow on trees
Money is no object
Something/someone is right on
the money
Pour money down the drain
Smell money in the air
Spend money like a drunken
sailor/Indian
Make/coin/mint money hand-
over-fist
A fool and his money are soon
parted
Something is money in the bank
Have money to burn

Someone is not made of money
Give someone a run for his
  money
See/not like the color of some-
  one's money
Throw good money after bad
Be rolling in money
Pour money into something
Put one's money on the line
Take the money and run
Put your money where your
  mouth is
Pay blood/conscience
Spend money like water
Time is money
Someone/something is as wel-
  come as money from home
Be in the money
Funny money
Mad/pin money
Seed money
Easy money
Front money
Bad money drives out good
Get one's money's worth
The smart money's on _____
It's only money!
If you've got the money, I've got
  the time!

Monkey

Monkey see, monkey do
Monkey business
Monkey suit
Grease monkey
Have a monkey on one's back
Throw a monkey wrench into
  something
There's a monkey in the woodpile
Make a monkey out of someone
More fun than a barrel of mon-
  keys
You pay peanuts, you get mon-
  keys

Well, I'll be a monkey's uncle!

Monster

Create a monster
Green-eyed monster
Monstrous injustice

Month

A month of Sundays
That time of the month

Moon

Cry/ask for the moon
Bay/howl/bark at the moon
Shoot/aim for the moon
Once in a blue moon
Promise someone the moon
Streaker's moon

Mop

Mop up the floor with someone

More

More than one way to skin a cat
More than you can shake a stick
  at
More than a grain of truth in
  something
More to something than meets
  the eye
More fun than a barrel of mon-
  keys
More or less
Get more into the bargain
Get more than one bargained for
Bite off more than one can chew
Have more in one's little finger
  than _____
Less is more
Couldn't agree with someone
  more
The more the merrier!
More power to you!
And there's more to boot!
More's the pity!

Morning

The morning after
Fresh as the morning dew
You have to get up pretty early
 in the morning to...
Monday-morning quarterback
Great day in the morning!

Moss

A rolling stone gathers no moss

Moth

Like a moth to the flame
Put something in mothballs
Moth-eaten

Mother

Necessity is the mother of inven-
 tion
Cluck like a mother hen
A face only a mother could love
Mother-hen someone/something
Mother's little helper
Be tied/hang onto one's mother's
 apron strings
Swear to something on one's
 mother's grave
Mama's boy
Pistol-packin' mama
Last of the red-hot mamas

Motion

Someone/something is poetry in
 motion
Go through the motions

Motor

Gun one's motor
Someone is a motor-mouth
Don't race your motor!

Mountain

Make a mountain out of a mole-
 hill
If Mohammad won't come to the
 mountain...

Move mountains for someone/
 something

Mouse

Be quiet as a mouse
Be timid as a mouse
Play cat and mouse with someone
Be poor as a churchmouse
When the cat's away, the mice
 will play

Mouth

Put your money where your
 mouth is
Foam at the mouth
By word of mouth
Keep one's mouth shut
Shoot off one's mouth
Button up one's mouth
Someone/something leaves a bad
 taste in one's mouth
Something makes one's mouth
 water
Get something straight from the
 horse's mouth
Butter wouldn't melt in someone's
 mouth
Run off at the mouth
Don't look a gift horse in the
 mouth
Be down in the mouth
Live hand to mouth
Have a big mouth
Born with a silver spoon in one's
 mouth
Put one's head in the lion's
 mouth
Put one's foot in one's mouth
Take the bread out of someone's
 mouth
Someone's taste is all in his
 mouth
Laugh out of the other side of
 one's mouth

Out of the mouths of babes
Give someone a mouthful of
    knuckles
Have foot-in-mouth disease
Bad-mouth someone/something
Someone is a motor-mouth
You said a mouthful!
You took the words right out of
    my mouth!
Wash your mouth out with soap!

Move

Move one's tail for someone/
    something
Move up the ladder of success
Move heaven and earth for some-
    one/something
Move mountains for someone/
    something
Won't move a muscle for some-
    one/something
Movers and shakers
Have/know all the moves
The moving finger writes
Someone/something is a moving
    force
A moveable feast
Get a move on!

Much

Someone/something is just too
    much
Something/someone is too much
    of a good thing
Something is too much of a
    muchness

Mud

Someone's name is mud
Something is clear as mud
Someone is as plain as a mud
    fence
Drag someone's name through

the mud
Mudslinging campaign
Muddy the waters
Be a stick-in-the-mud
Here's mud in your eye!

Mule

Stubborn as a mule
Kiss a mule, cure a cold

Mum

Mum's the word
The Queen Mum

Murder

Murder the language
Get away with murder
Scream bloody/blue murder

Muscle

Muscle in on someone/something
Put the muscle on someone
Won't move a muscle for some-
    one
Flex one's muscles

Music

Music hath charms to soothe the
    savage breast
Make beautiful music together
Face the music
Stop the music!

Must

It must be jelly, cuz jam don't
    shake like that
Into each life a little rain must
    fall

Mustard

Can/can't cut the mustard

Mystery

Mystery meat
Something is cloaked in mystery

N

Nail

Nail someone to the wall
Nail someone to the cross
Hit the nail right on the head
Go at it/fight tooth and nail
Another nail on one's coffin
Smoke coffin nails
Someone is hard as nails
Chew nails and spit rust
Steal anything that's not nailed down

Naked

Be naked as a jaybird
The naked truth
To the naked eye
Be buck/stark naked

Name

Name one's poison
Name the day
Something is someone's middle name
Know something like one's own name
Someone's name is mud
Take someone's name in vain
A bullet with one's name on it
The name of the game
In name only
Someone can't remember his own name
Call names
Name-dropper
Vanity, thy name is woman!
What in the name of heaven?

Nap

Catnap

Catch someone napping

Narrow

Keep on the straight and narrow
Be as narrow as an arrow

Native

Go native
The natives are restless

Nature

Nature abhors a vacuum
The nature of the beast
Call of nature
Be a child of nature
Big as life and twice as natural

Near

So near and yet so far
Sail too near to the wind
Search far and near for someone/something
Be near at hand
Something is a near miss
The nearer the bone, the sweeter the meat

Neat

Neat as a pin
Wear a neat set of threads

Necessity

Necessity is the mother of invention
Someone/something is a necessary evil
Have the bare necessities
It ain't necessarily so!

Neck

Break someone's neck
Someone/something is a pain in
the neck
Put one's neck in a noose
Break one's neck for someone/
something
This neck of the woods
Breathe down someone's neck
Catch/get it in the neck
Stick one's neck out for someone/
something
Wring someone's neck
Have a millstone/albatross
around one's neck
Necktie party
Be neck-and-neck with someone

Need

Need something/someone like a
hole in the head
A friend in need is a friend in-
deed
With friends like you, who needs
enemies?
Who needs it?

Needle

Needle someone
Give someone the needle
Like looking for a needle in a
haystack
Be on pins and needles

Neighbor

Good fences make good neighbors

Neither

Neither a borrower nor a lender
be
See neither hide nor hair of
someone/something
Something is neither fish nor fowl

Someone/something is neither
hot nor cold
Something is neither here nor
there

Nellie

Someone is a nice/nervous Nellie

Nerve

Get up one's nerve
Someone has a lot of nerve
Not have a nerve in one's body
Someone wears on one's nerves
War of nerves
Bundle of nerves
Be all nerves
As nervous as a long-tailed cat in
a roomful of rocking chairs
Someone is a nervous Nellie
Of all the nerve!
You've got a nerve!

Nest

Foul one's own nest
Feather one's nest
Stir up a hornet's nest
Have a nest egg
Mare's nest
Love nest
Empty-nester

Net

The old-boy network

Never

Never follow a trained dog act
Never a dull moment
Never say die
Never give a sucker an even
break
Someone never had it so good
It's now or never
Woman's work is never done
An elephant never forgets
Better late than never

You never miss the water till the
well runs dry
Lightning never strikes in the
same place twice
It never rains but what it pours

New

New wrinkle
Get a new lease on life
There's nothing new under the
sun
Be someone's new best friend
You can't teach an old dog new
tricks
Something is old wine in new
bottles
A new broom sweeps clean
Bright as a new penny
Something is a whole new ball
game
Turn over a new leaf
Feel like a new man
Be the new kid on the block
As good as new
Make a new beginning
Hire new blood
The new breed
Brand-spanking new
Innocent as a newborn babe
Out with the old, in with the
new!
What's new?

News

No news is good news
Be the bearer of bad news
Have a nose for news
Someone/something is bad news
Break the news
Be bursting with good news

Nice

Nice work if you can get it
Nice guys finish last

Someone is a nice Nellie
Nice weather for ducks!
Have a nice day!
No more Mister Nice Guy!

Nick

In the nick of time
Be full of the Old Nick

Nickel

Someone/something is not worth
a plugged nickel
Nickel-and-dime someone to
death
Don't take any wooden nickels!

Night

As different as night and day
Ships that pass in the night
Like a thief in the night
By dark of night
Dance the night away
Make a night of it
Fly-by-night operation
One-night stand

Nine

Nine/ninety-day wonder
Be on cloud nine
Possession is nine points of the
law
A stitch in time saves nine
A cat has nine lives
Go the whole nine yards
Dressed to the nines
Talk nineteen to the dozen

Nip

Nip something in the bud
Have a little nip
Something is nip and tuck

Nit

Nit-pick
Get down to the nitty-gritty

Nobody

There's nobody home upstairs
Be nobody's fool
Go like nobody's business
Ain't nobody here but us chickens!

Nod

A nod and a wink
Land of Nod
Have a nodding acquaintance
  with someone/something

None

Half a loaf is better than none
A bad excuse is better than none
Someone will have none of something
None of your beeswax!

Nonsense

Stuff and nonsense!

Noodle

Use one's noodle
Give someone forty lashes with a
  net noodle

Noose

Put one's neck/head in a noose

Nose

Nose around someone/something
Follow one's nose
Thumb one's nose at someone/
  something
As plain as the nose on one's face
Have a nose for news
Hit something right on the nose
Cut off one's nose to spite one's
  face
Lead someone around by the
  nose
Keep one's nose to the grindstone
Get/have one's nose out of joint

Poke/stick one's nose into some-
  thing
Not see beyond one's nose
Keep one's nose clean
Pay through the nose
Turn up one's nose at someone/
  something
Look down one's nose at some-
  one/something
Rub someone's nose in something
Have one's nose in the air
Something is right under one's
  nose
Win/lose by a nose
Something is no skin off one's
  nose
Keep one's nose out of something
Be a brown nose
Count noses
Take a nose-dive

Not

Not give a hoot
Not give two hoots in hell
Not have a leg to stand on
Not just another pretty face
Someone/something is not half
  bad
Not if I can help it!
Not for the world!
Not for all the tea in China!
Not on your life/tintype!

Nothing

Nothing ventured, nothing
  gained
Nothing succeeds like success
Nothing is forever
Someone/something is nothing to
  write home about
Someone/something is nothing to
  sneeze at
Someone/something is nothing to
  shake a stick at

All or nothing at all
Have nothing to fear but fear
  itself
Have next to nothing
Know the cost of everything and
  the value of nothing
Whisper sweet nothings
Here goes nothing!
You ain't seen/heard nothing yet!
Nothing doing!

Notice

Sit up and take notice of some-
  one/something
Put someone on notice

Now

Now you see it, now you don't
It's now or never

Nowhere

Go/get nowhere fast
Someone/something is nowhere
Be in the middle of nowhere
You're nowhere, man!

Number

Someone's number is up
Someone/something is a back
  number
Get/have someone's number
Do a number on someone
Someone is a hot number
Be number one
Look out for number one
Someone's days are numbered
Play the numbers game
There's safety in numbers
Go by the numbers
Concrete numbers

Nut

Someone/something is a hard/
  tough nut to crack
Make the nut
Be nuts about someone/some-
  thing
The nuts and bolts of something
From soup to nuts
In a nutshell
Nutty as a fruitcake

O

Oaks

Great oaks from little acorns
  grow

Oars

Rest on one's oars
Have both oars in the water

Oats

Feel one's oats

Sow one's wild oats

Odd

Odd man out
Odds and ends
By all odds
Against insurmountable odds
Be an odds-on favorite

Off

Be off the beam

Be off one's feed
Be off to a flying start
Be off one's trolley
Something is off the beaten track
Something is off the record
Get off on the wrong/right foot
Get off someone's back
Get off the hook
Get/be teed off
Get off on someone/something
Be off and running
Go off the deep end
Something is off the wall
Get something off one's chest
Go off one's rocker
Get something off the ground
Speak/talk off the top of one's head
A chip off the old block
Cut off someone's water
Like water off a duck's back
Call it off
Catch someone off balance
Sweep someone off his/her feet
Ease/back off on something
Get off to a good/bad start
On again, off again
Do something right off the bat
Talk/speak off the cuff
Be way off base
Pick someone off
Fall off the wagon
Bug/blow/buzz off!
Knock it off!
Blast off!
Jerk off!
Get off the dime!

Offense

The best defense is a good offense

Offer

Make someone an offer he can't refuse

Get a burnt offering

Office

Something/someone is big box office
Do a land-office business
I gave at the office!

Oil

Oil and water don't mix
Pour oil on troubled waters
Burn the midnight oil
Snake-oil salesman
Banana oil!

Ointment

A fly in the ointment

Okay

Okay by me!
A-ok!

Old

Old enough to know better
Old soldiers never die, they just fade away
Old habits die hard
Old wives' tale
For old times' sake
The same old grind
The good old days
You can't teach an old dog new tricks
Someone/something is as comfortable as an old shoe
Someone is an old bat/bag/coot
Be a good old boy
Someone/something is old hat
As old as the hills
Give something the old college try
There's no fool like an old fool
Too soon old, too late smart
Let the old cat die
Something is old wine in new bottles
A chip off the old block

Someone/something is as old as
    Adam
Be full of the Old Scratch/Old
    Nick
Live to a ripe old age
The same old song
Be an old hack
As tough as old boots
Give an old idea a new coat of
    paint
Something is older than God's dog
Respect your elders
Give someone the old one-two
The old-boy network
Out with the old, in with the
    new!
There'll be a hot time in the old
    town tonight!

Omen

A bird of ill omen

On

Be on the beam
Someone/something is right on
    the money

Once

Once in a blue moon
Opportunity knocks but once
Someone has been around the
    block once or twice
Give someone/something the
    once-over
For once and for all!

One

One man's meat is another man's
    poison
One hand washes the other
One and all
Have one too many
Back to square one
Take it one day/step at a time
Slip one over on someone

All in one piece
Be one brick short of a load
See one, you've seen 'em all
Have one foot in the grave
Someone/something is one for
    the books
Someone/something is one in a
    million
Have one for the road
Just one of those things
In one fell swoop
In one swell foop
There's more than one way to
    skin a cat
Sleep with one eye open
Since the year one
There's one in every crowd
Go in one ear and out the other
Two heads are better than one
Kill two birds with one stone
It takes one to know one
Be all one and the same
With one hand tied behind one's
    back
Pull a fast one on someone
Be one jump ahead of the sheriff
Tie one on
Be one of the boys
Look out for number one
Be number one
As busy as a one-armed paper-
    hanger
Have a one-track mind
One-armed bandit
Something is a one-way street
Something is a one-man band/
    show
On a scale of one-to-ten
Someone/something is A-one
Give someone the old one-two
One-night stand
One-horse town
Not one red cent!
All for one, one for all!

Onions

Know one's onions

Only

Only time will tell
The only game in town
A face only a mother could love
In name only
Someone is not the only fish in
the sea
Someone is not the only pebble
on the beach
It's only money!
You only live once!

Open

Open letter
Open a can of worms
Open the floodgates
Open Pandora's box
Open season on someone/some-
thing
Bring something out into the
open
Be open and aboveboard
Greet someone with open arms
Sleep with one eye open
Something is an open secret
With eyes wide open
One's life is an open book
When one door closes another
one opens
Something is an open-and-shut
case

Operate

Be a smooth operator
Someone is a two-bit operator
Fly-by-night operation
The operation was a success, but
the patient died

Opportunity

Opportunity knocks but once
A golden opportunity

Opposite

Opposites attract
Be on opposite sides of the fence

Orange

Compare apples and oranges

Orbit

Go into orbit over someone/
something

Order

Put one's house in order
The order of the day
Have everything in apple-pie
order
The pecking order
Just what the doctor ordered
Point of order!

Other

Look the other way
Go in one ear and out the other
One hand washes the other
Turn the other cheek
The other side of the coin
Have other fish to fry
Drop the other shoe
Laugh on the other side of one's
face
Six of one and half-a-dozen of the
other
Be at each other's throats

Ounce

An ounce of prevention is worth
a pound of cure
Get more bounce to the ounce

Out

Out on a limb
Out of sight, out of mind
Out of the mouths of babes

Out of a clear blue sky
Out of the frying pan and into
the fire
Cut the ground out from under
someone
Cut the wind out of someone's
sails
Go out on the town
Go in one ear and out the other
Knock oneself out for someone/
something
Let the cat out of the bag
Have someone eating out of one's
hand
Be out in left field
Be down and out
Be out of the woods
Be out like a light
Be out of one's right mind
Be out of the running
Be out of whack
Be out on the street
Be out to lunch
Be out on one's feet
Pull the chestnuts out of the fire
Someone/something is out of this
world
Take something out on someone
Have one's tongue hanging out
Jump out of one's skin
Stick one's neck out
Like a bolt out of the blue
Know someone/something inside
out
Get/be all bent out of shape
Have something coming out of
one's ears
Beat/scare the living daylights
out of someone
It'll all come out in the wash
Get out of the cold
Know enough to come in out of
the rain
Stick out like a sore thumb

Pull something out of thin air
From out of nowhere
Be out for blood
Tear out one's hair
Tell tales out of school
Pull rabbits out of a hat
Bottom out
Feel out of sorts
Freeze someone out
Odd man out
Look out for number one
Let it all hang out
Get a kick out of someone/some-
thing
Keep a weather eye out for some-
one/something
Someone's pilot light is out
Someone has a few lights out in
his marquee
Be left out in the cold
Have the bottom fall out of some-
thing
Make a big production/deal/
Federal case out of something
Beat/knock the stuffing out of
someone
Burn out
Branch out
Boot someone out
Be out on one's feet
Put someone out of his misery
Take something out on someone
Be on the outs with someone/
something
Know the ins and outs of some-
thing
Big as all outdoors
You took the words right out of
my mouth!
Call me out!
I'm outta here!
Time to get outta Dodge!
Out with the old, in with the
new!

Are you out of your gourd/
  tree?

Oven

Have a bun in the oven

Over

Over the long haul
Over and above the call of duty
Work someone over
Someone is over the hill
Go over the top
Someone/something goes over
  with a bang
Have someone over a barrel
The honeymoon is over
Don't cry over spilt milk
Get/be in something over one's
  head
Someone/something goes over
  like a lead balloon
Someone/something goes over
  big/like gangbusters
Hash something over
Something is over and done with
Fall head over heels in love
All over but the shouting
Something is enough to make
  someone turn over in his grave
It ain't over till the fat lady sings
It ain't over till it's over
Something will blow over
Kick over the traces
Not till hell freezes over
Someone/something is all over
  the lot
Look like death warmed over
Slip something over on someone
Go over something with a fine-
toothed comb
Go overboard for someone/some-
thing
Give someone the once-over
Over my dead body!

Owl

Screech like an owl
As wise as an owl

Own

Own up to something
Stand on one's own two feet
Be afraid of one's own shadow
Give someone a dose of his own
  medicine
Someone/something has a mind
  of its own
Carry one's own weight
Sign one's own death warrant
Know someone/something like
  one's own name
Be one's own worst enemy
Hold one's own
Keep one's own counsel
Take the law into one's own
  hands
Can't call your soul your own
Dig one's own grave
To each his own
To thine own self be true

Ox

Someone is clumsy/strong as an
  ox

Oyster

The world is one's oyster
Prairie oyster

P

P

Mind one's P's and Q's

Pace

Change of pace
Go at a snail's pace
Set one's own pace
Keep pace with someone/something
Put someone through his paces
Spot someone/something at twenty paces

Pack

Pack up one's troubles
Pack up one's tent and steal away
Pack it in
Someone/something packs a whallop/punch
Packed like sardines in a can
Good things come in small packages
Pistol-packin' mama

Paddle

Paddle one's own canoe
Be up the creek without a paddle

Page

Take a page from someone's book

Pain

No pain, no gain
Someone/something is a pain
Someone/something gives one a pain in the neck
Feeling no pain
Have growing pains

Paint

Paint oneself into a corner
Paint the town red
Give an old idea a new coat of paint
Put on one's war paint

Pair

Show a clean pair of heels
A peach of a pair
Baby needs a new pair of shoes!

Pajama

Pajama party
Someone/something is the cat's pajamas

Pale

Be as pale as a ghost
Go pale at the sight/thought of something/someone
Beyond the pale

Pall

Cast a pall over something

Palm

Palm something off on someone
Cross someone's palm with silver
Grease someone's palm
Have someone/something in the palm of your hand
Have an itchy palm

Pan

Something/someone is a flash in the pan
Hope something will pan out
Out of the frying pan and into the fire

As flat as a pancake

Panic

Panic city
Push the panic button

Pants

Scare the pants off someone
Have lead in one's pants
Have ants in the pants
Wear the pants in the family
Get/give a kick in the pants
Charm the pants off someone
Catch someone with his pants
  down
Someone is still in short pants
Beat the pants off someone
Fly by the seat of one's pants
Have hot pants for someone/
  something
Someone still gets into his pants
  one leg at a time
Fancy pants
Panty raid
Keep your pants on!

Paper

Pass bad paper
Something isn't worth the paper
  it's printed/written on
Someone can't punch/fight his
  way out of a paper bag
Put paper over the cracks
Something is a paper tiger
As busy as a one-armed paper-
  hanger
Give someone his walking papers
Be paper-rich and cash-poor
Paper-pusher
Go peddle your papers!
See you in the funny papers!

Par

Feel under par
Something is par for the course

Someone/something is up to/not
  up to par

Parade

Rain on someone's parade

Paradise

Trouble in paradise
Fools' paradise

Pardon

Pardon me for living!
Pardon my French!
Pardon my dust!

Park

Get/give a ballpark figure

Part

Something is part and parcel of
  something
Discretion is the better part of
  valor
For the most part
A man of parts
A fool and his money are soon
  parted
Have a parting of the ways
Parting is such sweet sorrow!

Party

Be the life of the party
Someone is a party animal
Necktie party

Pass

Pass the peace pipe
Pass out cold
Pass bad paper
Pass the buck
Pass the time of day
Pass the hat
Pass the acid test
Ships that pass in the night
Make a pass at someone

Cut 'em off at the pass
Take a pass on something
Come to pass
Someone/something passes muster
Have a passing acquaintance with someone/something
This too shall pass!

Pasture

Put someone/something out to pasture

Pat

Stand pat
Have something down pat
Have a pat answer for something
Give/get a pat on the back

Patch

Someone/something is tearing up the pea patch
Someone is not a patch on someone

Path

Cross one's path
Be off the beaten path
Beat a path to one's door
Lead someone down the garden/primrose path
Follow the well-traveled path

Patient

The operation was a success, but the patient died
Patience is a virtue
Have the patience of Job/a saint
Try/tax one's patience

Pave

Pave the way for someone
Find streets paved with gold
The road to hell is paved with good intentions
Pound the pavement

Paw

Be someone's cat's paw

Pay

Pay someone back in his own coin
Pay blood money
Pay cash on the barrelhead
Pay as you go
Pay someone back with interest
Pay a pretty penny for something
Pay one's dues
Pay through the nose
Pay a king's ransom
Pay the freight
Pay lip service to someone
Pay an arm and a leg for something
Pay court to someone
Pay conscience money
Pay the earth for something
Buy now, pay later
Crime does not pay
Have the devil/hell to pay
Rob Peter to pay Paul
Hit pay dirt
If you dance, you have to pay the piper/fiddler
You pay peanuts, you get monkeys
Be bound to pay
Wouldn't pay a dime for one's chances
Find a little something extra in your pay envelope
You get what you pay for
You pays your money and you takes your chances/choice

Pea

Fog like pea soup
Someone has a brain the size of a pea
As alike as two peas in a pod

Peace

Peace and quiet
Hold one's peace
Keep the peace
Rest in peace
Pass/smoke the peace pipe

Peach

A peach of a pair
Have a peaches-and-cream complexion
Peachy-keen
What a peach!

Peak

Widow's peak
Someone/something peaks too early

Peanut

Peanut gallery
Something is only peanuts
Work for peanuts
You pay peanuts, you get monkeys

Pearl

Pearls of wisdom
Cast pearls before swine
Pearly gates

Pebble

Someone is not the only pebble on the beach

Peck

Hunt and peck
Be in a peck of trouble
The pecking order
Peck's bad boy

Peddle

Go peddle your papers!

Peel

Keep one's eyes peeled

As bald as a peeled egg
Like peeling a grape with an axe
Peel me a grape!

Peep

Not hear a peep out of someone

Peg

Take someone down a peg or two
Be a square peg in a round hole
Have someone/something pegged

Pen/Pencil

Pen pal
The pen is mightier than the sword
A slip of the pen
Be waiting in the bull pen
Poison-pen letter
Something will put lead in your pencil
Pencil-pusher
Blue-pencil something out

Penny

In for a penny, in for a pound
Bright as a new penny
Turn up like a bad penny
Something costs a pretty penny
Pay a pretty penny
A penny saved is a penny earned
Pennies from heaven
Pinch pennies
Watch the pennies and the dollars will take care of themselves
Be penny-wise and pound-foolish
A penny for your thoughts?

People

People who live in glass houses shouldn't throw stones
Games people play

Percent

Be behind someone 110 percent

Play the percentages
Someone is a 10-percenter

Perfect

Someone is a perfect ten
Practice makes perfect
Be letter-perfect

Peter

Rob Peter to pay Paul
Something peters out
For Pete's sake
Honest to Pete!
For the love of Pete!

Pew

Sit in the wrong pew

Phone

Someone has more chins than a
  Chinese phone directory
Hold the phone!

Phony

As phony as a three-dollar bill

Phrase

To coin a phrase

Pick

Pick up on something
Pick someone's brains
Pick up all the marbles
Pick and choose
Pick 'em up and lay 'em down
Pick something over
Pick up the tab/check
Pick up someone's trail
Pick someone off
The pick of the litter
Someone/something is slim/easy
  pickings
Hand-pick someone/something
Keep your cotton-pickin' hands
  off!

Pickle

Pickle one's brains
Be in a pickle
Sit there like a wart on a pickle

Picnic

Something is no picnic

Picture

Picture this
Someone/something is not in the
  picture
A picture is worth a thousand
  words
Have to draw someone a pic-
  ture
Look at the big picture
Pretty as a picture
What's wrong with this picture?

Pie

Pie in the sky
Cut up the pie
Easy as pie
Sweet as pie
Eat humble pie
Have a finger in every pie
As American as apple pie
Miss American pie
Have everything in apple-pie
  order

Piece

Get/have a piece of the cake
Get/have a piece of the action
Give someone a piece of one's
  mind
Speak one's piece
All in one piece
Something is a conversation piece
Earn a nice piece of change
Tear someone to pieces
Someone/something goes to
  pieces

Pier

Take a long walk off a short pier!

Pig

Happy as a pig in clover
Bleed like a stuck pig
Buy a pig in a poke
Make a pig of oneself
Eat like a pig
Male chauvinist pig
In a pig's eye!

Pigeon

Set a cat among the pigeons
Someone is a clay pigeon
Someone is a stool pigeon

Pike

Come down the pike
Someone is a piker

Pile

You can only pile something on
  so high

Pill

Something is a bitter pill to swal-
  low
Someone is a real pill
Be on the pill
Sugar the pill

Pillar

Go from pillar to post
Someone is a pillar of the com-
  munity/society

Pillow

Pillow talk

Pilot

Someone's pilot light is out

Pin

Pin the rap on someone
Pin someone's ears back

Pin money
Stick a pin in someone's balloon
Quiet enough to hear a pin drop
Neat as a pin
Kingpin
Do something for two pins
Be on pins and needles

Pinch

Pinch pennies
Feel the pinch
Pinch-hit for someone

Pink

Be in the pink
Give/get the pink slip
Be tickled pink about something
Pink-collar job

Pint

Pint-sized

Pipe

Pipe dream
Pass/smoke the peace pipe
Take the gas pipe
Someone/something is a lead-pipe
  cinch
Someone has a great set of pipes
The piper calls the tune
If you dance, you have to pay the
  piper
Pipe down!
Put that in your pipe and smoke
  it!

Pistol

Hot as a two-dollar pistol
Pistol-packin' mama

Pit

Make a pit stop
Feel something in the pit of one's
  stomach
Bottomless pit

Snake pit
Someone/something is the pits

Pitch

Pitch woo
Black as pitch
Make a pitch for someone/something
Be in there pitching
Rain pitchforks
Little pitchers have big ears
Keep pitching!

Pity

More's the pity!

Place

Be between a rock and a hard
place
All dressed up and no place to go
Lightning never strikes in the
same place twice
There's no place like home
Have one's heart in the right
place
Turn the place upside down
Know one's place
Put/keep someone in his place
Have the run of the place
In the first place
Have one's place in the sun
A place for everything and every-
thing in its place
Jumping-off place
Have friends/juice in high places
Someone is going places
Your place or mine?

Plague

Avoid someone/something like
the plague
A plague on both your houses!

Plain

Plain and fancy

As plain as day
As plain as the nose on your face
As plain as a mud fence
Something comes in a plain
brown wrapper

Plank

Walk the plank

Plant

Plant the seeds of doubt
Plant you now, dig you later!

Platter

Have someone's head on a platter
Hand something to someone on a
silver platter

Play

Play with a cold deck
Play hard ball
Play in the big leagues
Play into someone's hands
Play the heavy
Play someone for a sucker
Play the percentages
Play dumb
Play the fool
Play the devil's advocate
Play catch-up ball
Play guts ball
Play heads-up ball
Play the beard
Play politics
Play ducks and drakes
Play something down
Play one's last card
Play both ends against the middle
Play ball with someone
Play it cool
Play footsie with someone
Play dirty pool
Play one's cards right
Play one's cards close to the vest/
chest

Play cat and mouse with someone
Play by the book
Play games/mind games with
  someone
Play around
Play one's trump card
Play the field
Play something by ear
Play possum
Play for keeps
Play fast and loose with someone/
  something
Play on words
Play the rubber match
Play it as it lays
Play second fiddle/banana
Play to the gallery
Play hob
Play someone like a violin
Play fair
Play with fire
Play the numbers game
Play havoc with someone/some-
  thing
Play into someone's hands
Play someone for a fool
Play the waiting game
Make a power play
It's not whether you win or lose,
  it's how you play the game
Call/bring someone/something
  into play
All work and no play makes Jack
  a dull boy
When the cat's away, the mice
  will play
Something comes into play
Make a grandstand play
Make a play for someone
Turnabout is fair play
Games people play
Something is child's play
Someone is not playing with a
  full deck

Can't tell the players without a
  scorecard
Playful as a kitten
Two can play that game!
Go play in traffic!

Plea

Cop a plea

Please

As pretty as you please
Pleased as punch
Pretty please?

Plow

Plow into something
Plow someone/something under
Put one's hand to the plow
Clean someone's plow
Beat one's swords into plow-
  shares

Pluck

Pluck up one's courage
Someone/something is ripe for
  the plucking

Plug

Pull the plug on someone/some-
  thing
Someone/something is not worth
  a plugged nickel

Plunge

Take the plunge

Pocket

Have someone/something in one's
  hip pocket
Money burns a hole in one's
  pocket
Fill/line one's pockets
Have a champagne taste on a
  beer pocketbook
Run a vest-pocket business

Pod

As alike as two peas in a pod

Poet

Someone is a poet and doesn't
  know it
Something/someone is poetry in
  motion
Wax poetic over someone/some-
  thing
Poetic justice

Point

Point the finger at someone
Drive home a point
Come to the point
Case in point
Someone/something is a sore
  point
Something is beside the point
Be at one's boiling point
Stretch a point
Be at sword's point
Reach the point of no return
At this point in time
Possession is nine points of the
  law
The shortest distance between
  two points is a straight line
Make brownie points
Do something point-blank
Point of order!

Poison

One man's meat is another man's
  poison
Hate someone/something like poi-
  son
Name one's poison
Poison-pen letter

Poke

Poke one's nose into something
Poke fun at someone/something

Poke around
Something is better than a sharp
  poke in the eye
Take a poke at someone/some-
  thing
Get a poke in the ribs
Wear a poker face

Pole

Be low man on the totem pole
Wouldn't touch someone/some-
  thing with a ten-foot pole
Be poles apart on something
Run something up the flagpole

Police

Police the area

Policy

Honesty is the best policy

Polish

Polish the apple
Spit and polish

Politics

Politics make strange bedfellows
Play politics

Pond

Be a big fish in a little pond

Pool

Play dirty pool
Last one in the pool is a rotten
  egg!

Poor

Be poor as a churchmouse
The rich get richer and the poor
  get poorer
Be paper-rich and cash-poor

Pop

Pop the question
Pop one's cork

Pop for the check/tab
Someone/something makes one's
 eyes pop
Too pooped to pop

Port

Any port in a storm
A girl in every port

Possess

Possession is nine points of the
 law
Like a man possessed

Possible

Something is within the realm of
 possibility
Anything's possible!

Post

Go from pillar to post
Be deaf as a post
Keep someone posted

Pot

Pot head
Go to pot
Sweeten the pot
Get off the pot/pity pot
The pot calling the kettle black
A watched pot never boils
Put something in the pot
Not have a pot to piss in
A chicken in every pot
Let the pot boil awhile
Smoke pot
Take potluck
Something is a potboiler
Something is a tempest in a tea-
 pot

Potato

Drop someone/something like a
 hot potato
Be a couch potato

Someone/something is small po-
 tatoes
Be a meat-and-potatoes man
All that meat and no potatoes!

Pound

Pound the pavement
Pound one's brains out
Pound some sense into someone
Get a pound of flesh
In for a penny, in for a pound
An ounce of prevention is worth
 a pound of cure

Pour

Pour on the juice
Pour money down the drain
Pour oil on troubled waters
Pour something on thick
It never rains but what it pours

Powder

Sit on a powder keg
Keep one's powder dry
Something is not worth the pow-
 der to blow it up
Take a powder!

Power

Power breakfast/lunch
Knowledge is power
The power behind the throne
Make a power play
Flower power
The powers that be

Practice

Practice makes perfect
Practice what you preach

Praise

Praise someone/something to the
 skies
Damn someone with faint praise

Prayer

Not have a prayer
Come in on a wing and a prayer
Someone/something is the answer
  to one's prayers

Preach

Practice what you preach

Present

No time like the present
All present and accounted for

Press

Press one's luck
Press the flesh

Pressure

Bring pressure to bear
Live in a pressure cooker

Pretty

Pretty as a picture
Sitting pretty
You have to get up pretty early
  in the morning to...
Not just another pretty face
As pretty as you please
Something costs/pay a pretty
  penny
Pretty, please?

Pretzel

Crooked as a pretzel
Life's not all beer and pretzels

Prevention

An ounce of prevention is worth
  a pound of cure

Price

Have a price on one's head
Every man has his price
The price is right
Something is cheap at twice the
  price

Want something/someone at any
  price
Beyond price
Rock-bottom price

Pride

Pride goeth before a fall
Swallow one's pride
Be someone's pride and joy

Prime

Prime the pump
Prime of life
Prime time
Be in one's prime

Prince

Someone is a prince of a guy
Someday your prince will come
Meet one's Prince Charming
Turn a frog into a prince

Print

Read the fine print
See it in print
Something is not worth the paper
  it's printed on
Print it!

Prison

Take no prisoners!

Prize

Be a prize fool
Someone is a real prize
Door/booby prize

Problem

Be saddled with a problem
You got a problem with that?

Production

Make a big production out of
  something

Promise

Promise someone a rose garden
Promise someone the moon
Give something a lick and a
  promise
Promises, promises!

Proof

The proof of the pudding is in
  the eating
The burden of proof is on some-
  one
Prove one's mettle
Innocent until proven guilty

Protect

Heaven will protect the working
  girl

Proud

Be proud as a peacock
Be so proud one could bust
Do someone proud

Prowl

Be out on the prowl

Prunes

Be full of prunes

Public

John Q. Public
Something is public knowledge
Be in the public eye
Wash/air one's dirty linen in pub-
  lic

Pudding

The proof of the pudding is in
  the eating
Puddin'-head

Pull

Pull oneself together
Pull one's punches

Pull something out of thin air
Pull one's own weight
Pull strings/wires
Pull the plug on someone/some-
  thing
Pull up stakes
Pull a fast one on someone
Pull someone's leg
Pull oneself up by the bootstraps
Pull something off
Pull someone to pieces
Pull the wool over someone's eyes
Pull rank on someone
Pull a boner
Pull in one's horns
Pull up one's socks
Pull chestnuts out of the fire
Pull the chicken switch
Pull rabbits out of a hat
Pull out all the stops .
Pull a cheap/dirty trick
Pull the rug out from under
  someone
Pull someone's chain
Have a lot of pull with someone
Have a lot more push than pull

Pulp

Beat someone to a pulp

Pulse

Keep a finger on the pulse of
  something

Pump

Pump someone
Prime the pump

Punch

Punch line
Punch someone's lights out
Someone/something packs a
  punch
Sunday punch
Beat someone to the punch

Can't punch one's way out of a
  paper bag
Be pleased as punch
Rabbit punch
Roll with the punches
Pull one's punches
Be punch-drunk

Punish

Be a bear/glutton for punishment
Let the punishment fit the crime

Pup

Not since Hector was a pup
Puppy love

Puppet

Someone is a puppet on a string

Pure

Pure and simple
As pure as the driven snow
Be Simon pure

Purpose

Do something on purpose
Be a man of purpose
Do something accidentally-on-
  purpose
Be at cross-purposes with some-
  one/something

Push

Push the panic button
Push someone around
Push someone too far
Push up daisies
If push comes to shove
Have a lot more push than pull
Know how to push someone's
  buttons
Pencil/paper pusher

Puss

Hit someone right in the puss

Someone is a sly puss
Sourpuss

Put

Put all one's eggs in one basket
Put someone through the mill
Put a bee in someone's bonnet
Put one's foot in it
Put one's foot in one's mouth
Put someone through the meat
  grinder
Put one's head on the chopping
  block
Put one's finger on something
Put someone in his place
Put one's head/neck in a noose
Put one's face on
Put one's house in order
Put one's best foot forward
Put one's two cents in
Put something over on someone
Put all one's cards on the table
Put the bite on someone
Put the skids to someone
Put the blocks to someone
Put on one's thinking cap
Put someone through his paces
Put the moves on someone
Put the clamps on someone
Put someone through the wringer
Put someone on notice
Put oneself in someone else's
  shoes
Put someone out of his misery
Put the squeeze on someone
Put our heads together
Put the arm on someone
Put the finger on someone/some-
  thing
Put a bug/flea in someone's ear
Put something in mothballs
Put the screws to someone
Put something across
Put on airs

Put on a happy face
Put in an appearance
Put one's back to something
Put something to bed
Put up one's dukes
Put out a contract on someone
Put something into the pot
Put your money where your
  mouth is
Put in one's licks
Put two and two together
Put someone's nose out of joint
Put someone down
Put someone/something to shame
Put in a good word for someone
Put the cart before the horse
Put words in someone's mouth
Put something on the map
Put something on ice
Put together with chewing gum
  and baling wire
Put on an act
Put on the dog

Put the kibosh on something/
  someone
Put something behind one
Put someone out to pasture
Put a bold face on something
Put daylight between you and
  someone/something
Put on a brave face
Put one's cash on the line
Put the fear of God into some-
  one
Put on a good/brave front
Put one's John Hancock on some-
  thing
Put one's money/cash on the line
Put on one's glad rags
Put no stock in something/some-
  one
Put a sock in it!
Put a cap/lid on it!   .

Putty

Be putty in someone's hands

Q

Q

Tell someone something on the
  Q.T.
Mind one's P's and Q's

Quarter

Draw and quarter someone
Give no quarter and ask none
Armchair quarterback
Monday-morning quarterback

Queen

Queen of the May

Drag/closet queen
The Queen Mum

Queer

Queer as a three-dollar bill
Someone is a queer duck
Come all over queer
Someone/something queers the
  deal

Question

Ask a silly question, get a silly
  answer

Pop the question
Something is out of the question
Beg the question
Ask a burning question
Call someone/something into
  question
Loaded question
The 64-dollar question
Ask me no questions, I'll tell you
  no lies

Quick

Quick on the trigger
Quick as a flash
Quick as a wink
Quick like a bunny
Someone is a quick study
Cut someone to the quick
Do the quick and dirty to some-
  one
Quicker than you can say Jack
Robinson
Quicker than you can shake a
  stick at
The hand is quicker than the eye
Candy is dandy, but liquor is
  quicker

Quiet

Quiet enough to hear a pin drop
Quiet as a tomb/mouse
Peace and quiet
It's quiet, too quiet!

Quit

Quit while one is ahead
Quit something cold turkey
Call it quits
Quit your bellyachin'!

Quote

Quote chapter and verse about
  something

R

Rabbit

Rabbit ears
Rabbit's foot
Rabbit punch
Run like a scared rabbit
Jackrabbit start

Race

Race against the clock
The race is/is not to the swift
Throw the race
Slow but steady wins the race
Drag race
Rat race

Off to the races
Don't race your motor!
That's what makes horse racing!

Rack

Rack one's brains
Go to rack and ruin
Tie someone to the rack
Buy something off the rack
Rack 'em and stack 'em!

Rafter

Raise the rafters
Hang from the rafters

Rag

A rag, a bone, a hank of hair
Be limp as a rag
Chew the rag
Something is like a red rag to a
  bull
Go from rags to riches
Put on one's glad rags
Run someone ragged

Rage

Be in a blind rage

Rail

Ride someone out of town on a
  rail
Someone is skinny as a rail
Ride the rails
Get railroaded into something

Rain

Rain cats and dogs
Rain on someone's parade
Rain pitchforks/buckets
Not know enough to come in out
  of the rain
Someone/something is as right as
  rain
Into each life a little rain must
  fall
Come rain or shine
Take a rain check
It never rains but what it pours
Save for a rainy day
Chase rainbows
The end of the rainbow

Raise

Raise the rafters/roof
Raise hell/Cain
Raise one's eyebrows
Raise hob with someone
Raise havoc with someone
Raise a big stink about something
Buck for a raise

Have a hair-raising experience

Rake

Rake someone over the coals

Rally

Rally around the flag

Rank

Pull rank on someone
The rank and file
Close the ranks

Rap

Rap music/session
Rap someone's knuckles
Someone/something is not worth
  a rap
Get a bum rap
Take the rap for someone
Not care a rap for someone/
  something
Beat the rap
Pin the rap on someone

Rare

Someone is a rare bird
Be rarin' to go
What is so rare as a day in June?

Rat

Rat on someone
Rat race
Smell a rat
Look like a drowned rat
Someone is a rat fink
Caught like a rat in a trap
Flee like rats from a sinking ship
You dirty rat!

Rattle

Rattle one's tongue
Rattle skeletons
Rattle someone's cage
Rattle sabers
Shake, rattle and roll

Raw

Get a raw deal
Have raw courage

Ray

Ray of hope
See a ray of light at the end of
 the tunnel
Catch some rays

Razor

Be sharp as a razor
Be on the razor's edge

Reach

Reach the point of no return
Reach for the stars
Reach/be at the end of one's
 rope/tether
Let your reach exceed your grasp
Boardinghouse reach
Reach for the sky!

Reaction

Chain reaction

Read

Read the bottom line
Read the fine print
Read between the lines
Read someone the riot act
Read someone like a book
Read someone loud and clear
Read someone's mind
Read the handwriting on the wall
Read something into something
Don't believe everything you read
Read 'em and weep!
Read my lips!

Ready

Ready for anything
Ready for Freddie
Be ready, willing and able
Rough and ready

Here I come, ready or not!

Real

The real McCoy
Get real!
Are you for real?
It's been a real slice!

Realm

Coin of the realm
Something is in the realm of possibility

Ream

Ream someone out

Reap

As ye sow, so shall ye reap

Rear

Bring up the rear
Get one's rear in gear
Something rears its ugly head

Reason

Reason something out
No rhyme or reason to something
It stands to reason

Reckon

Someone/something is a force to
 be reckoned with
Day of reckoning

Recognize

A spark of recognition

Record

Set the record straight
Something is a matter of record
Something is off the record
Stand on one's record
Sound like a broken record
Look at someone's track record

Red

Red alert

Something is like a red rag to a
  bull
Paint the town red
Roll out the red carpet
As red as a beet
Be awash in red ink
See red
One's little red wagon
Better dead than Red
Something is a red herring
Something is full of red tape
Red-letter day
Catch someone red-handed
Last of the red-hot mamas
Not one red cent!

Refuse

Make someone an offer he can't
refuse

Regular

Be a regular guy
Something is as regular as clockwork

Remark

Cutting remark

Remember

Someone can't remember his own
  name

Repeat

Repeat oneself
History repeats itself

Respect

Respect your elders
With all due respect

Rest

Rest on one's laurels
Rest on one's oars
Rest in peace
There's no rest for the wicked

Lay something to rest
Today is the first day of the rest
  of your life
The natives are restless
Give it a rest!

Retreat

Beat a hasty retreat
Sound retreat!

Return

Return to the fold
Return the compliment
Reach the point of no return
I shall return!

Revenge

Living well is the best revenge

Reward

Honesty/virtue is its own reward
Go to one's reward

Rhyme

No rhyme or reason to something
False rhyme

Rib

Rib someone
Get a poke in the ribs
Something sticks to one's ribs
Something tickles one's ribs

Rich

Strike it rich
Something is too rich for one's
  blood
The rich get rich and the poor
  get poorer
Be filthy rich
Be rich as Croesus
You can't be too rich or too thin
Go from rags to riches
Have an embarrassment of riches
Be paper-rich and cash-poor
That's rich!

Ride

Ride for a fall
Ride shank's mare
Ride shotgun on someone/something
Ride herd on someone/something
Ride something out
Ride tall in the saddle
Ride someone out of town on a rail
Ride the rails
Ride roughshod over someone
Take someone for a ride
Thumb a ride
Go along for the ride
Let something ride
Go for a joyride
Ride 'em, cowboy!

Ridiculous

From the ridiculous to the sublime

Right

Be in/out of one's right mind
Someone/something is right up to the minute
The price is right
The customer is always right
Be someone's right arm
Something rolls right off one's back
Play one's cards right
Live on the right side of the tracks
Do something right off the bat
Someone/something is right as rain
Give one's right arm for something
Be right up one's alley
Have one's heart in the right place
Get hit right between the eyes

Someone/something is right on the money
Hit the nail right on the head
Something is right under one's nose
One's left hand doesn't know what one's right hand is doing
Get off on the right foot
Someone/something is a bit of all right
Be right on the dot
Have the right stuff
Get on the right track
Meet Mister Right
Two wrongs don't make a right
Have someone dead to rights
By all rights
Right on!
It gets me right here!

Ring

Ring someone up
Ring the changes
Ring down the curtain on something
Someone/something doesn't ring true
Throw/toss one's hat into the ring
Catch the brass ring
Something rings a bell
Run rings around someone
Someone is a dead ringer for someone
Send in a ringer
Something is a three-ring circus
Ring-a-ding-ding!

Riot

Read someone the riot act
Run riot over something/someone
Someone's imagination runs riot
Be a laff-riot

Rip

Rip someone off
Rip someone/something to shreds
Sleep like Rip Van Winkle
Rip-snortin'
Rip-roarin'
Something is a rip-snorter
Let 'er rip!

Ripe

The time is ripe for something
Something/someone is ripe for
    plucking
Live to a ripe old age

Rise

Rise to the occasion
Rise above something
Rise to the bait
Get a rise out of someone
If the Lord be willin' and the
    creek don't rise
Early to bed and early to rise
    makes a man healthy, wealthy
    and wise
Cream rises to the top
A rising tide lifts all boats
Rise and shine!

Risk

Risk life and limb for someone/
    something
Something is a risky business

River

Sell someone down the river
Send someone up the river

Road

Road hog
Hit the road
Have one for the road
Burn up the road
Get the show on the road
The road to hell is paved with
    good intentions
Take the high road
Middle of the road
All roads lead to Rome

Roar

Roar like a lion
Get roaring drunk
Be a roaring success
Rip-roarin'

Rob

Rob someone blind
Rob the cradle
Rob Peter to pay Paul
Highway robbery

Rock

Rock the cradle
Hit rock bottom
Hard as a rock
Between a rock and a hard place
Be a Rock of Gibraltar
Steady as a rock
Be on the rocks
Have rocks in one's head
Someone/something is dumber
    than a box of rocks
Go off one's rocker
As nervous as a long-tailed cat in
    a roomful of rocking chairs
Rock-bottom price
Don't rock the boat!

Rod

Spare the rod and spoil the child

Roll

Roll the big dice
Roll with the punches
Roll out the red carpet
Roll out the welcome mat
Roll up one's sleeves
Roll in clover
Roll up the sidewalks at sunset

A roll big enough to choke a
  horse
Someone is on a roll
Heads will roll
Let the good times roll
Something rolls right off one's
  back
A rolling stone gathers no moss
Start/get/keep the ball rolling
Be rolling in money
Someone is a high roller

Rome

Rome wasn't built in a day
When in Rome, do as the
  Romans do
Fiddle while Rome burns
Roman collar

Roof

Raise the roof
Hit the roof
Have the roof fall/cave in on
  someone/something
Busy as a cat on a hot tin roof
Have a roof over one's head
Shout something from the roof-
  tops

Room

Room at the top
Have/not have room to breathe
Not have enough room to turn
  around
Not enough room to swing a cat
Elbow room
Work in a boiler room
As nervous as a long-tailed cat in
  a roomful of rocking chairs

Roost

Rule the roost
Chickens come home to roost

Root

Money is the root of all evil

Rope

Rope someone in on something
Be at the end of one's rope
Give someone enough rope and
  he'll hang himself
Learn/know the ropes
Be on the ropes

Rose

Come out smelling like a rose
Promise someone a rose garden
Something is no bed of roses
Everything's coming up roses
Have roses in one's cheeks
Stop and smell the roses
Gather rosebuds while ye may
Look at the world through rose-
  colored glasses

Rotten

There's a rotten apple in every
  barrel
Be rotten to the core
Something is rotten in the State
  of Denmark!
Last one in the pool is a rotten
  egg!
Dumb, rotten luck!

Rough

Rough someone up
Rough and ready
Cut up rough
Someone/something is a diamond
  in the rough
Ride roughshod over someone

Round

Round something out/off
Be a square peg in a round hole
Love/money makes the world go
  'round
Make the rounds
Heading for the last roundup

Row

Get one's ducks in a row
Something is a hard/tough row
  to hoe
Skid row
Kick up a row

Royal

Have a battle royal

Rub

Rub salt in the wound
Rub it in
Rub elbows with someone
Rub someone the wrong way
Rub someone's nose/face in some-
  thing
Ah, there's the rub!

Rubber

Burn rubber
Write a rubber check
Play the rubber match
Rubberneck at someone

Rude

Get a rude awakening

Ruffle

Ruffle someone's feathers

Rug

Snug as a bug in a rug
Sweep the dirt under the rug
Pull the rug out from under
  someone
Cut a rug

Ruin

Go to rack/wrack and ruin

Rule

Rule the roost
Rule someone/something out
Rule with an iron hand

The Golden Rule
Hard-and-fast rule
The exception proves the rule
Know the ground rules
Bend the rules

Run

Run out of gas
Run off at the mouth
Run scared
Run something up the flagpole
Run circles/rings around someone
Run into a brick wall
Run something into the ground
Run into a dead-end
Run the gamut/gauntlet
Run like a scared rabbit
Run like a clock/clockwork
Run to seed
Run riot over someone/some-
  thing
Run dry
Run around every which way
Run around in circles
Run someone ragged
Run that by once again
Run around like a chicken with
  its head cut off
Give someone a run for his
  money
Be run down at the heels
Something/someone makes one's
  blood run cold
In the long run
Have the run of the place
Make a run for the border
Be on the run
Make a run for it
Take the money and run
Still waters run deep
Cut and run
Turn tail and run
Dry run
Let something run its course

You can run, but you can't hide
Something runs like a top
One's imagination runs riot
True love never runs smooth
You never miss the water till the
  well runs dry
Someone/something runs hot and
  cold
Something runs in one's family/
  blood
Be off and running
Hit the ground running
Get a running start
Be out of the running

One's cup runneth over
Give someone the runaround
Run-of-the-mill

Runt

The runt of the litter

Rush

Fools rush in where angels fear to
  tread
Give/get the bum's rush

Rust

Chew nails and spit rust

S

Saber

Rattle sabers

Sack

Sack out
Give/get the sack
Hit the sack
Someone is a sadsack
Wear sackcloth and ashes

Sacred

Sacred cow
Is nothing scared?

Saddle

Sit/ride tall in the saddle
Be back in the saddle
Be saddled with a problem

Safe

Safe and sane

Safe and sound
Better safe than sorry
There's safety in numbers
Safety first!
Your secret is safe with me!

Said

Easier said than done
No sooner said than done
Least said, soonest mended
After/when all is said and done
You said it!
You said a mouthful!
Enough said!

Sail

Sail too close to the wind
Sail into someone
Sail under false colors
Sail off into the sunset
Trim one's sails

Take/cut the wind out of someone's sails
Smooth sailing
Spend money like a drunken
  sailor

Saint

Have the patience of a saint
Saints preserve us!

Sake

Art for art's sake
For old times' sake
For corn's sake!
For Pete's sake!
For pity's sake!
For lands' sake!
For God's/heaven's sake!
For goodness sake!
Sakes alive!

Salad

Salad days

Salt

Salt something away
Sit above/below the salt
Take something with a grain of
  salt
Be the salt of the earth
Back to the salt mines
Earn/be worth one's salt
Rub salt in the wound

Same

Same difference
Someone/something is cast in the
  same mold
The same old grind
All in the same boat
Be all one and the same
Cut from the same bolt of cloth
The same, but different
All in the same breath
The same old song

By the same token
Be on the same side of the fence
Be on the same wavelength
Same here!

Sand

Build castles in the sand
Bury/hide one's head in the sand

Sardine

Packed like sardines in a can

Sassy

Fat and sassy

Sauce

Hit the sauce
What's sauce for the goose is
  sauce for the gander
Flying saucer
Have eyes like saucers

Save

Save the best for last
Save one's/someone's skin/neck
Save for a rainy day
Save face
To save one's soul/life
Someone/something saves the
  day
A stitch in time saves nine
Saved by the bell
A penny saved is a penny earned
Something is a saving grace
Save your breath!
Save it!

Saw

Saw wood
Have sawdust in one's head

Say

Say uncle
Do as I say, not as I do
Quicker than one can say Jack
  Robinson

Just say the word
Just say when
Something goes without saying
After/when all is said and done
The devil you say!
You can say that again!
You don't say!

Scale

Scale something down
On a scale of one-to-ten
Tip the scales

Scarce

Scarce as hens' teeth
Make oneself scarce

Scare

Scare someone out of his wits
Scare the living daylights out of
  someone
Scare something up
Scare the pants off someone
Scared silly/stiff
Scared as a jackrabbit
Run scared
Run like a scared rabbit
Scaredy-cat

Scene

Change of scene
Make the scene
Make a scene
Bad scene
Be behind the scenes
Chew the scenery

Scent

Scent something from afar
Throw someone off the scent

Scheme

Outlandish scheme
Something is/isn't in the scheme
  of things

The best-laid schemes...

School

School of hard knocks
Tell tales out of school
Have a schoolgirl complexion
As bashful as a schoolgirl

Scoop

What's the scoop?

Scope

Scope something out
Something is beyond one's scope

Score

Score a hit
Know the score
Settle an old score
Something is a real score
Can't tell the players without a
  scorecard

Scorn

Hell hath no fury like a woman
  scorned

Scot

Go scot-free

Scout

Scout around for something
Scout something/someone up
Be a good scout
Scout's honor!

Scrape

Scrape the bottom of the barrel
Scrape by
Bow and scrape
Get into a scrape

Scratch

Scratch one's way to the top
Barely scratch the surface
Get some scratch together

You scratch my back, I'll scratch
  yours
Someone/something doesn't come
  up to scratch
Be full of the Old Scratch

Scream

Scream bloody murder
Someone/something is a scream
You scream, I scream, we all
  scream for ice cream!

Screech

Screech like an owl
Come to a screeching halt

Screw

Screw something up
Screw someone out of something
Screw around with someone/
  something
Screw up one's courage
Have a screw loose
Put the screws to someone
Couldn't find one's head if it
  wasn't screwed on
Someone/something is screwy
Someone is a screwball

Sea

Sea dog
Someone is not the only fish in
  the sea
Between the devil and the deep
  blue sea
A sea of troubles
Go down to the sea in ships

Seal

Sealed with a kiss
Signed, sealed and delivered
One's lips are sealed

Seam

Sew a fine seam

Come apart/burst at the seams
See the seamy side of something/
  someone

Search

Search high and low for some-
  one/something
Search me!

Season

It's open season on someone/
  something

Seat

Fly by the seat of one's pants
Be in the hot seat
Be in the driver's seat
Be in the catbird seat
Take a backseat to someone/
  something
Backseat driver

Second

Get one's second wind
Have second thoughts
The second time around
Play second fiddle/banana to
  someone
Be in one's second childhood
Come off second-best/string
Second-guess someone

Secret

Something is top secret
Something is an open secret
Be in on the secret
Your secret is safe with me!

Security

Need a security blanket

See

See something in black and white
See which way the wind blows
See red

See stars
See eye-to-eye with someone
See the color of someone's money
See the light of day/daylight
See one's way clear to do some-
thing
See the light
See double
See no evil
See a ray of light at the end of
the tunnel
See how the land lies
See the seamy side of something/
someone
See one, you've seen 'em all
As far as the eye can see
Not see beyond one's nose
Have to see a man about a dog
Can't see the forest for the trees
Monkey see, monkey do
So mad one can't see straight
Could see something with half an
eye
Can see right through someone
What you see is what you get
Now you see it, now you don't
Someone is blind in one eye and
can't see out of the other
Come up and see someone's etch-
ings
Look like one's seen a ghost
Wouldn't be seen dead in some-
thing
Children should be seen and not
heard
Someone/something has seen bet-
ter days
Not seen someone in a coon's
age/donkey's years
Not seen neither hide nor hair of
someone/something
Seeing is believing
Have a look-see
See you in church!

See you in the funny papers!
See you later, alligator!
See you in court!
Long time no see!
See you in hell first!
You ain't seen nothin' yet!

Seed

Seed money
Run/go to seed
Plant the seed of something

Seek

Seek and ye shall find
Water seeks its own level

Self

Be a shadow/shell of one's former
self
Make a fool of oneself
Suit yourself!

Sell

Sell one's soul/birthright
Sell the sizzle, not the steak
Sell someone a bill of goods
Sell someone down the river
Sell out
Sell someone/something short
Sell like hotcakes
Buy and sell someone
Still trying to sell buggy-whips

Send

Send a fox to guard the henhouse
Send up a trial balloon
Send someone up the river
Something/someone sends shivers
down one's spine

Sense

Have/not have any horse sense
Pound some sense into someone
Common sense
Have a sixth sense

Be out of/lose one's senses
Come to one's senses
Bring someone to his senses
Take leave of one's senses

Separate

Separate the men from the boys
Separate the sheep from the goats
Separate the wheat from the chaff

Serve

Serve something up to someone
on a silver platter
First come, first served
Pay lip service to someone

Session

Bull/rap session
Jam session
Brainstorming session

Set

Set a good example
Set eyes on someone/something
Set one's cap for someone
Set someone back on his heels/
ears
Set the world on fire
Set one's hand to something
Set up shop
Have one's heart set on some-
thing
The truth shall set you free
Wear a neat set of threads
Someone is dead-set on/against
something
Someone/something sets one's
teeth on edge

Settle

Settle an old score
Have an account to settle with
someone
When the dust settles
This'll settle your hash!

Seven

Be at sixes and sevens over some-
thing/someone
Be in seventh heaven
Get the seven-year itch
The seventh-inning stretch

Sew

Sew a fine seam
Have something all sewn/sewed
up

Shack

Shack up with someone

Shadow

Cast a long shadow
Be afraid of one's own shadow
Be a shadow of one's former self
Beyond the shadow of a doubt

Shaft

Get/give someone the shaft

Shake

Shake in one's boots
Shake like a leaf
Shake someone down
Shake one's fist at someone
Shake the dust from one's feet
Shake, rattle and roll
Give/get a fair shake
Quicker/more than you can
shake a stick at
Someone/something is nothing to
shake a stick at
It must be jelly, cuz jam don't
shake like that
Someone/something is no great
shakes
In two shakes of a lamb's tail
Movers and shakers
Bet/be all shook up over some-
one/something
Shake a leg!

Let's shake on it!
We've howdied, but we ain't
    shook!

Shame

Shrink back in shame
Put someone/something to shame
Something is a crying shame
Shame on you!
For shame!

Shank

The shank of the evening
Ride shank's mare

Shape

Shape up or ship out
The shape of things to come
Get into shape
Get/be all bent out of shape
Lick someone into shape

Share

Share and share alike
Share the wealth
Get the lion's share of something
Kick in one's share
Beat one's swords into plowshares

Sharp

As sharp as a tack/razor
Better than a sharp poke in the
    eye
Look sharp!

Shave

Shave the dice
Have a close shave with some-
    one/something
Little shaver
Shave and a haircut, six bits!

Sheep

Separate the sheep from the goats
Someone is the black sheep in
    the family

Count sheep
Follow someone like sheep
A wolf in sheep's clothing
Make sheep's eyes at someone

Sheet

Be white as a sheet
Scandal sheet
Be three sheets to the wind

Shelf

Put someone/something on the
    shelf

Shell

Shell out
Come out of one's shell
Play the shell game
Someone is just a shell of his
    former self
Drop a bombshell

Shift

Shift into high gear
Shift for oneself
Work the graveyard/swing shift
Shiftless bum

Shine

Shine someone on by
Shine up to someone
Take a shine to someone/some-
    thing
Cram something where the sun
    don't shine
Come rain or shine
Make hay while the sun shines
One brief, shining moment
Knight in shining armor

Shingle

Hang up one's shingle

Ship

Go down with the ship

Shape up or ship out
Abandon the ship
Flee like rats from a sinking ship
When one's ship comes in
Don't give up the ship
Ships that pass in the night
Go down to the sea in ships
Loose lips sink ships
The face that launched a thou-
  sand ships

Shirt

Give someone the shirt off one's
  back
Lose one's shirt
Wear a hair shirt
Bet one's shirt
Be a stuffed shirt
Shirt-sleeve shop
Keep your shirt on!

Shiver

Something/someone sends shivers
  up one's spine
Shiver me timbers!

Shoe

If the shoe fits, wear it
The shoe is on the other foot
Someone/something is as com-
  fortable as an old shoe
Wait for the other shoe to drop
Step into dead men's shoes
Fill someone's shoes
Put oneself into someone else's
  shoes
Put on one's dancing shoes
Close only counts in horseshoes
Be a goody-two-shoes
Baby needs a new pair of shoes!

Shoot

Shoot blanks
Shoot the breeze/bull with some-
  one
Shoot one's wad
Shoot one's cuffs
Shoot off one's mouth/face
Shoot the moon
Shoot for the moon
Shoot up
Shoot one's bolt
Shoot oneself in the foot
Shoot from the hip
Be a straight/square shooter
Like shooting fish in a barrel
The whole shooting match
Sure as shootin'!

Shop

Shop till you drop
Shop the street
Talk shop
Set up/close up shop
Window shop
Like a bull in a china shop
Shirt-sleeve shop
Sweatshop

Short

Short and sweet
Have a short fuse
Keep someone on a short leash
Be caught short
The long and short of something
Bring someone up short
Make short work of someone/
  something
Sell someone/something short
Get the short end of the stick
Someone is still in short pants
Have someone by the short hairs
Get short shrift
A day late and a dollar short
Be one brick short of a load
To cut a long story short
Fall short of the mark
Get down to the short strokes
Have the shorts

The shortest distance between
  two points is a straight line
Cut off my legs and call me
  Shorty!
Take a long walk off a short pier!

Shot

Take a long shot
Someone is a big shot
Give someone/something one's
  best shot
Take a shot in the dark
Get a shot in the arm
Take a cheap shot at someone/
  something
Be shot at dawn
Call the shots
Someone is a hotshot
Ride shotgun on someone/some-
  thing
Shotgun wedding
Not by a long shot!

Shoulder

Put one's shoulder to the wheel
Have a chip on one's shoulder
Talk straight from the shoulder
Give/get the cold shoulder
Need a shoulder to lean/cry on
Have a good head on one's
  shoulders
Carry the weight of the world on
  one's shoulders
Have broad shoulders
Work shoulder-to-shoulder with
  someone
Be head-and-shoulders above
  someone/something

Shout

Shout something from the roof/
  housetops
Twist and shout
All over but the shouting

Shove

Shove something down someone's
  throat
If push comes to shove
Shove off!

Show

Show a clean pair of heels
Show one's face
Show someone the door
Show one's true colors
Show the white feather/flag
Show someone a thing or two
Show someone the ropes
Show one's teeth
Something is a one-man show
Put on a dog-and-pony show
It just goes to show you
Get the show on the road
There's no business like show
  business
Steal the show
The show must go on
Give the show away
That's show business/biz!
I'm from Missouri, show me!

Shrink

Shrink back in shame
Shrinking violet

Shrug

Shrug someone/something off
Shrug one's shoulders

Shuffle

Someone/something gets lost in
  the shuffle
Get a fast shuffle
Get the double shuffle

Shut

Keep one's mouth shut
Something is an open-and-shut
  case

Grab some shut-eye
Shut your face/mouth/trap!
Put up or shut up!

Shy

Shy away from something
Once bitten/burned, twice shy

Sick

Be sick as a dog
Be sick to death of someone/
    something
Be sick in the head
Make someone sick

Side

Look on the bright side
Know which side one's bread is
    buttered on
Born on the wrong side of the
    blanket
Get up on the wrong side of the
    bed
Be a thorn in someone's side
Get on one's good/bad side
Live on the wrong side of the
    tracks
The sunny side of the street
The other side of the coin
Be on the side of the angels
Can't hit the broad side of a barn
The grass is always greener on
    the other side of the fence
Keep someone on the side
Laugh out of the other side of
    one's mouth
Laugh on the other side of one's
    face
Bread always falls on its buttered
    side
Born on the sunny side of the
    hedge
Be on the same/opposite side of
    the fence

See the seamy side of something
Two sides to the coin
Split one's sides laughing
Butter one's bread on both sides
Choose up sides
There are two sides to every
    story
Work both sides of the street
Sidewalk superintendent
Roll up the sidewalks at sunset

Sight

Love at first sight
Someone/something is a sight for
    sore eyes
Out of sight, out of mind
Buy something sight unseen
Lose/catch sight of someone/
    something
Go pale at the sight of someone/
    something
Have 20/20 hindsight
Outta sight!

Sign

Sign of the times
Sign off on something
Sign one's own death warrant
Give someone the high sign
Signed, sealed and delivered

Signal

Get a clear signal from someone/
    something
Get one's signals crossed

Silent

Silent as a cigar-store Indian
Silence is golden

Silk

Smooth/soft as silk
You can't make a silk purse out
    of a sow's ear
Hit the silk!

Silly

Slap someone silly
Laugh oneself silly
Be scared silly
Ask a silly question, get a silly answer

Silver

Silver threads among the gold
Cross someone's palm with silver
Speak with a silver tongue
Every cloud has a silver lining
Born with a silver spoon in one's mouth
Serve/hand someone something on a silver platter

Simple

Simple as ABC
Pure and simple
Someone is simple in the head

Sin

Earn the wages of sin
Someone is sorry/guilty as sin
Something/someone is as ugly as sin

Sing

Sing one's swan song
Sing like an angel
Sing for one's supper
Sing like a bird/canary
Sing a different tune
Sing the blues
It ain't over till the fat lady sings

Sink

Sink to the bottom
Sink one's teeth into something
Sink or swim
Everything but the kitchen sink
Loose lips sink ships
Let something sink in

Swallow something hook, line and sinker
Sinking sensation
Flee like rats from a sinking ship

Sister

Sob sister
Weak sister
Be sisters under the skin

Sit

Sit on the edge of one's chair
Sit above/below the salt
Sit tall in the saddle
Sit on one's hands
Sit tight
Sit on a powder keg
Sit on the fence
Sit there like a bump on a log/wart on a pickle
Sit up and take notice of someone/something
Sit on the bench
Sit in the catbird seat
Sit in judgment on someone
Sit in the wrong pew
Not sit still for something
Sitting pretty
Sitting on top of the world
Sitting on high cotton
Someone is a sitting duck
Go sit on a tack!

Six

Six ways to Sunday
Hit on all six
Something is six of one and half-a-dozen of the other
Be at sixes and sevens over someone/something
Go like sixty
Have a sixth sense
The sixty-four dollar question
Deep-six someone
Shave and a haircut, six bits!

Size

Size someone/something up
Cut someone down to size
Try something on for size
One size fits all
Pint-sized
That's about the size of it!

Sizzle

Sell the sizzle, not the steak

Skate

Skate on thin ice
Be a good skate
Cheapskate

Skeleton

Have a skeleton in one's closet
Rattle skeletons

Skid

Skid row
Wear a skid lid
Be on the skids
Put the skids to someone
Hit the skids

Skin

Skin someone alive
Save one's own/someone's skin
Something is no skin off one's
  nose
Beauty is only skin deep
Be all skin and bones
Jump out of one's skin
Get under someone's skin
By the skin of one's teeth
More than one way to skin a cat
Be sisters under the skin
Skinny Minnie
Someone is skinny as a rail
Go skinny-dipping
Thin/thick-skinned
Give/slip me some skin!

Skip

Skip town
A hop, skip and a jump away
Make one's heart skip a beat

Skull

Get something through one's
  thick skull

Skunk

Skunk someone
Be drunk as a skunk

Sky

Out of a clear blue sky
Pie in the sky
Praise someone to the skies
Blow something sky-high
Reach for the sky!
The sky's the limit!

Slant

Get/have a fresh slant on something

Slap

Slap someone silly
Slap something together
Slap someone down
Something is a slap in the face
Give someone a slap on the wrist
Slap-happy

Slate

Have a clean slate

Slave

Be a slave to fashion
Slave-driver

Sleep

Sleep on it
Sleep like a log/baby/top
Sleep with one eye open
Sleep around

Sleep like Ran Van Winkle
Sleep over
Get one's beauty sleep
Can't sleep a wink
Not lose any sleep over someone/
  something
Let sleeping dogs lie
Asleep in the arms of Morpheus

Sleeve

Laugh up one's sleeve
Have an ace/card up one's sleeve
Have something up one's sleeve
Wear one's heart on one's sleeve
Have a trick up one's sleeve
Roll up one's sleeves
Shirt-sleeve shop

Slice

Slice near the bone
Any way you slice it
Take a slice at someone
Get a slice of the cake
Someone/something is the best
  thing since sliced bread
Something is a slice-of-life
It's been a real slice!

Slick

Someone/something is slick as a
  whistle
City slicker

Slim

Something is slim pickings

Sling

Sling hash
Sling the bull
Suffer the slings and arrows of
  someone/something
Mudslinging campaign

Slip

Slip a rung lower on the ladder

Slip something over on someone
Slip through one's fingers
Slip a cog/gear
Slip into something more com-
  fortable
Give someone the slip
A slip of the pen
A slip of the lip/tongue
There's many a slip between the
  cup and the lip
Give/get the pink slip
A mere slip of a girl
Slippery as an eel
Slippin' around
Slip me some skin!
Slip me five!

Slow

Slow but steady wins the race
Slow as molasses in January
Do a slow burn
Someone is slow to anger
Be slow on the uptake
Make haste slowly
The mills of god grind slowly
Let something twist slowly in the
  wind

Slump

Fall into a slump

Sly

Sly as a fox
Someone is a sly-puss

Smack

Smack someone silly
Be smack dab in the middle of
  something
Give someone a big smackeroo

Small

Small fry
It's a small world
Someone/something is small po-
  tatoes/beer

The wee, small hours
Good things come in small pack-
ages
Someone is small-time
Small wonder!

Smart

Smart Alec
Someone is a smart cookie
Be smart as a whip
Too soon old and too late smart
The smart money's on _____
Have street smarts
Ooooh, that smarts!

Smear

Smear campaign

Smell

Smell blood
Smell a rat
Smell money in the air
The sweet smell of success
Wake up and smell the coffee
Stop and smell the roses
Someone/something smells fishy
Come out smelling like a rose

Smile

Smile like a Cheshire cat
Not crack a smile
Let a smile be your umbrella
Break into a smile
Have a winning smile
Be all smiles

Smoke

Smoke like a chimney/fiend
Smoke a cancer stick
Smoke coffin nails
Smoke a joint
Smoke someone/something out
Someone is just blowing smoke
Where there's smoke, there's fire
Something goes up in smoke

Put up a smokescreen
Chain-smoke
Holy smoke!
Watch my smoke!
Put that in your pipe and smoke
it!
Someone/something is smokin'!

Smooth

Smooth sailing
As smooth as silk/glass
Be a smooth operator
True love never runs smooth
Be an old smoothie

Snail

Go at a snail's pace

Snake

Snake in the grass
Snake eyes
Snake pit
Someone is lower than a snake's
belly

Snap

Snap one's fingers
Snap something up
Snap out of it!
Snap it up!
Snap to it!
Make it snappy!

Sneeze

Someone/something is nothing to
sneeze at

Snort

Snort lines/tracks
Rip-snorter/snortin'

Snow

Snow someone under
Be white as snow
Give someone a snow job

As pure as the driven snow
Be snowed over by someone
Something starts to snowball
Not have a snowball's chance in
 hell

Snuff

Snuff someone/something out
Come/be up to snuff

Snug

Snug as a bug in a rug

So

So far, so good
So to speak
So be it
So far as it goes
So much for that!
So help me!
So what?

Soak

Soak up something like a sponge
Old soak
Go soak your head!

Soap

Soft-soap someone
No soap!
Wash your mouth out with soap!

Sob

Sob sister
Sob story

Sober

As sober as a judge
Be stone-cold sober
Sober up!

Sock

Sock something away
Something suits someone right
 down to the socks
Pull up one's socks

Knock someone's socks off
Put a sock in it!
Sock it to me!

Soft

Soft as a whisper
Soft as a kitten/silk/satin
Be a soft touch
Someone is soft in the head
Have a soft spot for someone/
 something
Speak softly and carry a big stick
Be an old softie
Soft-soap someone

Soldier

Old soldiers never die, they just
 fade away

Solemn

Be as solemn as a judge

Some

Some like it hot
Win some, lose some
Have something going on with
 someone
Have something on someone
Have something on the ball
Be something else again
Somebody up there likes someone
Wanna start something?
Wanna make something of it?

Son

Like father, like son
Go like a son of a gun
Son of a gun!

Song

Burst into song
Buy/get something for a song
Give someone a song and dance
The same old song
Sing one's swan song

Soon

Sooner or later
The sooner the better
No sooner said than done
Least said, soonest mended

Sore

Someone/something is a sore
    spot/point
Someone/something is a sight for
    sore eyes
Someone/something stands out
    like a sore thumb
Be a sore loser

Sorrow

Drown one's sorrows
Parting is such sweet sorrow!

Sorry

Better safe than sorry
Someone is sorry as sin

Soul

Be the captain of one's soul
Bare one's soul
Sell one's soul
Brevity is the soul of wit
Keep body and soul together
To save one's soul
Can't call your soul your own
Eyes are the windows to the soul
Heart and soul
Bless my soul!

Sound

Sound and fury
Sound like a broken record
A sound mind in a healthy body
Be safe and sound
Be sound as a dollar
Something sounds as clear as a
    bell
Sound retreat!

Soup

Be in the soup
Everything from soup to nuts
Something is duck soup
Fog like pea soup
Be all souped up

Sour

Sour grapes/apples
Sourpuss

Source

Consider the source

Sow

Sow one's wild oats
As ye sow, so shall ye reap

Space

Space cadet
Need one's space
Black hole in space
Be all spaced out

Spade

Call a spade a spade
As black as the ace of spades
Give something to someone in
    spades
Do all the spadework

Spank

Something is brand-spanking new

Spanner

Throw a spanner in the works

Spare

Spare no expense
Spare the rod and spoil the child
Don't spare the horses!
Brother, can you spare a dime?

Spark

Spark to someone/something

A spark of recognition
Make sparks fly

Sparrow

Keep your eye on the sparrow

Speak

Speak no evil
Speak softly and carry a big stick
Speak with forked tongue
Speak someone's language
Speak off the top of one's head
Speak of the devil and he's sure
  to appear
Speak one's piece/mind
Speak with silver tongue
Speak with tongue in cheek
Speak off the cuff
So to speak
Actions speak louder than words
Children and fools speak the
  truth
A look that speaks volumes
Speak up!
Speak for yourself, John!

Speed

Go at breakneck speed
Get up to speed
Bring someone up to speed
Put on speed
Faster than a speeding bullet
Watch my speed!

Spend

Spend money like water
Spend money like a drunken
  sailor/Indian
Last of the big spenders

Spice

Variety is the spice of life

Spider

Would steal a dead fly from a
  blind spider

Spill

Spill the beans/one's guts
Don't cry over spilt milk

Spin

Spin one's wheels
Put a spin on something
Make one's eyes spin around in
  one's head
Go into a tailspin

Spine

Someone/something sends shivers
  down one's spine
Someone is a spineless wonder

Spirit

Someone is the spirit and image
  of someone
Get into the spirit of the thing
The spirit is willing, but the flesh
  is weak
Dampen one's spirits
That's the spirit!

Spit

Spit and polish
Spit in the wind
So mad one could spit
Chew nails and spit rust
Someone is the spittin'/spit and
  image of someone

Spite

Cut off one's nose to spite one's
  face

Splash

Make a splash

Split

Split hairs
Split the difference
Split one's sides laughing
Splitting headache

Lickety-split
I gotta split!

Spoil

Spare the rod and spoil the child
Too many cooks spoil the broth
To the victor go the spoils
Be spoiling for a fight
Spoilsport

Sponge

Sponge off someone
Throw in the sponge
Soak up something like a sponge

Spoon

Born with a silver spoon in one's
    mouth
Greasy spoon
Spoon-feed something to someone

Sport

Not have a sporting chance
Have sporting blood
Sporting house
Spoilsport

Spot

Spot something at twenty paces
Something hits the spot
Be/put someone on the spot
Be in a tight spot
X marks the spot
Someone/something is a sore spot
Have a blind spot about some-
    one/something
Have a soft spot for someone/
    something
Hit the high spots
A leopard can't change its spots
Knock someone's spots off
Hog/steal the spotlight
Be in the spotlight
Johnny-on-the-spot

Spread

Spread something on thick
Spread something far and wide
Middle-age spread
Secretary spread
Something spreads like wildfire

Spree

Be on a spree

Spring

Spring for the check/tab
Someone is no spring chicken
Something springs a leak
Hope springs eternal

Spur

Spur someone on
Do something on the spur of the
    moment
Earn one's spurs

Square

Square off with someone
Square accounts with someone
Square meal
Back to square one
Call it square
Be a square peg in a round hole
Beat someone fair and square
Give/get a square deal
Be on the square with someone/
    something
Be kidding on the square
Someone is a real square
Someone lights up like Times
    Square
Be on the square with someone/
    something
Have three squares a day
Get something all squared away
Be a square-shooter

Squeak

The squeaky wheel gets the grease

Squeeze

Put the squeeze on someone
Someone is one's main squeeze

Stab

Stab someone in the back
Take a stab at something

Stack

Blow one's stack
Someone/something doesn't stack
  up
Swear to something on a stack of
  Bibles
Have the cards/deck stacked
  against one
Like looking for a needle in a
  haystack
Rack 'em and stack 'em!

Staff

Bread is the staff of life

Stage

Set the stage for someone
Get stage fright
All the world's a stage
At this stage of the game
Be stagestruck

Stake

Stake a claim on someone/some-
  thing
Pull up stakes

Stand

Stand on one's record
Stand on ceremony
Stand the test of time
Stand by one's guns
Stand pat
Stand out like a sore thumb
Stand in one's way
Stand in good stead
Stand on one's own two feet
Stand up and be counted
Stand up and cheer
Stand on one's dignity
Not have a leg to stand on
Someone/something makes one's
  hair stand on end
If you can't stand the heat, stay
  out of the kitchen
Can't stand the gaff
One-night stand
One's heart stands still
Be left standing at the altar/gate
Mexican standoff
Be a stand-up guy

Star

Born under a lucky/dark star
Hitch one's wagon to a star
One's star is on the wane
Wish upon a star
Have stars in one's eyes
See stars
Thank one's lucky stars
Reach for the stars
Something is in the stars for
  someone
Be star-struck
Bless my stars!

Stare

Stare a hole through someone
Stare daggers at someone
Have something staring one right
  in the face

Stark

Be stark naked
Go/be stark raving mad

Start

Start from scratch
Start the ball rolling
Start a fire under someone
Get a running start
Get a head start

Get off to a flying start
Get off to a good/bad start
Jackrabbit start
By fits and starts
Just try and start something!

Starve

Feed a cold, starve a fever

Stay

Stay on middle ground
Stay in one's own backyard
Stay on one's toes
Stay to the bitter end
Stay put
If you can't stand the heat, stay
  out of the kitchen
Should have stayed/stood in bed

Steady

Steady as a rock
Slow but steady wins the race
Going steady
Steady as you go!

Steak

Sell the sizzle, not the steak

Steal

Steal someone's thunder
Steal the spotlight/limelight
Steal the show
Steal anything that's not nailed
  down
Steal a march on someone
Steal someone blind
Would steal a dead fly from a
  blind spider
Fold up one's tent and steal away
Beg, borrow or steal something
Lock the barn door after the
  horse is stolen

Steam

Build up a full head of steam

Go with a full head of steam
Under one's own steam
Blow/let off steam
Be all steamed up about some-
  thing
Full steam ahead!

Steel

Steel oneself for something
Have nerves of steel
Have a mind like a steel trap
Steely-eyed

Steer

Steer clear of someone/something
Steer someone wrong
Get a bum steer

Stem

Stem the tide
Do something from stem to stern

Step

Step on someone's toes
Step all over someone
Step on the gas
Step into dead men's shoes
One step beyond
Look like one just stepped out of
  a bandbox
Step on it!
Step lively!

Stern

Do something from stem to stern

Stew

Stew in one's own juice
Get/be stewed to the gills

Stick

Stick up for someone/something
Stick to one's guns
Stick to one's knitting
Stick one's neck/chin out for
  someone/something

Stick out like a sore thumb
Stick a pin in someone's balloon
Smoke a cancer stick
Speak softly and carry a big stick
Someone/something is nothing to
    shake a stick at
Get the short end of the stick
Quicker than you can shake a
    stick
Someone/something is more than
    you can shake a stick at
Get on the stick
Not enough to stick in one's eye
A cobbler should stick to his last
Be a stick in the mud
Jazz stick
Joystick
Be as cross as two sticks
Something sticks to one's ribs
Something sticks in one's craw/
    throat
Live out in the sticks
Something is a sticky situation/
    wicket
Have sticky fingers
Jump over the broomstick

Stiff

Stiff someone
Stiff as a board
Keep a stiff upper lip
Someone is a lucky stiff
Scared stiff
Bored stiff
Have a good stiff belt

Still

Still waters run deep
One's heart stands still
Not sit still for something

Stilt

Someone is higher than Jesus on
    stilts

Stink

Stink to high heaven
Raise a big stink about something

Stir

Stir up trouble
Stir up a hornet's nest
Go stir crazy

Stitch

A stitch in time saves nine
Have someone in stitches

Stock

Take stock of someone/something
Something is one's stock in trade
Buy something lock, stock and
    barrel
Put/take no stock in someone/
    something
Blue-chip stock

Stomach

Have one's stomach tied up in
    knots
Have no stomach for someone/
    something
Someone/something turns one's
    stomach
Have eyes bigger than one's stom-
    ach
An army marches/travels on its
    stomach
Feel something in the pit of one's
    stomach
Have butterflies in one's stomach
Have a strong stomach
Have a cast-iron stomach
The way to a man's heart is
    through his stomach

Stone

Kiss the blarney stone
Cast the first stone
Be stone broke
Can't get blood from a stone

Run into/be up against a stone
  wall
Leave no stone unturned
A rolling stone gathers no moss
Kill two birds with one stone
Beat one's head against a stone
  wall
Have a heart of stone
Something is/isn't written/etched
  in stone
Be stone deaf
Be stoned out of one's gourd
Be a stone's throw away from
  something
People who live in glass houses
  shouldn't throw stones
Stonewall someone
Stone-cold dead in the market
Be stone-cold sober

Stool

Someone is a stool pigeon/stoolie

Stop

Stop dead in one's tracks
Stop on a dime
Stop cold/cold turkey
Stop and smell the roses
Someone has a face that would
  stop a clock
Make a pit stop
Whistle stop
Pull out all the stops
The buck stops here
Stop the music!

Store

Set store by something
Like a kid in a candy store
Chain store
Keep someone/something in cold
  storage
Silent as a cigar-store Indian
Who's minding the store?

Stork

Date the stork

Storm

Any port in a storm
The lull before the storm
Take someone/something by
  storm

Story

There are two sides to every story
As the story goes
Sob story
Fish story
Shaggy dog story
The same old story
Get the inside story
Buy/not buy someone's story
Cut a long story short
Cover story
Leak a story
Hard-luck story
Cock-and-bull story
Second-story man
A likely story!

Straddle

Straddle the fence

Straight

Set the record straight
Get something straight from the
  horse's mouth
Be a straight arrow
Get/go straight
Keep a straight face
Keep on the straight and narrow
Talk straight from the shoulder
So mad one can't see straight
Walk a straight line
Give it to someone straight
Straighten someone out
Straighten up and fly right
Be a straight-shooter
Straight ahead and strive for tone!

Strange

Politics make strange bedfellows
Truth is stranger than fiction

Straw

Something is the last straw
The straw that broke the camel's
  back
Try to make bricks without straw
Clutch at straws in the wind

Streak

Talk/swear a blue streak
Have a yellow streak down one's
  back
Have a streak of good/bad luck
Streaker's moon

Street

Work both sides of the street
Have street smarts
Be on easy street
The word on the street
Be out on the street
Something is a one/two-way
  street
Shop the street
On the sunny side of the street
Find streets paved with gold

Stretch

Stretch a point
Stretch the truth
Seventh-inning stretch

Stride

Hit one's stride
Take someone/something in one's
  stride

Strike

Strike it rich
Strike a balance
Strike a bargain with the devil
Strike while the iron is hot

Strike an attitude
Strike a balance
Someone/something strikes a
  chord
Have two strikes against one
Lightning never strikes in the
  same place twice
Three strikes and you're out
Be within striking distance of
  something
Be star/stage struck
Strike me blind/dead!

String

String someone along
String along with someone/some-
  thing
Have the world on a string
Play out a string
Someone is a puppet on a string
Draw the purse strings
With no strings attached
Be tied to one's mother's apron
  strings
Pull strings
Someone/something tugs at one's
  heartstrings
Be all strung out
Be second-string

Stripe

Have a yellow stripe down one's
  back
A zebra can't change its stripes

Stroke

Have a stroke of bad/good luck
With one bold stroke
Give someone some strokes
Different strokes for different
  folks
Get down the short/fine strokes

Strong

Come on strong

Someone is as strong as a bull/ox
Have a strong stomach
Something is strong medicine
Someone is a tower of strength
Strong-arm someone

Stubborn

Stubborn as a mule

Study

Be in a brown study
Someone is a quick study

Stuff

Stuff the ballot box
Stuff oneself
Know one's stuff
Someone/something is hot stuff
Do/strut one's stuff
Be a stuffed shirt
Beat/knock the stuffing out of
    someone
Stuff and nonsense!

Stumble

Hit a stumbling block

Stump

Something has one stumped

Style

Cramp someone's style
Do something like it's going out
    of style

Sublime

From the ridiculous to the sub-
    lime

Success

Move up the ladder of success
Nothing succeeds like success
The sweet smell of success
Be a howling/roaring success
The operation was a success, but
    the patient died

Dress for success
If at first you don't succeed, try,
    try again

Suck

Suck up to someone
Suck someone into something
Something/someone sucks
Sucker list
Sucker bet
Never give a sucker an even
    break
There's a sucker born every min-
    ute
Go suck eggs!

Sudden

Feel a sudden chill
This is so sudden!

Suffer

Suffer the slings and arrows of
    someone/something
Not suffer fools gladly

Sugar

Sugar the pill
Sugar daddy
Give someone some sugar
Sugarcoat something

Suit

Something is someone's long suit
Be in one's birthday suit
Monkey suit
Ice-cream suit
Follow suit
Something suits someone right
    down to the socks
Something suits someone to a T
Suit yourself!

Summer

One swallow does not a summer
    make

The boys of summer
Indian summer

Sun

Have one's moment in the sun
Make hay while the sun shines
Have one's place in the sun
There's nothing new under the sun
Cram something where the sun don't shine
Man works from sun to sun, but woman's work is never done
Be on the sunny side of the street
Born on the sunny side of the hedge
Sail off into the sunset
Roll up the sidewalks at sunset

Sunday

Sunday punch
Sunday driver
Wear one's Sunday best/Sunday go-to-meeting clothes
Six ways to Sunday
A month of Sundays

Supper

Sing for one's supper

Sure

As sure as death and taxes
As sure as God made little green apples
Something is a sure thing
Something is surefire
Be cock-sure
Sure enough!
Sure as shootin'!
Sure as eggs is eggs!

Suspicion

Someone/something is above suspicion

Swallow

Swallow one's pride
Swallow one's words
Swallow something hook, line and sinker
Swallow the bait
Something is a bitter pill to swallow
One swallow does not a summer make
Look like the cat that swallowed the canary

Swan

Sing one's swan song

Swear

Swear off of something
Swear to something on a stack of Bibles
Swear to something on one's mother's grave
Swear a blue streak

Sweat

Sweat something out
Sweat blood
By the sweat of one's brow
Blood, sweat, toil and tears
Flop sweat
Break out into a cold sweat
Sweatshop
Don't sweat it!
No sweat!

Sweep

Sweep someone of his/her feet
Sweep something under the carpet
Sweep the boards
Sweep the dirt under the rug
Make a clean sweep of something
A new broom sweeps clean

Sweet

Sweet as pie
Take one's own sweet time
Short and sweet
Take the bitter with the sweet
Have a sweet tooth
Home, sweet home
In the sweet bye and bye
The sweet smell of success
Whisper sweet nothings
Sweeten the pot
All sweetness and light
Give/get a sweetheart deal
The blacker the berry, the
  sweeter the juice
The nearer the bone, the sweeter
  the meat
Sweet-talk someone
Sweets for the sweet!
Parting is such sweet sorrow!

Swell

Have a swelled head

Swift

The race is/is not to the swift

Swim

Swim like a fish
Swim against the current
Sink or swim
Get in the swim of something
So fast it makes one's head swim

Swine

Cast pearls before swine
You can't make a purse out of a
  swine's/sow's ear

Swing

Swing like a gate
Swing one's weight around
Be in full swing with something
It don't mean a thing if it ain't
  got that swing
Not enough room to swing a cat
Work the swing shift
The door swings both ways
Go down swinging

Swoop

In one fell swoop

Sword

Be put to the sword
The pen is mightier than the
  sword
He who lives by the sword, dies
  by the sword
Be at sword's point
Beat one's swords into plowshares
Cross swords with someone

System

You can't beat the system
Use the buddy system
All systems are go

T

T

Someone/something suits/fits one
  to a T/tee

Cross the T's and dot the I's
Tell someone something on the
  Q.T.

Tab

Spring for/pick up the tab
Keep tabs on someone/something

Table

Drink someone under the table
Do something under the table
Put/lay all one's cards on the
  table
Hands across the table
Have both hands on the table
Don't dance on the table where
  you eat
Turn the tables on someone
Table-hopper

Tack

Take a different tack
Be sharp as a tack
Get down to brass tacks
Go sit on a tack!

Tail

Turn tail and run
Have the world by the tail
In two shakes of a lamb's tail
Can't make head nor tail out of
  someone/something
Drag one's tail
Have one's tail between one's legs
Move one's tail for someone/
  something
Case of the tail wagging the dog
Have a bear/tiger by the tail
Chase one's own tail
Heads I win, tails you lose
Hang on to someone's coattails
Go into a tailspin
Be bright-eyed and bushy-tailed

Take

Take a bath on something
Take someone to the cleaners
Take someone for a ride
Take a bow
Take someone/something by
  storm
Take one's hat off to someone
Take someone down a peg or two
Take leave of one's senses
Take one's own sweet time
Take one's breath away
Take one's life into one's own
  hands
Take someone under one's wing
Take five
Take someone at his word
Take it on the chin
Take a meeting
Take a gander at something
Take a dim view of someone/
  something
Take the fifth
Take a stab at something
Take something lying down
Take the air
Take a different tack
Take the law into one's own
  hands
Take something in one's stride
Take the bit in one's teeth
Take one's medicine
Take a long shot
Take to the tall timber
Take the acid test
Take it on the lam
Take the wind out of someone's
  sails
Take it out on someone
Take the rap for someone
Take the bull by the horns
Take a load off one's feet
Take to one's heels
Take a shine to someone/some-
  thing
Take a backseat to someone
Take up the cudgels for someone/
  something

Take something with a grain of salt
Take a flyer
Take the bitter with the sweet
Take the cure
Take a dive/nosedive
Take a fancy to someone/something
Take one's final curtain
Take French leave
Take the gas pipe
Take the high road
Take someone's measure
Take the money and run
Take someone's name in vain
Take a poke at someone/something
Take something into account
Take a bad turn
Take a leap in the dark
Take a turn for the worse/better
Take it or leave it
Take no stock in someone/something
Take to the woods/hills
Take a fling at something
Take something for granted
Take a leaf/page from someone's book
Take one's lumps
Take the plunge
Take advantage of someone/something
Take the bait
Take a trimming
Take it one day/step at a time
Take a slice at someone
Take something out in trade
Someone is on the take
You can't take it with you
Give someone an inch and he'll take a mile
Have all one can take
Give and take

Sit up and take notice of someone/something
If you can't take the heat, stay out of the kitchen
Do a double take
It takes one to know one
Have what it takes
It takes a thief to catch a thief
It takes two to tango
Someone/something takes the cake
Easy as taking candy from a baby
Don't take any wooden nickels!
Take a powder!
Take me to your leader!
Take care!
Take a hike!
Take no prisoners!
You can't take it with you!

Tale

Thereby hangs a tale
Old wives' tale
Tell tall tales
Dead men tell no tales
Tell tales out of school

Talk

Talk straight from the shoulder
Talk in circles
Talk someone's ear off
Talk one's head off
Talk through one's hat
Talk off the top of one's head
Talk big/big talk
Talk someone's language
Talk off the cuff
Talk turkey
Talk shop
Talk a blue streak
Talk out of turn
Talk till one is blue in the face
Talk someone/something up
Talk nineteen to the dozen

Talk a mile a minute
Talk down to someone
Talk the hind leg off a donkey
Talk is cheap
Someone is all talk
Give someone a pep talk
Chalk talk
Be the talk of the town
Have a heart-to-heart talk
Have a man-to-man talk
Sweet-talk someone
Now you're talkin'!
What are we talkin'?

Tall

Tall, dark and handsome
Sit/ride tall in the saddle
Tell tall stories/tales
Feel ten feet tall
Take to the tall timber

Tan

Tan someone's hide/britches
Black-and-tan joint

Tape

Something is full of red tape
Have something taped

Tar

Tar and feather someone
Knock/beat the tar out of some-
one
Be tarred with the same brush

Taste

Someone's taste is all in his
mouth
There's no accounting for taste
Want something so bad you can
taste it
Something/someone leaves a bad
taste in one's mouth
Have a champagne taste on a
beer pocketbook

Something tastes like dishwater

Tat

Tit for tat

Tax

Tax someone's patience
As sure as death and taxes

Tea

Someone/something is/isn't one's
cup/dish of tea
Not for all the tea in China
Something is a tempest in a tea-
pot/teacup

Teach

Teach someone a lesson
You can't teach an old dog new
tricks
Those who can't do, teach
Experience is the best teacher

Tear

Tear someone's heart out
Tear one's hair out
Tear someone/something to
shreds
Wear and tear
Someone is tearing up the pea
patch

Tears

Be bored to tears
Cry alligator/crocodile tears
Blood, sweat, toil and tears
Burst/break into tears
Tear-jerker

Tee

Someone/something suits one to
a tee/T
Get/be teed off

Teeth

Give/get a kick in the teeth

Something has teeth in it
Be fed up to the back teeth with
    someone/something
Scarce as hens' teeth
Grit one's teeth
Get/sink one's teeth into some-
    thing
Throw something in someone's
    teeth
Take the bit in one's teeth
Lie through one's teeth
By the skin of one's teeth
Be armed to the teeth
Someone/something sets one's
    teeth on edge
Like pulling teeth
Gnash one's teeth
Show one's teeth
Cut one's eyeteeth on something
Give one's eyeteeth for something

Tell

Tell someone a thing or two
Tell the world
Tell it like it is
Tell someone where to get off
Tell tales out of school
Tell tall tales/stories
Tell someone something on the
    Q.T.
Tell someone something flat out
Tell little white lies
Ask me no questions, I'll tell you
    no lies
Only time will tell
Dead men tell no tales
Class will tell
To tell the truth
No telling apart
A little bird told me
Tell it to the Marines!
Tell ya what I'm gonna do!
That's tellin' 'em!
I told you so!

Temper

Hold one's temper
Try one's temper
Have a hair-trigger temper

Tempest

Something is a tempest in a tea-
    pot/teacup

Ten

Count to ten
Five will get you ten
Someone/something is a perfect
    ten
Feel ten feet tall
On a scale of one-to-ten
Wouldn't touch something with a
    ten-foot pole

Tent

Fold up one's tent and steal away

Term

In no uncertain terms
Come to terms with someone/
    something
Get on good terms with someone
Something is a contradiction in
    terms

Terror

Someone is a holy terror
The terrible two's

Test

Test the waters
Stand the test of time
Best by test
Take/fail/pass the acid test
Time-tested

Thank

Thank one's lucky stars
Thank God it's Friday
Thanks for nothing

Something is a thankless task
Thank heavens/goodness/God!

That

That is to say
That goes without saying
That's that
That's show business/biz/Holly-
wood!
That's all she wrote!

Then

Right then and there
And then some!

There

There, but for the grace of God,
go I
Right then and there
Someone is not all there
Something is neither here nor
there
Somebody up there likes someone
Ay, there's the rub
Thereby hangs a tale

Thick

Thick as ticks on a hound dog
Thick and fast
Through thick and thin
Pour/spread something on thick
Be thick as thieves
Get something through one's
thick skull/head
Something is so thick you could
cut it with a knife
Lay something on a bit thick
Something is a bit thick
Blood is thicker than water
The plot thickens
Be thick-skinned

Thief

Like a thief in the night
It takes a thief to catch a thief

Be thick as thieves
No honor among thieves

Thin

Through thick and thin
Vanish into thin air
Skate on thin ice
Pull something out of thin air
Someone/something wears a bit
thin
Tread a thin line
As thin as a boardinghouse blan-
ket
You can't be too rich or too thin
Be thin-skinned

Thing

Do one's own thing
Make a big thing out of some-
thing
Tell someone a thing or two
First thing you know
A little knowledge is a dangerous
thing
It don't mean a thing if it ain't
got that swing
A thing of beauty is a joy forever
Something/someone is too much
of a good thing
Just one of those things
Be all things to all men
All good things must come to an
end
Things are looking up
First things first
The best things in life are free
The play's the thing!

Think

Think twice about something
Think the world of someone/
something
Think on one's feet
Think better of something
Think out loud

Great minds think alike
Can't hear oneself think
Put on one's thinking cap
Wishful thinking
Think nothing of it!
You've got another think coming!

This

This, that or the other
This and that
This won't hurt a bit!
This will hurt me more than it
  will hurt you!
Now hear this!
What is this?
What's the meaning of this?

Thorn

Be a thorn in one's side/flesh

Thought

Be lost in thought
Food for thought
It's the thought that counts
Train of thought
Have second thoughts
Perish the thought!
A penny for your thoughts?

Thousand

Bat a thousand
The face that launched a thousand ships
A picture is worth a thousand
  words

Thread

Hang by a thread
Silver threads among the gold
Wear a neat set of threads

Three

Three strikes and you're out
Three on a match is bad luck
Have three squares a day

Be three sheets to the wind
Give three cheers for someone/
  something
Give/get the third degree
Third time's a charm
Something is a three-ring circus
As phony/queer as a three-dollar
  bill

Thrill

The thrill is gone
Someone/something is a thrill a
  minute
Get a cheap thrill
The thrill of victory, the agony of
  defeat
Be thrilled to bits

Throat

Go for the throat
Jump down someone's throat
Have a lump in one's throat
Have a frog in one's throat
Force/cram/shove something
  down someone's throat
Something sticks in one's throat
Be at each other's throats

Throne

The power behind the throne

Through

Through thick and thin
Go through hell and high water
  for something/someone
Jump through hoops for some-
  one
Talk through one's hat
Go through the mill
Pay through the nose
Go through the motions
Get something through one's
  thick skull/head
Come through with flying colors

Throw

Throw a fit
Throw the bull
Throw in the towel/sponge
Throw cold water on something/
someone
Throw the race/fight/game
Throw someone a curve
Throw caution to the wind
Throw good money after bad
Throw a spanner in the works
Throw the book at someone
Throw someone over
Throw someone to the wolves/
lions
Throw one's weight around
Throw a wet blanket on some-
thing
Throw a monkey wrench into
something
Throw someone out on his ear
Throw someone a bone
Throw one's hat into the ring
Throw the baby out with the
bathwater
Throw something in someone's
face/teeth
Throw in one's hand
Throw someone off the scent
Throw up one's hands
Throw oneself on the mercy of
the court
Throw someone in the clink
Throw discretion to the wind
Throw water on a drowning man
Throw oneself at someone's feet
Throw light on something
Throw something out of gear/
whack/kilter
Throw someone a kiss
Throw down the gauntlet
Trust someone as far as you can
throw him
People who live in glass houses
shouldn't throw stones
Be a stone's throw away from
something
Be thrown for a loss/loop

Thumb

Thumb a ride
Thumb one's nose at someone/
something
By rule of thumb
Be under someone's thumb
Someone/something sticks/stands
out like a sore thumb
Have a green thumb
Twiddle one's thumbs
Turn thumbs down/up on some-
one/something

Thunder

Steal someone's thunder
Blood and thunder
Be thunderstruck by someone/
something

Tick

Tight as a tick
Thick as ticks on a hound dog

Ticket

Write one's own ticket
Get a ticket to nowhere
Meal ticket
Someone/something is just the
ticket
That's the ticket!

Tickle

Tickle the ivories
Tickle someone's funny bone
Something tickles one's fancy
Something tickles one's ribs
Be tickled to death

Tide

Tide someone over

Stem the tide
Time and tide wait for no man
Turn the tide
A rising tide lifts all boats

Tie

Tie the knot
Tie one on
Tie someone to the rack
Have one's stomach tied up in
 knots
Be tied to one's mother's apron
 strings
With one hand tied behind one's
 back
One's hands are tied

Tiger

Have a tiger by the tail
Something is a paper tiger

Tight

Tight as a bedbug/tick
Something/someone is tight as a
 drum
Be in a tight spot
Sit tight
Tighten one's belt
Walk a tightrope
Someone is not too tightly
 wrapped
Be tight-fisted

Till

Dip into the till
Catch someone with his hand in
 the till

Timber

Take to the tall timber
Shiver me timbers!

Time

Time is money
Time is of the essence

Time heals all wounds
Time wounds all heels
Time flies
Time hangs heavy on one's hands
Time and tide wait for no man
Time to close the books
Something is like feeding time at
 the zoo
Someone is a legend in his own
 time
Pass the time of day
Stand the test of time
At this point in time
Do time/hard time
Take it one day/step at a time
Be ahead of one's time
Have time to burn/kill
Take one's own sweet time
Give someone a hard time
Beat someone's time
Third time is a charm
The time is ripe for something
Do something in jig time
Kill/mark time
Live on borrowed time
A stitch in time saves nine
The time is right
You're a long time dead
Prime time
In the nick of time
Make up for lost time
In less than no time
Not know what time it is
Have the time of one's life
Every time one turns around
All in good time
Give someone a bad time
In no time flat
The second time around
There's a first time for everything
That time of the month
Wouldn't give someone the time
 of day
No time like the present

Have time on one's hands
Only time will tell
Bide one's time
Make time
Someone lights up like Times
  Square
Trying times
Fall on hard times
Be behind the times
For old times' sake
Let the good times roll
Half-past kissing time, time to kiss
  again
Someone/something is small-time
If you've got the money, I've got
  the time!
Long time no see!
Time to get outta Dodge!
There'll be a hot time in the old
  town tonight!
It's about time!
Better luck next time!

Tin

Tin Pan Alley
Have a tin ear
Busy as a cat on a hot tin roof
Tinhorn

Tinker

Not worth/give a tinker's damn

Tip

Tip one's hand
Tip the scales
Tip the wink to someone
Something is on the tip of one's
  tongue
Something is only the tip of the
  iceberg

Tired

Be sick and tired of someone/
  something
Be bone/dog/dead tired

Tit

Tit for tat

Today

Today is the first day of the rest
  of your life
Here today, gone tomorrow
Live for today
Tomorrow, today will be yester-
  day
Don't put off till tomorrow what
  you can do today

Toe

Toe the line
Keep/stay on one's toes
Step on someone's toes
Have a toehold on something

Together

All in something together
Get one's act together
Keep body and soul together
Put two and two together
Make beautiful music together
Put our heads together
Get it all together

Toil

Blood, sweat, toil and tears

Token

A token of one's esteem
By the same token

Tomorrow

Tomorrow, today will be yester-
  day
There's no tomorrow
Eat, drink and be merry, for
  tomorrow you may die
Don't put off till tomorrow what
  you can do today
Here today, gone tomorrow
Tomorrow's another day

Ton

Something hits someone like a
  ton of bricks
Fall for someone like a ton of
  bricks
Come down on someone like a
  ton of bricks

Tone

Tone something down
Be tone deaf
Straight ahead and strive for
  tone!

Tongue

Speak with a silver tongue
Speak with a forked tongue
Keep a civil tongue in one's head
Something is on the tip of one's
  tongue
Have an acid tongue
Hold one's tongue
Have one's tongue hanging out
A slip of the tongue
Rattle one's tongue
Speak with tongue in cheek
Tongues will wag
Be tongue-tied
Give someone a tongue-lashing
Bite your tongue!
Cat got your tongue?

Toot

Toot one's own horn
Go on a toot
You're darn tootin'!

Tooth

An eye for an eye, a tooth for a
  tooth
Go over something with a fine-
  toothed comb
Fight/go at something tooth and
  nail
Getting long in the tooth

Have a sweet tooth
As clean as a hound's tooth

Top

Be top banana
Go over the top
Something runs like a top
Blow one's top
Sitting on top of the world
Sleep like a top
The top of the heap
Room at the top
Speak/talk off the top of one's
  head
It's lonely at the top
Scratch one's way to the top
Be top dog/gun
Cream rises to the top
Someone is top brass
Something is top secret
At the top of one's lungs
Be at the top of one's form
You're the top!

Torch

Torch a building
Carry a torch for someone

Torpedo

Damn the torpedoes!

Toss

Toss one's cookies
Toss one's hat into the ring
Toss a coin

Totem

Be low man on the totem pole

Touch

Touch all the bases
Touch wood
Have the common touch
Have the Midas touch
Something is touch and go

Put the touch on someone
Be a soft touch
Wouldn't touch something/some-
  one with a ten-foot pole
Something/someone touches a
  chord

Tough

Tough it out
Someone/something is a tough
  act to follow
Someone/something is a tough
  nut to crack
Something is a tough row to hoe
Something is tough sledding
Hang tough
As tough as old leather/boots
Someone is a tough customer/
  cookie
When the going gets tough, the
  tough get going
Tough tomatoes!

Tour

Take a Cook's tour
Take the 25¢ tour

Towel

Throw in the towel
Crying towel

Tower

Sit in an ivory tower
Someone is a tower of strength

Town

Ride someone out of town on a
  rail
The only game in town
Go to town
Go/get out on the town
Paint the town red
Blow/breeze into town
Skip town
Be the talk/toast of the town

One-horse town
Jerk-water town
Boomtown
Man-about-town

Trace

Disappear without a trace
Kick over the traces

Track

Lose track of someone/something
Off the beaten track
Get on the right track
Have the inside track
Something doesn't track
Look at someone's track record
Cover one's tracks
Make tracks
Live on the wrong side of the
  tracks
Drop/stop dead in one's tracks
Have a one-track mind

Trade

Take something out in trade
Know all the tricks of the trade
Something is one's stock in trade
Carriage trade
Someone is a horse-trader

Traffic

Someone stops traffic
All the traffic will bear
Go play in traffic!

Trail

Pick up someone's trail
Leave a trail of broken hearts
Blaze new trails

Train

Train of thought
Get on the gravy train

Trap

Caught like a rat in a trap

Have a mind like a steel trap
Booby trap
Shut your trap!

Travel

Travel light
Have tux, will travel
An army travels on its stom-
ach
He travels fastest who travels
alone
Fellow traveler
Follow a well-traveled path

Tread

Tread water
Tread a thin line
Tread on someone's corns
Fools rush in where angels fear to
tread

Treat

Treat someone like dirt/a dog
Dutch treat

Tree

Be up a tree
Someone lights up like a Christ-
mas tree
Chase/bark up the wrong tree
The apple doesn't fall far from
the tree
As the twig is bent, so grows the
tree
Charm the birds out of the trees
Can't see the forest for the trees
Money doesn't grow on trees
Go climb a tree!
Are you out of your tree?

Trial

Trial run
By trial and error
Send up a trial balloon
Trials and tribulations

Trick

Have a trick up one's sleeve
Pull a dirty/cheap trick
Have a trick knee
Turn/do a trick
Confidence trick
Something does/turns the trick
Know all the tricks of the trade
You can't teach an old dog new
tricks

Trigger

Quick on the trigger
Trigger-happy
Have a hair-trigger temper

Trim

Trim one's sails
Be in fine trim
Take a trimming

Trip

Trip the light fantastic
Trip someone up
Take a trip down memory lane
Have a bad trip
Be all tripped out
Wouldn't know someone/some-
thing if one tripped over it

Trot

Trot someone/something out
Hot to trot

Trouble

Trouble in paradise
Stir up trouble
Ask for trouble
Borrow trouble
Be in a pack/peck of trouble
Get a girl in trouble
Pack up your troubles
Drown one's troubles
A sea of troubles
Pour oil on troubled waters

Fish in troubled waters

Truck

Look like one was hit by a truck
Keep on truckin'!

True

True to life
True love never runs smooth
True grit
Someone/something is true blue
To thine ownself be true
Someone/something is too good
    to be true
Someone/something doesn't ring
    true
Tried and true
Show one's true colors
Truth is stranger than fiction
More than a grain of truth in
    something
Stretch the truth
The truth shall set you free
The truth hurts
Children and fools speak the
    truth
The naked truth
The truth will out
To tell the truth
The bitter truth
Truth is beauty
The unvarnished truth
Ain't it the truth?
Is it true what they say about
    Dixie?

Trump

Play one's trump card
Hold all the trumps
Something is a trumped-up
    charge

Trust

Trust someone as far as you can
    throw him

Brain trust

Try

Try one's hand at something
Try something on for size
Try one's luck
Try one's wings
Try someone's temper
If at first you don't succeed, try,
    try again
Give something the old college
    try
Someone/something tries one's
    patience
Someone/something is tried and
    true
Trying times
Just try and start something!

Tub

Someone is a tub of lard

Tube

Boob tube
Something goes down the tubes

Tuck

Something is nip and tuck
One's best bib and tucker
Be all tuckered out

Tug

Something tugs at one's heart-
    strings

Tumble

Not tumble to something
Give/not give someone a tumble
Have a tumble in the sack
Rough-and-tumble

Tune

Tune someone/something out
Change one's tune
Call the tune

Whistle/sing a different tune
Can't carry a tune in a bucket/
  wheelbarrow
Belt out a tune
Dance to a different/another tune
The piper/fiddler calls the tune
Tune in, turn on, drop out!
And that's the name of that tune!

Tunnel

See a ray of light at the end of
  the tunnel
Have tunnel vision

Turkey

Go/quit/stop cold turkey
Talk turkey
What a turkey!

Turn

Turn the corner
Turn up the heat on something
Turn a blind eye to something
Turn something inside out
Turn the place upside down
Turn one's back on someone/
  something
Turn up one's nose at someone/
  something
Turn a deaf ear to someone/
  something
Turn back the clock
Turn the tables on someone
Turn the other cheek
Turn someone's head
Turn tail and run
Turn thumbs down/up on some-
  thing/someone
Turn over a new leaf
Turn up like a bad penny
Turn on one's heel
Turn/do a trick
Turn the tide
Turn in one's chips

Turn someone off
Turn on the waterworks
Enough to make someone turn
  over in his grave
Take a bad turn
Something is done to a turn
At each and every turn
Not turn a hair
One good turn deserves another
Talk out of turn
Not know which way to turn
Give someone a turn
Take a turn for the worse/better
Someone/something turns the
  trick
Every time one turns around
The worm turns
Be turned on/off by someone/
  something
Leave no stone unturned
Turnabout is fair play
Tune in, turn on, drop out!

Twenty

Spot something/someone at
  twenty paces
Take the 25¢ tour
Have 20/20 hindsight

Twice

Big as life and twice as natural
Once bitten/burned twice shy
Think twice about something
Lightning never strikes in the
  same place twice
Something is cheap at twice the
  price
Always chew your cabbage twice
Someone has been around the
  block once or twice

Twig

As the twig is bent, so grows the
  tree

Twinge

Have a twinge of conscience

Twist

Twist someone's arm
Let something twist slowly in the wind
Get one's knickers into a twist
Brain twister
Tongue twister

Two

Two of a kind
Two heads are better than one
Two wrongs don't make a right
Two sides of the coin
In two shakes of a lamb's tail
Born into the world owing two dollars
As alike as two peas in a pod
Stand on one's own two feet
Have two strikes against one
Have two left feet
Take someone down a peg or two

Kill two birds with one stone
A bird in the hand is worth two in the bush
Put one's two cents in
Tell someone a thing or two
Put two and two together
Feel like two cents
No two ways about it
It takes two to tango
Choose the lesser of two evils
Do something for two cents/pins
Not care two hoots in hell
There are two sides to every story
The terrible two's
Two's company, three's a crowd
A gruesome twosome
Two-time someone
As hot as a two-dollar pistol
Someone is a two-bit operator
Something is a two-way street
Someone is two-faced
Give someone the old one-two
Be two-fisted
Two can play that game!

U

Ugly

Ugly duckling
Someone/something is ugly as sin
Something rears its ugly head
Someone has an ugly disposition
Something could get ugly

Uncle

Cry/say uncle
Have/be a Dutch uncle
I'll be a monkey's uncle!

Under

Be under a cloud
Be under the weather
Be under the influence
Sweep something under the carpet
Cut the ground out from under someone
Snow someone under
Have something under one's belt
Something is right under one's nose

Be under one's own steam
Take someone under one's wing
Do something under the table/
  counter
Keep something/someone under
  wraps
Hide one's light under a bushel
Keep something under one's hat
Get under someone's skin
Be under someone's thumb
Be/get hot under the collar
There's nothing new under the
  sun
Something is water under the
  bridge
Drink someone under the table
Just under the wire
Feel under par
Knuckle under
Sweep the dirt under the rug
Plow someone under
Pull the rug out from under
  someone
Someone/something is underfoot

Up

Be up to par/scratch/snuff
Be up against it
Be on the up and up
Be up in arms about something
Be up against a brick wall
Be up to one's ears in something
Be up a tree
Be up the creek without a paddle
Be all dressed up and no place to
  go
Be/get all shook up
Be/get all fired up about some-
  thing
Be/get all uptight
Be all buttoned up
Pull oneself up by one's boot-
  straps
Not know which end is up

Something is right up one's alley/
  street
Go up a blind alley
Get up on the wrong side of the
  bed
Dry up and blow away
Have something all wrapped up
Go belly up
Belly up to the bar
Get/have one's back/hackles up
Have an ace/card up one's sleeve
Something is up for grabs
Hurry up and wait
Someone's number is up
Stand up and cheer
Turn thumbs up on something
Everything's coming up roses
Laugh up one's sleeve
Laugh it up
Live it up
Act up
Give someone a leg up
Not know which end is up
Scare something up
Things are looking up
Someone up there likes someone
Jack up the ante
Be down so long it looks like up
Something/someone is right up to
  the minute
Upset the applecart
The upper crust
Be on one's uppers
Something is an uphill battle
The Man upstairs
Ante up!
Bottoms up!
Put up or shut up!
Brighten up!
The jig is up!

Urge

The urge to kill
The urge to merge

Use

Use one's bean/noodle
Use it or lose it!

Usual

Business as usual

V

Valet

No man is a hero to his valet

Vacuum

Nature abhors a vacuum

Vain

Take someone's name in vain

Valor

Discretion is the better part of valor

Value

Take something/someone at face value
Know the cost of everything and the value of nothing

Vanish

Vanish into thin air

Vanity

Vanity, thy name is woman!

Variety

Variety is the spice of life
Common garden variety

Veins

Someone has ice-water in his veins

Velvet

Iron fist in a velvet glove

Vessel

Break a blood vessel

Vest

Play one's cards close to the vest
Run a vest-pocket business

Vibes

Get good/bad vibes from someone/something

Vicious

Vicious circle

Victor

To the victor go the spoils
Landslide victory
Snatch victory from the jaws of defeat
The thrill of victory, the agony of defeat

View

Take a dim view of someone/something
Bird's-eye view

Vine

Die on the vine
Someone is a clinging vine

Hear something through/by the grapevine

Vinegar

You can catch more flies with honey than with vinegar

Violet

Shrinking violet

Violin

Play someone like a violin

Virtue

Virtue is its own reward

Patience is a virtue

Vision

Have tunnel vision
Someone is a vision of loveliness

Void

Feel an aching void

Volume

A look that speaks volumes

Vote

Vote early and often
Give/get a vote of confidence
You've got my vote!

W

Wad

Have a wad big enough to choke a horse
Shoot one's wad

Wag

Tongues will wag
A case of the tail wagging the dog

Wage

Earn the wages of sin

Wagon

Fix someone's wagon
Fall off the wagon
Go on the wagon
Hitch one's wagon to a star
One's little red wagon
Meat wagon
Climb/jump on the bandwagon

Wait

Wait for the other shoe to drop
Wait with bated breath
Wait on someone hand and foot
Time and tide wait for no man
Hurry up and wait
Play the waiting game
Be waiting in the wings/bullpen
Wait till next year!
Just you wait!

Wake

Wake up and smell the coffee
Loud enough to wake the dead

Walk

Walk down the aisle
Walk on eggs/eggshells
Walk a thin line
Walk a straight line

Walk the plank
Walk the floor over someone/
  something
Walk on air
Walk a tightrope
Walk the chalk
Walk a mile in another man's
  mocassins
Win in a walk
You have to crawl before you can
  walk
Cock of the walk
Don't walk under a ladder
Worship the ground someone
  walks on
Give someone his walking papers
Someone is a walking encyclo-
  pedia
Take a long walk off a short pier!

Wall

Have one's back against/to the
  wall
Live in a hole in the wall
Run up against/into a brick/
  stone wall
Beat/bang/butt one's head
  against the wall
Hit the wall
Read the handwriting on the wall
Drive someone up the wall
Something/someone is off the
  wall
Nail someone to the wall
Walls have ears
Bounce off the walls
Climb the walls

Waltz

Waltz right in

Want

Want an egg in one's beer
Want something in the worst way

Want someone so bad you can
  taste it
Waste not, want not
What do you want, blood?
Want to make something of it?

War

War of nerves
War is hell
Win the battle but lose the war
All's fair in love and war
Make love, not war
Go/be on the warpath
Put on one's warpaint
This means war!

Warm

Warm the bench
Warm the cockles of one's heart
Warm as toast
Cold hands, warm heart
Someone/something warms one's
  blood
Look like death warmed over

Warrant

Sign one's own death warrant

Wart

Sit there like a wart on a pickle

Wary

Be wary as a cat

Wash

Wash one's hands of someone/
  something
Wash one's dirty linen in public
It'll all come out in the wash
Something won't wash
One hand washes the other
Be all washed up
Be chief cook and bottlewasher
Something is eyewash
Whitewash someone/something

Brainwash someone
The great unwashed
Wash your mouth out with soap!

Waste

Waste not, want not
Haste makes waste
Get wasted
Don't waste your breath!

Watch

Watch your pennies and the dol-
lars will take care of themselves
Watch someone/something like a
hawk
A watched pot never boils
Big Brother is watching
Clock-watcher
Watch my smoke/dust/speed!

Water

Water something down
Water seeks its own level
Be in deep water
Be dead in the water
Something/someone is of the first
water
Cut off someone's water
Get blown out of the water
Come hell or high water
Get into hot water
Tread water
Something is water under the
bridge
Something is water over the dam
Oil and water don't mix
Like a duck takes to water
Like a fish out of water
Something makes one's mouth
water
Dash/throw cold water on some-
one/something
Blood is thicker than water
Something won't/doesn't hold
water

Someone has ice water in his
veins
You never miss the water till the
well runs dry
Like water off a duck's back
You can lead a horse to water,
but you can't make him drink
Have both oars in the water
Spend money like water
Keep one's head above water
Throw water on a drowning man
Go through fire and water for
someone/something
Pour oil on troubled waters
Cast bread upon the waters
Muddy the waters
Still waters run deep
Fish in troubled waters
Test the waters
Dull as dish/ditchwater
Throw the baby out with the
bathwater
Cover the waterfront
Turn on the waterworks
Jerk-water town

Wave

Wave the flag for something
The wave of the future
Be on the same wavelength as
someone
Don't make waves!

Wax

Wax poetic over someone/some-
thing
The whole ball of wax
None of your beeswax!

Way

The way to a man's heart is
through his stomach
Look the other way
Look like an accident on its way
to happen

Know which way the cat will
jump
The American way
Scratch one's way to the top
Know one's way around
Be in the family way
Have one's way with someone
Cry/laugh all the way to the
bank
Go/run around every which way
Rub someone the wrong way
Go out of one's way for some-
one/something
There's more than one way to
skin a cat
Any way you slice it
Have a way with words
Be in a bad way
Find out/do something the hard
way
Go for someone/something in a
big way
See one's way clear
Where there's a will there's a way
Go all the way
Pave the way for someone
Be in/out of harm's way
Not know which way to jump
Want something in the worst way
Stand in one's way
See which way the wind blows
Lead the way
Can't punch one's way out of a
paper bag
The way of all flesh
Ways and means
Have a parting of the ways
See the error of one's ways
One can't have something both
ways
Something cuts both ways
Change one's ways
Six ways to Sunday
Someone/something falls by the

wayside
Something is a one/two-way
street
That's the way the cookie crum-
bles!
That's the way the wind blows!
Way out!

Weak

Weak sister
Be weak in the knees
The spirit is willing, but the flesh
is weak
Be weak as a kitten
Be the weak link in the chain

Wealth

Share the wealth
Early to bed and early to rise,
makes a man healthy, wealthy
and wise

Wear

Wear a hair shirt
Wear concrete boots
Wear one's heart on one's sleeve
Wear and tear
Wear the pants in the family
Wear out one's welcome
Wear many hats
Wear sackcloth and ashes
Wear one's Sunday best
Wear a poker face
Wear a skid-lip/brain bucket
Wear a neat set of threads
Wear one's glad rags
Wear one's Sunday-go-to-meeting
clothes
If the shoe fits, wear it
Be none the worse for wear
Someone/something wears on
one's nerves
Uneasy lies the head that wears
the crown
Something wears a bit thin

Weary

Be bone weary

Weather

Be under the weather
Keep a weather eye out/open
Someone is a fair-weather friend
Nice weather for ducks!
How's the weather up there?

Weave

Oh, what a tangled web we
weave, when first we practice to
deceive
Weave me a fancy on your loom!

Web

Oh, what a tangled web we
weave, when first we practice to
deceive

Wedding

Shotgun wedding

Wee

The wee small hours

Weed

Grow like a weed

Week

Any day of the week

Weep

Read 'em and weep
Finders keepers, losers weepers

Weight

Carry the weight of the world on
one's shoulders
Carry/pull one's own weight
Throw one's weight around
Someone/something is dead
weight
Something carries some weight
with someone

Someone/something is worth its
weight in gold

Welcome

Welcome someone with open
arms
Roll out the welcome mat
Wear out one's welcome
Someone/something is as wel-
come as money from home
Welcoming committee
Welcome to the club!

Well

All's well that ends well
Living well is the best revenge
Leave well enough alone
Alive and well and living in

You never miss the water till the
well runs dry
Anything worth doing is worth
doing well
Something is all well and good
Hale fellow, well met
Love not wisely but too well
Go back to the well again
Someone is well-connected

West

East is east and west is west

Wet

Wet one's whistle
Someone is all wet
Be a wet blanket
Throw a wet blanket on some-
one/something
Mad as a wet hen
Be still wet behind the ears
Get one's feet wet
Give someone forty lashes with a
wet noodle

Whack

Throw something out of whack

Whale

Have a whale of a time
As big as a whale

What

What you see is what you get
You are what you eat
It's not what you know, it's who
    you know
Know what's what
What's good/sauce for the goose
    is good/sauce for the gander
What's up?
What's new?
What's the big idea?
What's eating you?
What's cooking?

Wheat

Separate the wheat from the chaff

Wheel

Wheel and deal
Reinvent the wheel
Someone is a big wheel
The squeaky wheel gets the grease
Put one's shoulder to the wheel
Grease the wheels of something
Spin one's wheels
Be hell on wheels
Can't carry a tune in a wheel-
    barrow

When

When all is said and done
Just say when

Where

Where it's at
Where there's a will, there's a way
Where there's smoke there's fire
Where's the fire?

Whip

Be smart as a whip

Crack the whip
Have the whip hand on some-
    thing
Be someone's whipping boy
Still trying to sell buggy-whips

Whisker

Lose/win by a whisker
Someone/something is the cat's
    whiskers

Whisky

Cigarettes, whisky and wild, wild
    women

Whisper

Whisper sweet nothings
Soft as a whisper
Whispering campaign

Whistle

Whistle in the dark
Whistle a different tune
Whistle stop
Be clean as a whistle
Be slick as a whistle
Blow the whistle on someone/
    something
Wet one's whistle
Go whistle for something
You ain't just whistling Dixie!

White

White elephant
Have white knuckles
Be white as a sheet
Be white as snow
Bleed someone white
Tell little white lies
See something in black and white
Show the white feather/flag
Be someone's white knight
Be free, white and twenty-one
Have a white-color job
Someone is lily-white

Who

It's not what you know, it's who
  you know
Sez who?

Whole

Go the whole nine yards
The whole ball of wax
The whole shooting match
Go whole hog over someone/
  something
The whole shebang
The whole kit and caboodle
Something is a whole new ball
  game
Something is a whole 'nother
  world
Cut/made up from whole cloth

Wicked

There's no rest for the wicked

Wide

High, wide and handsome
All wool and a yard wide
With eyes wide open
Give a wide berth to someone/
  something
Search for/spread something far
  and wide

Widow

Widow's mite
Widow's peak
Grass widow
Golf/football widow

Wife

Old wives' tale

Wig

Wig out
Flip one's wig
Bigwig

Wild

Wild horses couldn't drag one
  away from something
Someone/something is the wild
  card in the deck
Be wild and woolly
Sow one's wild oats
Call of the wild goose
Cigarettes, whisky and wild, wild
  women
Something spreads like wildfire
Go hog-wild over someone/some-
  thing
Go on a wild-goose chase

Will

Bend someone to one's will
Anything that can go wrong, will
Of one's own free will
Where there's a will, there's a way
Be ready, willing and able
If the Lord be willing and the
  creek don't rise
The spirit is willing but the flesh
  is weak

Win

Win some, lose some
Win the battle but lose the war
Win, lose or draw
Win hands down
Win in a walk
Win by a country mile
Win one's spurs/wings
Win in a breeze
Win by a hair/nose/whisker
Win a few, lose a few
Can't win for losing
Heads I win, tails you lose
It's not whether you win or lose,
  it's how you play the game
You can't win them all
Slow but steady wins the race
Hold the winning hand

Have a winning smile

Wind

Clutch at straws in the wind
Get wind of something
Spit in the wind
Take/cut the wind out of some-
  one's sails
It's an ill wind that blows nobody
  good
See which way the wind blows
Sail too close to the wind
Be three sheets to the wind
Throw caution to the wind
Throw discretion to the wind
Get one's second wind
Something/someone is gone with
  the wind
Something is in the wind
Let something/someone twist
  slowly in the wind
The winds of change
Tilt at windmills
That's the way the wind blows!

Window

When the wolf is at the door,
  love flies out the window
Eyes are the windows of the soul
Window-shop

Wine

Wine and dine someone
Something is old wine in new
  bottles
A jug of wine, a loaf of bread
  and thou

Wing

Wing it
Take someone under one's wing
Come in on a wing and a prayer
Earn one's wings
Be waiting in the wings
Try one's wings

Wink

Can't sleep a wink
Quick as a wink
Tip the wink to someone
A nod and a wink
Catch forty winks

Wipe

Wipe up the floor with someone
Wipe someone out
Be/get wiped out

Wire

Just under the wire
Go down to the wire
Someone is a live wire
Put together with chewing gum
  and baling wire
Have someone/something wired
Get/be wired
Go haywire

Wise

Wise guy/wiseacre
Wise up to someone
As wise as an owl
A word to the wise
Put someone wise to someone/
  something
Early to bed and early to rise,
  makes a man healthy, wealthy
  and wise
Sadder but wiser
Love not wisely, but too well
Be penny-wise and pound-foolish

Wish

Wish upon a star
Be careful what you wish for, you
  just might get it
Make a birthday wish
Wishing will/will not make it so
Wishful thinking
Your wish is my command!

Wit

Brevity is the soul of wit
Be at wits' end
Be scared out of one's wits
Keep one's wits about one
Live by one's wits

Witch

Witch hunt

Within

Within an inch of one's life
Within an ace of something

Without

Without benefit of clergy
Without batting an eye
Be up the creek without a paddle

Witness

Bear false witness
With God as my witness!

Wolf

Wolf down one's food
A wolf in lamb's/sheep's clothing
Keep the wolf from the door
When the wolf is at the door,
  love flies out the window
Cry wolf
Lone wolf
Who's afraid of the big, bad wolf?

Woman

Make an honest woman of some-
  one
Hell hath no fury like a woman
  scorned
Man works from sun to sun, but
  woman's work is never done
The other woman
A fine figure of a woman
Cigarettes, whisky and wild, wild
  women
Women and children first!

Vanity, thy name is woman!

Wonder

Someone is a spineless wonder
Nine/ninety-day wonder
Will wonders never cease?

Wood

Knock on/touch wood
Saw wood
This neck of the woods
Be out of the woods
Be a babe in the woods
Take to the woods
Crawl/come out of the woodwork
There's a monkey in the woodpile
Don't take any wooden nickels!

Wool

All wool and a yard wide
Pull the wool over someone's eyes
Be wild and woolly
Woolgathering
Something is a dyed-in-the-wool
  something

Word

Someone's word is law
Someone/something is the last
  word in something
Break one's word
Not breathe a word of something
By word of mouth
Be as good as one's word
A word to the wise
Put in a good word for someone
The Greeks have a word for it
Can't get a word in edgewise
From the word go
Mum's the word
Just say the word
The "F" word
Have the last word
The word on the street
Take someone at his word

Four-letter word

One picture is worth a thousand words

Do/don't mince words

Clip one's words

Actions speak louder than words

In so many words

Put words in someone's mouth

Famous last words

Be a man of few words

Be at a loss for words

Play on words

You took the words right out of my mouth!

Words fail me!

Mark my words!

What's the good word?

Work

Work one's butt off

Work like a dog/horse/beaver

Work under cover

Work in a boiler-room

Work someone over

Work both sides of the street

Work one's fingers to the bone

Work the graveyard/swing shift

Work for peanuts

Work on one's image

Nice work if you can get it

All in a day's work

Have one's work cut out for one

All work and no play makes Jack a dull boy

Make short work of someone/ something

Do someone's dirty work

Many hands make light work

Do the spadework

Do legwork

Throw a spanner in the works

Give someone the works

Shoot the works

Gum up the works

Something works like a charm

Man works from sun to sun, but woman's work is never done

Turn on the waterworks

Make busywork

Get/be all worked up over some-one/something

Heaven will protect the working girl

Something goes/is as regular as clockwork

Idle fingers/hands are the devil's workshop

Write if you get work!

World

Carry the weight of the world on one's shoulders

Come up in the world

Sitting on top of the world

It's a small world

Something is a whole 'nother world

Something does someone a world of good

Be dead to the world

The world is one's oyster

Look at the world through rose-colored glasses

Be born into the world owing two dollars

Set the world on fire

Someone/something is out of this world

Have the world by the tail/on a string

Money/love makes the world go around

Tell the world

Wouldn't miss something for the world

Think the world of someone/ something

Not have a care in the world

A man of the world
Dog-eat-dog world
All the world's a stage
Have the best of both worlds
Not for the world!

Worm

The worm turns
The early bird gets/catches the
  worm
Open a can of worms
Go eat worms!

Worse

For better or worse
Go from bad to worse
A fate worse than death
Someone's bark is worse than
  one's bite
If worse comes to worst
Take a turn for the worse
Be none the worse for wear
Someone/something is far and
  away the worst
Be one's own worst enemy
Want something in the worst way
Get the worst of something

Worth

Anything worth doing is worth
  doing well
For all one is worth
Someone/something is worth its
  weight in gold
Something is not worth a plugged
  nickel
Something is not worth a tinker's
  damn
A bird in the hand is worth two
  in the bush
Be worth one's salt
Something is not worth the paper
  it's printed on
For what it's worth

Something is not worth a hill of
  beans/a fig
One picture is worth a thousand
  words
The game is/isn't worth the can-
  dle
An ounce of prevention is worth
  a pound of cure
Get one's money's worth
Something is not worth a rap
Something is not worth the pow-
  der to blow it up
Milk something for all its worth

Wound

Rub salt in the wound
Time heals all wounds
Time wounds all heels
Lick one's wounds
It's only a flesh wound!

Wrack

Wrack one's brains
Go to wrack and ruin

Wrap

Wrap someone around one's little
  finger
Wrap something up
Keep something under wraps
Someone is not too tightly
  wrapped
Be all wrapped up in someone/
  something
Have something all wrapped up
That's a wrap!

Wring

Wring someone's neck
Put someone through the wringer

Wrist

Give someone a slap on the wrist
Limp-wristed
It's all in the wrist!

Write

Write one's own ticket
Write a rubber check
Someone/something is nothing to write home about
The moving finger writes
Suffer writer's cramp
Have something written all over it/one's face
Something is not worth the paper it's written on
Something is/isn't written in stone
Someone wrote the book/bible on something
Read the handwriting on the wall
Write if you get work!
That's all she wrote!

Wrong

Live on the wrong side of the tracks
Rub someone the wrong way
Bark/chase up the wrong tree
Get up on the wrong side of the bed
Born on the wrong side of the blanket
Back/bet on the wrong horse
Steer someone wrong
Anything that can go wrong, will
Get off on the wrong foot
Sit in the wrong pew
Fifty million Frenchmen can't be wrong
Two wrongs don't make a right

X

X

"X" marks the spot

Have X-ray eyes

Y

Yard

All wool and a yard wide
Go the whole nine yards
Stay in one's own backyard

Year

Year in and year out

Since the year one
A moment on the lips, a year on the hips
Not see someone in donkey's years
Getting along/get on in years

Get/have the seven-year itch
Wait till next year!

Yellow

Have a yellow streak/stripe down
  one's back
Yellow-bellied/livered

Yesterday

Someone was not born yesterday
Tomorrow today will be yesterday

You

Let me tell you!
You can say that again!
All right for you!
I'm telling you!
The laugh's on you!
You're telling me?

Youth

The blush of youth

Z

Z

From A to Z
Catch some Zzzzz's

Zebra

A zebra can't change its stripes

Zero

Zero in on something
Zero hour
Batting zero
Big fat zero

Zip

Not worth zip
Put a little zip into your life
Zip your lip!

Zone

Dead zone
Zone out

Zonk

Zonk out